Adobe®

Flash® Professional CC

CLASSROOM IN A BOOK®

The official training workbook from Adobe Systems

Adobe Press books are published by Peachpit, a division of Pearson Education located in San Francisco, California. For the latest on Adobe Press books, go to www.adobepress.com. To report errors, please send a note to errata@peachpit.com. For information on getting permission for reprints and excerpts, contact permissions@peachpit.com.

Acquisitions Editor: Rebecca Gulick
Writer: Russell Chun
Development and Copy Editor: Stephen Nathans-Kelly
Production Coordinator: David Van Ness
Compositor: Danielle Foster
Technical Reviewer: Keith Gladstien
Keystroker: H. Paul Robertson
Proofreader: Patricia Pane
Indexer: Valerie Haynes Perry
Cover Designer: Eddie Yuen
Interior Designer: Mimi Heft

Printed and bound in the United States of America

ISBN-13:   978-0-321-92785-9
ISBN-10:   0-321-92785-0

9 8 7 6 5 4 3 2 1

WHERE ARE THE LESSON FILES?

Purchasing this Classroom in a Book gives you access to the lesson files that you'll need to complete the exercises in the book, as well as other content to help you learn more about Adobe software and use it with greater efficiency and ease. The diagram below represents the contents of the lesson files directory, which should help you locate the files you need. Please see the Getting Started section for full download instructions.

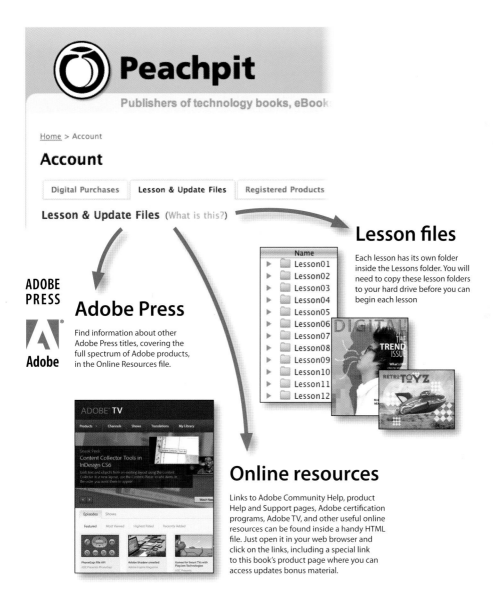

Adobe Press

Find information about other Adobe Press titles, covering the full spectrum of Adobe products, in the Online Resources file.

Lesson files

Each lesson has its own folder inside the Lessons folder. You will need to copy these lesson folders to your hard drive before you can begin each lesson

Online resources

Links to Adobe Community Help, product Help and Support pages, Adobe certification programs, Adobe TV, and other useful online resources can be found inside a handy HTML file. Just open it in your web browser and click on the links, including a special link to this book's product page where you can access updates bonus material.

CONTENTS

11 PUBLISHING FLASH DOCUMENTS 330

GETTING STARTED

Adobe Flash Professional CC provides a comprehensive authoring environment for creating interactive and media-rich applications. Flash is widely used to create engaging projects integrating video, sound, graphics, and animation. You can create original content in Flash or import assets from other Adobe applications such as Photoshop or Illustrator, quickly design animation and multimedia, and use Adobe ActionScript 3.0 to integrate sophisticated interactivity.

Use Flash Professional to build innovative and immersive Web sites, to create standalone applications for the desktop, or to create apps to distribute to mobile devices running on the Android or the iOS system.

With extensive controls for animation, intuitive and flexible drawing tools, and a powerful, object-oriented coding language, Flash delivers one of the few robust authoring environments that let your imagination become reality.

About Classroom in a Book

Adobe Flash Professional CC Classroom in a Book is part of the official training series for Adobe graphics and publishing software developed with the support of Adobe product experts. The lessons are designed so you can learn at your own pace. If you're new to Flash, you'll learn the fundamental concepts and features you'll need to use the program. Classroom in a Book also teaches many advanced features, including tips and techniques for using the latest version of this application.

What's New

The lessons in this book provide opportunities to use some of the updated features and improvements in Flash Professional, including:

- A fresh, modern user interface
- Working in full-screen mode
- Distributing symbols and bitmaps to keyframes
- Swapping multiple symbols or bitmaps
- A powerful Find and Replace panel
- Improved Photoshop and Illustrator file import
- A re-engineered Actions panel
- Smoother, more responsive drawing and editing
- Exporting videos with Adobe Media Encoder
- Resizing the Stage relative to an anchor point
- An integrated Toolkit for CreateJS, which publishes animation to HTML5 and JavaScript
- Comprehensive testing tools, such as device testing via USB and SWF analysis with Adobe Scout
- Synchronizing preferences on multiple machines with Creative Cloud

Streamlined Feature Set

In order to provide a more focused creative environment, Adobe Flash Professional CC has streamlined its feature set. The following is a list of the notable tools that have been dropped from the previous version:

- Support for ActionScript 1 and 2
- TLF text
- Motion Editor for motion tweens
- Bone tool for inverse kinematics
- Deco tool
- Project panel
- Printing
- Strings panel

- Behaviors panel

- Object-level undo

- Spelling panel

- Movie Explorer

- Bandwidth profiler in Test Movie mode

- FXG file import or export

- Kuler panel

- Video Cue Points (but still available in Media Encoder and through ActionScript)

- Closed captioning

- Video playback on Stage with FLV playback component

- Device Central

- Importing SWFs

- Pick whip in the Code Snippets panel

- Auto-Save

- File Info (XMP Metadata)

- Import support for some bitmap formats (BMP, TIFF, AutoCad) and some sound formats (AIFF, Sound Designer, Around AU, Adobe Sounds Document)

- Publishing projectors

Prerequisites

Before you begin using *Adobe Flash Professional CC Classroom in a Book*, make sure your system is set up correctly and that you've installed the required software. You should have a working knowledge of your computer and operating system. You should know how to use the mouse and standard menus and commands, and also how to open, save, and close files. If you need to review these techniques, see the printed or online documentation included with your Microsoft Windows or Apple Mac OS software.

If you're working on Microsoft Windows, you need to download Apple's QuickTime software, free from http://www.apple.com/quicktime/download/ in order to work with the videos in Lesson 7.

In addition, you need to download the free Adobe AIR runtime, available at http://get.adobe.com/air/ to publish desktop applications in Lesson 11.

Installing Flash

You must purchase the Adobe Flash Professional application as part of the Adobe Creative Cloud. The following specifications are the minimum required system configurations.

Windows

- Intel® Pentium 4, Intel Centrino®, Intel Xeon®, or Intel Core™ Duo (or compatible) processor
- Microsoft® Windows® 7 64-bit and Microsoft® Windows® 8 64-bit
- 2GB of RAM (4GB recommended)
- 1024x768 display (1280x800 recommended)
- Java Runtime Environment 1.7 (included)
- QuickTime 10.x software recommended
- 2GB of available hard-disk space for installation; additional free space required during installation (cannot install on removable flash storage devices)
- Broadband Internet connection and registration are necessary for required software activation, validation of subscriptions, and access to online services.

Mac OS

- Multicore Intel® processor
- Mac OS X v10.7 64-bit and 10.8 64-bit
- 2GB of RAM (4GB recommended)
- 1024x768 display (1280x800 recommended)
- Java™ Runtime Environment 1.7
- QuickTime 10.x software recommended
- 2.5GB of available hard-disk space for installation; additional free space required during installation (cannot install on a volume that uses a case-sensitive file system or on removable flash storage devices)
- Broadband internet connection and registration are necessary for required software activation, validation of subscriptions, and access to online services.

For updates on system requirements and complete instructions on installing the software, visit http://www.adobe.com/products/flash/tech-specs.html.

Install Flash from the Adobe Creative Cloud at https://creative.adobe.com/ and make sure that you have your login and password accessible.

Copying the Lesson Files

The lessons in *Adobe Flash Professional CC Classroom in a Book* use specific source files, such as image files created in Adobe Illustrator, video files created in Adobe After Effects, audio files, and prepared Flash documents. To access the Classroom in a Book files:

1 On a Mac or PC, go to www.peachpit.com/redeem and enter the code found at the back of your book.

2 If you do not have a Peachpit.com account, you will be prompted to create one.

3 The downloadable files will be listed under Lesson & Update Files tab on your Account page.

4 Click the lesson file links to download them to your computer.

5 On your hard drive, create a new folder in a convenient location and name it **FlashProCC,** following the standard procedure for your operating system:

   • If you're running Windows, right-click and choose New > Folder. Then enter the new name for your folder.

   • If you're using Mac OS, in the Finder, choose File > New Folder. Type the new name and drag the folder to the location you want to use.

   Now you can download the lesson files onto your hard drive.

6 Drag the Lessons folder (which contains folders named Lesson01, Lesson02, and so on) that you downloaded onto your hard drive to your new FlashProCC folder.

When you begin each lesson, navigate to the folder with that lesson number to access all the assets, sample movies, and other project files you need to complete the lesson.

If you have limited storage space on your computer, you can copy each lesson folder as you need it, and then delete it after you've completed the lesson if desired. Some lessons build on preceding lessons; in those cases, a starting project file is provided for you for the second lesson or project. You do not have to save any finished project if you don't want to or if you have limited hard drive space.

Copying the sample movies and projects

You will create and publish SWF animation files in some lessons in this book. The files in the End folders (01End, 02End, and so on) within the Lesson folders are samples of completed projects for each lesson. Use these files for reference if you want to compare your work in progress with the project files used to generate the sample movies. The end project files vary in size from relatively small to a couple of megabytes, so you can either copy them all now if you have ample storage space or copy just the end project file for each lesson as needed. Then you can delete it when you finish that lesson.

How to Use the Lessons

Each lesson in this book provides step-by-step instructions for creating one or more specific elements of a real-world project. Some lessons build on projects created in preceding lessons; most stand alone. All the lessons build on one another in terms of concepts and skills, so the best way to learn from this book is to proceed through the lessons in sequential order. In this book, some techniques and processes are explained and described in detail only the first few times you perform them.

The organization of the lessons is also project-oriented rather than feature-oriented. That means, for example, that you'll work with symbols on real-world design projects over several lessons rather than in just one chapter.

Additional Resources

Adobe Flash Professional CC Classroom in a Book is not meant to replace documentation that comes with the program or to be a comprehensive reference for every feature. Only the commands and options used in the lessons are explained in this book. For comprehensive information about program features and tutorials, refer to these resources:

Adobe Flash Professional CC Help and Support: www.adobe.com/support/flash is where you can find and browse Help and Support content on Adobe.com. Adobe Flash Professional Help and Adobe Flash Professional Support Center are accessible from Flash Professional's Help menu.

Adobe Creative Cloud Learning: For inspiration, key techniques, cross-product workflows, and updates on new features, go to the Creative Cloud Learn page https://helpx.adobe.com/creative-cloud/tutorials.html. Available only to Creative Cloud members.

Adobe Forums: forums.adobe.com lets you tap into peer-to-peer discussions, questions, and answers on Adobe products. The Flash Professional forum is accessible from Flash Professional's Help menu.

Adobe TV: tv.adobe.com is an online video resource for expert instruction and inspiration about Adobe products, including a How To channel to get you started with your product.

Adobe Design Center: www.adobe.com/designcenter offers thoughtful articles on design and design issues, a gallery showcasing the work of top-notch designers, tutorials, and more.

Resources for educators: www.adobe.com/education and http://edex.adobe.com offer a treasure trove of information for instructors who teach classes on Adobe software. Find solutions for education at all levels, including free curricula that use an integrated approach to teaching Adobe software and can be used to prepare for the Adobe Certified Associate exams.

Also check out these useful links:

Adobe Marketplace & Exchange: www.adobe.com/cfusion/exchange is a central resource for finding tools, services, extensions, code samples, and more to supplement and extend your Adobe products.

Adobe Flash Professional CC product home page: www.adobe.com/products/flash

Adobe Labs: labs.adobe.com gives you access to early builds of cutting-edge technology, as well as forums where you can interact with both the Adobe development teams building that technology and other like-minded members of the community.

Adobe Certification

The Adobe training and certification programs are designed to help Adobe customers improve and promote their product-proficiency skills. There are four levels of certification:

- Adobe Certified Associate (ACA)
- Adobe Certified Expert (ACE)
- Adobe Certified Instructor (ACI)
- Adobe Authorized Training Center (AATC)

The Adobe Certified Associate (ACA) credential certifies that individuals have the entry-level skills to plan, design, build, and maintain effective communications using different forms of digital media.

The Adobe Certified Expert program is a way for expert users to upgrade their credentials. You can use Adobe certification as a catalyst for getting a raise, finding a job, or promoting your expertise.

If you are an ACE-level instructor, the Adobe Certified Instructor program takes your skills to the next level and gives you access to a wide range of Adobe resources.

Adobe Authorized Training Centers offer instructor-led courses and training on Adobe products, employing only Adobe Certified Instructors. A directory of AATCs is available at partners.adobe.com.

For information on the Adobe Certified programs, visit www.adobe.com/support/certification/main.html.

1

GETTING ACQUAINTED

Lesson Overview

In this lesson, you'll learn how to do the following:

- Create a new file in Flash

- Adjust Stage settings and document properties

- Add layers to the Timeline

- Manage keyframes in the Timeline

- Work with imported images in the Library panel

- Move and reposition objects on the Stage

- Open and work with panels

- Select and use tools in the Tools panel

- Preview your Flash animation

- Save your Flash file

- Access online resources for Flash

 This lesson will take less than 1 hour to complete. Copy the Lesson01 folder, which contains the images you'll use in this lesson, onto your hard drive if it's not already there. Download the project files for this lesson from the Lesson & Update Files tab on your Account page at www.peachpit.com and store them on your computer in a convenient location, as described in the Getting Started section of this book. Your Accounts page is also where you'll find any updates to the chapters or to the lesson files. Look on the Lesson & Update Files tab to access the most current content.

In Flash, the Stage is where the action takes place,
the Timeline organizes frames and layers, and other
panels let you edit and control your creation.

Starting Flash and Opening a File

● **Note:** If you have not already downloaded the project files for this lesson to your computer from your Account page, make sure to do so now. See "Getting Started" at the beginning of the book.

● **Note:** You can also start Flash by double-clicking a Flash file (*.fla or *.xfl), such as the 01End.fla file that is provided to show you the completed project.

The first time you start Flash you'll see a Welcome screen with links to standard file templates, tutorials, and other resources. In this lesson, you'll create a simple animation to showcase a few vacation snapshots. You'll add photos and a title, and in the process you'll learn about positioning elements on the Stage and placing them along the Timeline. You'll begin learning how to use the Stage to organize your visual elements spatially, and how to use the Timeline to organize your elements temporally.

1   Start Adobe Flash Professional. In Windows, choose Start > Programs > Adobe Flash Professional CC. In Mac OS, click Adobe Flash CC in the Adobe Flash CC folder in the Applications folder.

2   Choose File > Open. In the Open dialog box, select the 01End.fla file in the Lesson01/01End folder and click Open to see the final project.

3   Choose File > Publish.

Flash creates the necessary files (an HTML file and a SWF) to display the final animation in a browser. The files are saved in the same folder as an .fla file.

4   Double-click the HTML file.

An animation plays. During the animation, several overlapping photos appear one by one, ending with a title.

5   Close the browser.

Creating a New Document

You'll create the simple animation that you just previewed by starting a new document.

1   In Flash, choose File > New.

The New Document dialog box opens.

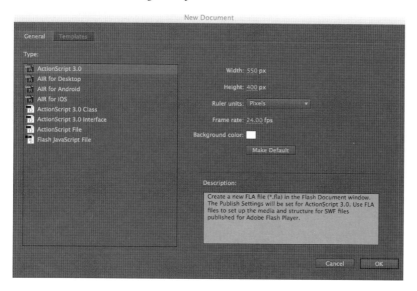

2   Under the General tab, choose ActionScript 3.0.

ActionScript 3.0 is the latest version of Flash's scripting language, which you use to add interactivity. In this lesson, you will not be working with ActionScript, but choosing ActionScript 3.0 creates a new document configured for playback in a desktop browser (such as Chrome, Safari, or Firefox) with Flash Player.

The other options target alternative playback environments. For example, AIR for Android and AIR for iOS create new documents configured for playback with AIR on an Android or an Apple mobile device.

3   On the right-hand side of the dialog box, you can choose the dimensions of the Stage by entering new pixel values for the Width and Height. Enter **800** for Width and **600** for Height. Keep the Ruler units as Pixels.

Leave the Frame rate and Background color for the Stage at their default settings. You can always edit these document properties, as explained later in this lesson.

● **Note:** This latest version of Flash supports only ActionScript 3.0. If you need ActionScript 1.0 or 2.0, you must work with previous versions of the software.

4 Click OK.

Flash creates a new ActionScript 3.0 file with all the specified settings.

5 Choose File > Save. Name the file **01_workingcopy.fla**, and from the File Format/Save as type pull-down menu, choose Flash document (*.fla). Save it in the 01Start folder. Saving your file right away is a good working habit that ensures your work won't be lost if the application or your computer crashes. You should always save your Flash file with the extension .fla (or .xfl if you save it as a Flash Uncompressed Document) to identify it as the Flash source file.

Getting to Know the Workspace

The Adobe Flash Professional work area includes the command menus at the top of the screen and a variety of tools and panels for editing and adding elements to your movie. You can create all the objects for your animation in Flash, or you can import elements you've created in Adobe Illustrator, Adobe Photoshop, Adobe After Effects, or other compatible applications.

By default, Flash displays the menu bar, Timeline, Stage, Tools panel, Properties inspector, Edit bar, and a few other panels. As you work in Flash, you can open, close, dock, undock, and move panels around the screen to fit your work style or your screen resolution.

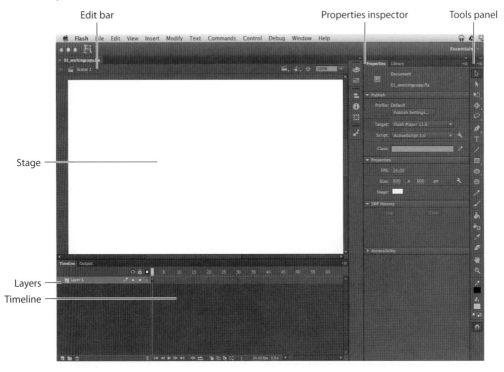

Choosing a new workspace

Flash also provides a few preset panel arrangements that may better suit the needs of particular users. The various workspace arrangements are listed in a pull-down menu at the top right of the Flash workspace or in the top menu under Window > Workspaces.

1　Click the Essentials button at the top right of the Flash workspace and choose a new workspace.

The various panels are rearranged and resized according to their importance in the chosen workspace. For example, the Animator and Designer workspaces put the Timeline at the top for easy and frequent access.

2　If you've moved some of the panels around and want to return to one of the prearranged workspaces, choose Window > Workspaces > Reset and the name of the preset workspace.

3　To return to the default workspace, choose Window > Workspaces > Essentials. In this Classroom in a Book, we'll be using the Essentials workspace.

Saving your workspace

If you find an arrangement of panels that suits your style of work, you can save it as a custom workspace and return to it at a later date.

1　Click the Essentials button at the top-right corner of the Flash workspace and choose New Workspace.

The New Workspace dialog box appears.

2 Enter a name for your new workspace. Click OK.

Flash saves the current arrangement of panels and adds it to the options in the Workspace pull-down menu, which you can access at any time.

About the Stage

The big white rectangle in the middle of your screen is called the Stage. As with a theater stage, the Stage in Flash is the area that viewers see when a movie is playing. It contains the text, images, and video that appear on the screen. Move elements on and off the Stage to place them in and out of view. You can use the rulers (View > Rulers) or grids (View > Grid > Show Grid) to help you position items on the Stage. Additionally, you can use the Align panel and other tools you'll learn about in the lessons in this book.

By default, you'll see the gray area off the Stage where you can place elements that won't be visible to your audience. The gray area is called the Pasteboard. To just see the Stage, choose View > Pasteboard to deselect the option. For now, leave the option selected.

To scale the Stage so that it fits completely in the application window, choose View > Magnification > Fit in Window. You can also choose different magnification view options from the pop-up menu just above the Stage.

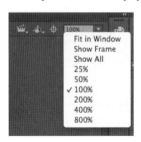

Changing the Stage properties

Now you'll change the color of the Stage. The Stage color, along with other document properties such as the Stage dimensions and frame rate, are available in the Properties inspector, which is the vertical panel just to the right of the Stage.

1 At the bottom of the Properties inspector, note that the dimensions of the current Stage are set at 800 x 600 pixels, which you chose when you created the new document.

2 Click the Background color button next to Stage and choose a new color from the color palette. Choose dark gray (#333333).

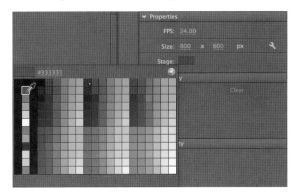

Your Stage is now a different color. You can change the Stage properties at any time.

Working with the Library Panel

The Library panel is accessible from a tab just to the right of the Properties inspector. The Library panel is where you store and organize symbols created in Flash, as well as imported files, including bitmaps, graphics, sound files, and video clips. Symbols are graphics used frequently for animation and for interactivity.

● **Note:** You'll learn much more about symbols in Lesson 3.

About the Library panel

The Library panel lets you organize library items in folders, see how often an item is used in a document, and sort items by type. When you import items into Flash, you can import them directly onto the Stage or into the library. However, any item you import onto the Stage is also added to the library, as are any symbols you create. You can then easily access the items to add them to the Stage again, edit them, or see their properties.

To display the Library panel, choose Window > Library, or press Ctrl+L (Windows) or Command+L (Mac).

Importing an item to the Library panel

Often, you'll create graphics directly with Flash's drawing tools and save them as symbols, which are stored in the library. Other times you'll import media such as JPEG images or MP3 sound files, which are also stored in the library. In this lesson, you'll import several JPEG images into the library to be used in the animation.

1   Choose File > Import > Import to Library. In the Import to Library dialog box, select the background.jpg file in the Lesson01/01Start folder, and click Open.

Flash imports the selected JPEG image and places it in the Library panel.

2   Continue importing photo1.jpg, photo2.jpg, and photo3.jpg from the 01Start folder. Don't import the last image, photo4.jpg. You'll use that image later in this lesson.

You can also hold down the Shift key to select multiple files and import all of the images at once.

3   The Library panel displays all the imported JPEG images with their filenames and a thumbnail preview. These images are now available to be used in your Flash document.

Adding an item from the Library panel to the Stage

To use an imported image, simply drag it from the Library panel onto the Stage.

1 Choose Window > Library to open the Library panel if it isn't already open.

2 Select the background.jpg item in the Library panel.

3 Drag the background.jpg item onto the Stage and place it approximately in the center of the Stage.

● **Note:** You can also choose File > Import > Import to Stage, or press Ctrl+R (Windows) or Command+R (Mac) to import an image file to the Library and put it on the Stage all in one step.

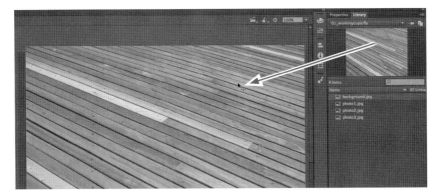

Understanding the Timeline

The Timeline is located below the Stage. Like films, Flash documents measure time in frames. As the movie plays, the playhead, shown as a red vertical line, advances through the frames in the Timeline. You can change the content on the Stage for different frames. To display a frame's content on the Stage, move the playhead to that frame in the Timeline.

At the bottom of the Timeline, Flash indicates the selected frame number, the current frame rate (how many frames play per second), and the time that has elapsed so far in the movie.

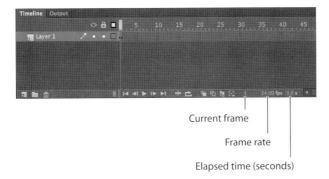

Current frame

Frame rate

Elapsed time (seconds)

The Timeline also contains layers, which help you organize the artwork in your document. At the moment, your project only has one layer, which is called Layer 1. Think of layers as multiple film strips stacked on top of one another. Each layer can contain a different image that appears on the Stage, and you can draw and edit objects on one layer without affecting objects on another layer. The layers are stacked in the order in which they overlap each other, so that objects on the bottom layer in the Timeline are on the bottom of the stack on the Stage. You can hide, lock, or show the contents of layers as outlines by clicking the dots in the layer under the layer option icons.

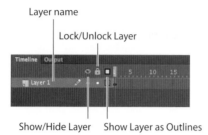

Renaming a layer

It's a good idea to separate your content on different layers and name each layer to indicate its contents so that you can easily find the layer you need later.

1 Select the existing layer in the Timeline, called Layer 1.

2 Double-click the name of the layer to rename it and type **background**.

3 Click outside the name box to apply the new name.

4 Click the dot below the lock icon to lock the layer. Locking a layer prevents you from accidentally making changes to it.

The pencil icon with a diagonal slash that appears after the layer name indicates that you can't make edits to the layer because it is locked.

Adding a layer

A new Flash document contains only one layer, but you can add as many layers as you need. Objects in the top layers will overlap objects in the bottom layers.

1   Select the background layer in the Timeline.

2   Choose Insert > Timeline > Layer. You can also click the New Layer button below the Timeline. A new layer appears above the background layer.

3   Double-click the new layer to rename it and type **photo1**. Click outside the name box to apply the new name.

Your Timeline now has two layers. The background layer contains the background photo, and the newly created photo1 layer above it is empty.

4   Select the top layer called photo1.

5   Choose Window > Library to open the Library panel if it isn't already open.

6   Drag the library item called photo1.jpg from the library onto the Stage.

The photo1 JPEG appears on the Stage and overlaps the background JPEG.

7   Choose Insert > Timeline > Layer, or click the New Layer button () below the
     Timeline to add a third layer.

8   Rename the third layer **photo2**.

Working with Layers

If you don't want a layer, you can easily delete it by selecting it, and then clicking
the Delete button below the Timeline.

If you want to rearrange your layers, simply click and drag any layer to move it to a
new position in the layer stack.

Inserting frames

So far, you have a background photo and another overlapping photo on the Stage,
but your entire animation exists for only a single frame. To create more time on the
Timeline, you must add additional frames.

1   Select frame 48 in the background layer.

2 Choose Insert > Timeline > Frame (F5). You can also right-click/Ctrl-click and choose Insert Frame from the context menu that pops up.

Flash adds frames in the background layer up to the selected frame, frame 48.

3 Select frame 48 in the photo1 layer.

4 Choose Insert > Timeline > Frame (F5). You can also right-click/Ctrl-click and choose Insert Frame from the context menu.

Flash adds frames in the photo1 layer up to the selected frame, frame 48.

5 Select frame 48 in the photo2 layer and insert frames on this layer.

You now have three layers, all with 48 frames on the Timeline. Since the frame rate of your Flash document is 24 frames per second, your current animation lasts 2 seconds.

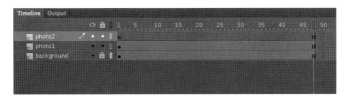

Selecting Multiple Frames

Just as you can hold down the Shift key to select multiple files on your desktop, you can hold down the Shift key to select multiple frames on the Flash Timeline. If you have several layers and want to insert frames into all of them, hold down the Shift key and click and drag where you want to add frames. Then choose Insert > Timeline > Frame.

Creating a keyframe

A keyframe indicates a change in content on the Stage. Keyframes are indicated on the Timeline as a circle. An empty circle means there is nothing in that particular layer at that particular time. A filled-in black circle means there is something in that particular layer at that particular time. The background layer, for example, contains a filled keyframe (black circle) in the first frame. The photo1 layer also contains a filled keyframe in its first frame. Both layers contain photos. The photo2 layer, however, contains an empty keyframe in the first frame, indicating that it is currently empty.

Empty keyframe

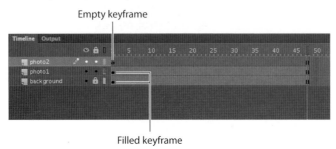

Filled keyframe

You'll insert a keyframe in the photo2 layer at the point in time when you want the next photo to appear.

1 Select frame 24 on the photo2 layer. As you select a frame, Flash displays the frame number beneath the Timeline.

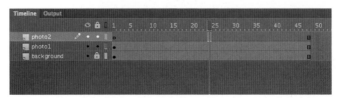

2 Choose Insert > Timeline > Keyframe (F6).

A new keyframe, indicated by an empty circle, appears in the photo2 layer in frame 24.

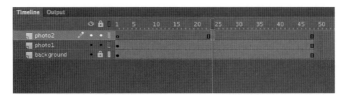

3 Select the new keyframe at frame 24 in the photo2 layer.

4 Drag photo2.jpg from your library onto the Stage.

The empty circle at frame 24 becomes filled, indicating that there is now content in the photo2 layer. At frame 24, your photo appears on the Stage. You can click and drag the red playhead from the top of the Timeline to "scrub," or show what's happening on the Stage at any point along the Timeline. You'll see that the background photo and photo1 remain on the Stage throughout the Timeline, but photo2 appears only at frame 24.

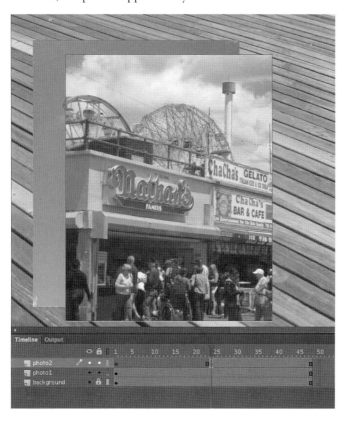

Understanding frames and keyframes is essential for mastering Flash. Be sure you understand how the photo2 layer contains 48 frames with 2 keyframes—an empty keyframe at frame 1 and a filled keyframe at frame 24.

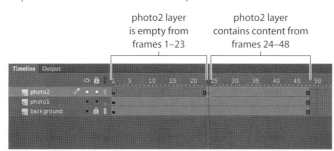

Moving a keyframe

If you want your photo2.jpg to appear later or earlier, you need to move the keyframe in which it appears later or earlier along the Timeline. You can easily move any keyframe along the Timeline by simply selecting it, and then dragging it to a new position.

1   Select the keyframe in frame 24 on the photo2 layer.

2   Move your mouse cursor slightly, and you'll see a box icon appear near your cursor indicating that you can reposition the keyframe.

3   Click and drag the keyframe to frame 12 in the photo2 layer.

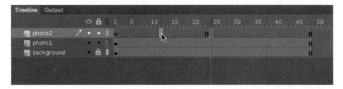

The photo2.jpg now appears on the Stage much earlier in the animation.

Removing Keyframes

If you want to remove a keyframe, do not press the Delete key! Doing so will delete the contents of that keyframe on the Stage. Instead, select the keyframe and choose Modify > Timeline > Clear Keyframe (Shift+F6). Your keyframe will be removed from the Timeline.

Organizing Layers in a Timeline

At this point, your working Flash file has only three layers: a background layer, a photo1 layer, and a photo2 layer. You'll be adding additional layers for this project, and as in most other projects, you'll end up having to manage multiple layers. Layer folders help you group related layers to keep your Timeline organized and manageable, just like you make folders for related documents on your desktop. Although it may take some time to create the folders, you'll save time later because you'll know exactly where to look for a specific layer.

Creating layer folders

For this project, you'll continue to add layers for additional photos, and you'll place those layers in a layer folder.

1 Select the photo2 layer and click the New Layer button at the bottom of the Timeline ().

2 Name the layer **photo3**.

3 Insert a keyframe at frame 24.

4 Drag the photo3.jpg from the library onto the Stage.

   You now have four layers. The top three contain photos of scenes from Coney Island that appear at different keyframes.

5 Select the photo3 layer and click the New Folder icon at the bottom of the Timeline ().

   A new layer folder appears above the photo3 layer.

6 Name the folder **photos**.

Adding layers to layer folders

Now you'll add the photo layers to the photo folder. As you arrange layers, remember that Flash displays the content in the layers in the order in which they appear in the Timeline, with the top layer's content at the front and the bottom layer's content at the back.

1 Drag the photo1 layer into the photos folder.

Notice how the bold line indicates the destination of your layer. When you place a layer inside a folder, Flash indents the layer name.

2 Drag the photo2 layer into the photos folder.

3 Drag the photo3 layer into the photos folder.

All three photo layers should be in the photos folder.

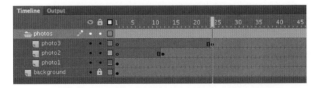

You can collapse the folder by clicking the arrow just to the left of the folder name. Expand the folder by clicking the arrow again. Be aware that if you delete a layer folder, you delete all the layers inside that folder as well.

Changing the appearance of the Timeline

You can adjust the Timeline's appearance to accommodate your workflow. When you want to see more layers, select Short from the Frame View pop-up menu in the upper-right corner of the Timeline. The Short option decreases the height of frame cell rows. The Preview and Preview in Context options display thumbnail versions of the contents of your keyframes in the Timeline.

You can also change the width of the frame cells by selecting Tiny, Small, Normal, Medium, or Large.

Cut, Copy, Paste, and Duplicate Layers

When managing multiple layers and layer folders, you can rely on cut, copy, paste, and duplicate layer commands to make your workflow easier and more efficient. All the properties of the selected layer are copied and pasted, including its frames, keyframes, any animation, and even the layer name and type. You can also copy and paste layer folders and their contents.

To cut or copy any layer or layer folder, simply select the layer and right-click/Ctrl-click the layer. In the contextual menu that appears, choose Cut Layers or Copy Layers.

Right-click/Ctrl-click on the Timeline again, and choose Paste Layers. The layer or layers that you cut or copied are pasted into the Timeline. Use Duplicate Layers to copy and paste in one operation.

You can also Cut, Copy, Paste, or Duplicate layers from the top Flash menu. Choose Edit > Timeline > and choose Cut Layers, Copy Layers, Paste Layers, or Duplicate Layers.

Using the Properties Inspector

The Properties inspector gives you quick access to the attributes you're most likely to need. What appears in the Properties inspector depends on what you've selected. For example, if nothing is selected, the Properties inspector includes options for the general Flash document, including changing the Stage color or dimensions; if you've selected an object on the Stage, the Properties inspector shows its x and y coordinates and its width and height, among other information. You'll use the Properties inspector to move your photos on the Stage.

Positioning an object on the Stage

You'll begin by moving the photos with the Properties inspector. You'll also use the Transform panel to rotate the photos.

1 At frame 1 of the Timeline, select the photo1.jpg image that you dragged onto the Stage in the photo1 layer. A blue outline indicates that the object is selected.

● **Note:** If the Properties inspector is not open, choose Window > Properties, or press Ctrl+F3 (Windows)/ Command+F3 (Mac OS).

2 In the Properties inspector, type **50** for the X value and **50** for the Y value. Press Enter (Windows)/Return (Mac OS) to apply the values. You can also click and drag your mouse cursor over the X and Y values to change their values. The photo moves to the left side of the Stage.

The X and Y values are measured on the Stage from the top-left corner. X begins at 0 and increases to the right, and Y begins at 0 and increases downward. The registration point (the point from which Flash makes measurements) for imported photos is at the top-left corner.

3 Choose Window > Transform to open the Transform panel.

4 In the Transform panel, select Rotate, and type **-12** in the Rotate box, or click and drag over the value to change the rotation. Press Enter (Windows)/Return (Mac OS) to apply the value.

The selected photo on the Stage rotates 12 degrees counterclockwise.

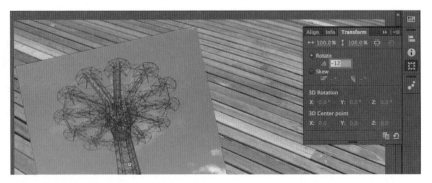

5 Select frame 12 of the photo2 layer. Now click on the photo2.jpg on the Stage.

6   Use the Properties inspector and Transform panel to position and rotate the second photo in an interesting way. Use X=**80**, Y=**50**, and a Rotate of **6** to give it some contrast with the first photo.

7   Select frame 24 in the photo3 layer. Now click on photo3.jpg on the Stage.

8   Use the Properties inspector and Transform panel to position and rotate the third photo in an interesting way. Use X=**120**, Y=**55**, and a Rotate of **−2** so all your photos have visual variety.

● **Note:** When images are scaled or rotated in Flash, they may appear jagged. You can smooth them out by double-clicking the bitmap icon in the Library panel. In the Bitmap Properties dialog box that appears, select the Allow Smoothing option.

Working with Panels

Just about everything you do in Flash involves a panel. In this lesson, you use the Library panel, Tools panel, Properties inspector, Transform panel, History panel, and the Timeline. In later lessons, you'll use the Actions panel, the Color panel, the Align panel, and other panels that let you control various aspects of your project. Because panels are such an integral part of the Flash workspace, it pays to know how to manage them.

To open any panel in Flash, choose its name from the Window menu.

By default, the Properties inspector, Library panel, and Tools panel appear together at the right of the screen; the Timeline is at the bottom; and the Stage is on the top. However, you can move a panel to any position that is convenient for you.

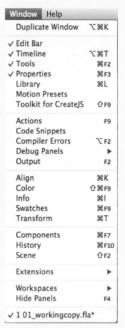

- To undock a panel from the right side of the screen, drag it by its tab to a new location.

- To dock a panel, drag it by its tab into the dock at a new position on the screen. You can drag it to the top, bottom, or in between other panels. A blue highlight indicates where you can dock a panel.

- To group a panel with another, drag its tab onto the other panel's tab.

- To move a panel group, drag the group by its dark gray top bar.

You also have the option of displaying most of the panels as icons to save space but still maintain quick access. Click the double arrowheads at the upper right to collapse the panels to icons. Click the double arrowheads again to expand the panels.

Using the Tools Panel

The Tools panel—the long, narrow panel on the far right side of the work area—contains selection tools, drawing and type tools, painting and editing tools, navigation tools, and tool options. You'll use the Tools panel frequently to switch to tools designed for the task at hand. Most often, you'll use the Selection tool, which is the black arrow tool at the top of the Tools panel, for selecting and clicking on items on the Stage or the Timeline. When you select a tool, check the options area at the bottom of the panel for more options and other settings appropriate for your task.

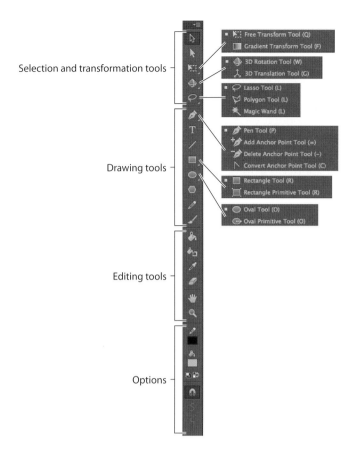

Selection and transformation tools

- Free Transform Tool (Q)
- Gradient Transform Tool (F)
- 3D Rotation Tool (W)
- 3D Translation Tool (G)
- Lasso Tool (L)
- Polygon Tool (L)
- Magic Wand (L)

Drawing tools

- Pen Tool (P)
- Add Anchor Point Tool (=)
- Delete Anchor Point Tool (-)
- Convert Anchor Point Tool (C)
- Rectangle Tool (R)
- Rectangle Primitive Tool (R)
- Oval Tool (O)
- Oval Primitive Tool (O)

Editing tools

Options

Selecting and using a tool

When you select a tool, the options available at the bottom of the Tools panel and the Properties inspector change. For example, when you select the Rectangle tool, the Object Drawing mode and Snap To Objects options appear. When you select the Zoom tool, the Enlarge and Reduce options appear.

The Tools panel contains too many tools to display all at once. Some tools are arranged in hidden groups in the Tools panel; only the tool you last selected from a group is displayed. A small triangle in the lower-right corner of the tool's button indicates that there are other tools in the group. Click and hold the icon for the visible tool to see the other tools available, and then select one from the pop-up menu.

You'll use the Text tool to add a title to your animation.

1 Select the top layer folder in the Timeline, and then click the New Layer button.

2 Name the new layer **text**.

3 Lock the other layers below it so you don't accidentally move anything into them.

4 In the Timeline, move the playhead to frame 36 and select frame 36 in the text layer.

5 Choose Insert > Timeline > Keyframe (F6) to insert a new keyframe at frame 36 in the text layer.

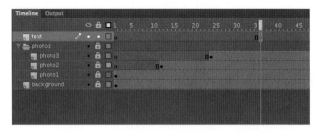

You will create text to appear at frame 36 in this layer.

6 In the Tools panel, select the Text tool, which is indicated by the large capital letter T ( ).

7 In the Properties inspector, choose Static Text from the pull-down menu.

Static Text is a mode for adding simple text used for display (read-only) purposes. Dynamic and Input Text are special text options for more interactive purposes and can be controlled with ActionScript.

8 Select a font and size in the Properties inspector. Your computer may not have the same fonts as those shown in this lesson, but choose one that is close in appearance.

9 Click the colored square in the Properties inspector to choose a text color. You can click on the color wheel at the upper right to access the Adobe Color Picker, or you can change the Alpha percentage at the upper right, which determines the level of transparency.

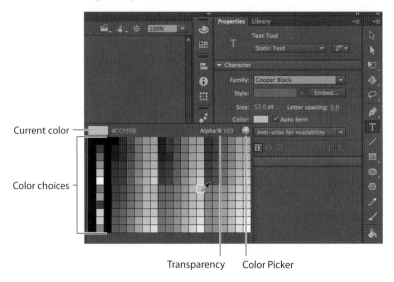

10 Make sure the empty keyframe in frame 36 of the title layer is selected, and then click on the Stage where you want to begin adding text. You can either click once and begin typing, or you can click and drag to define the width of your text field.

11 Type a title that describes the photos that are being displayed on the Stage.

12 Exit the Text tool by selecting the Selection tool (🔖).

13 Use the Properties inspector or the Transform panel to reposition or rotate your text on the Stage, if desired. Or, choose the Selection tool and simply drag your text to a new position on the Stage. The X and Y values in the Properties inspector update as you drag the text around the Stage.

14 Your animation for this lesson is finished! Compare Timeline in your file with the Timeline in the final file, 01End.fla.

Undoing Steps in Flash

In a perfect world, everything would go according to plan. But sometimes you need to move back a step or two and start over. You can undo steps in Flash using the Undo command or the History panel.

To undo a single step in Flash, choose Edit > Undo or press Ctrl+Z (Windows)/ Command+Z (Mac OS). To redo a step you've undone, choose Edit > Redo.

The easiest way to undo multiple steps in Flash is to use the History panel, which displays a list of all the last 100 steps you've performed. Closing a document clears its history. To access the History panel, choose Window > History.

For example, if you aren't satisfied with the newly added text, you can undo your work and return your Flash document to a previous state.

1   Choose Edit > Undo to undo the last action you made. You can choose the Undo command multiple times to move backward as many steps as are listed in the History panel. You can change the maximum number of Undo commands by selecting Flash > Preferences.

2   Choose Window > History to open the History panel.

3   Drag the History panel slider up to the step just before your mistake. Steps below that point are dimmed in the History panel and are removed from the project. To add a step back, move the slider back down.

● **Note:** If you remove steps in the History panel and then perform additional steps, the removed steps will no longer be available.

Previewing Your Movie

As you work on a project, it's a good idea to preview it frequently to ensure that you're achieving the desired effect. To quickly see how an animation or movie will appear to a viewer, choose Control > Test Movie > in Flash Professional. You can also press Ctrl+Enter (Windows) or Command+Return (Mac OS) to preview your movie.

1 Choose Control > Test Movie > in Flash Professional.

   Flash creates a SWF file in the same location as your FLA file and opens and plays the file in a separate window. A SWF file is the compressed, published file that you would upload to the Web to play in a browser on the desktop.

   Flash automatically loops your movie in this preview mode. If you don't want the movie to loop, choose Control > Loop Playback to deselect the option.

2 Close the preview window.

3 Click on the Stage with the Selection tool. Note at the bottom of the Properties inspector that the SWF History displays and keeps a log of the file size, date, and time of the most recent SWF file published. This will help you keep track of your work progress and revisions.

Modifying the Content and Stage

When you first started this lesson, you created a new file with the Stage set at 800 pixels by 600 pixels. However, your client may later tell you that they want the animation in several different sizes to accommodate different layouts. For example, they'd like to create a smaller version with a different aspect ratio for a banner ad. Or, they may want to create a version that will run on AIR for Android devices, which has specific dimensions.

Fortunately, you can modify the Stage even after all your content is put in place. When you change the Stage dimensions, Flash provides the option of scaling the content with the Stage, automatically shrinking or enlarging all your content proportionally.

Stage resizing and content scaling

You'll create another version of this animated project with different Stage dimensions.

1   At the bottom of the Properties inspector, note that the dimensions of the current Stage are set at 800 x 600 pixels. Click the Edit button next to the Stage size (the wrench icon).

The Document Settings dialog box appears.

2   In the Width and Height boxes, enter new pixel dimensions. Enter **400** for the Width and **300** for the Height.

Notice that as you enter new values for the Width and the Height, the option to Scale content with Stage becomes enabled.

3   Check the option to Scale content with Stage.

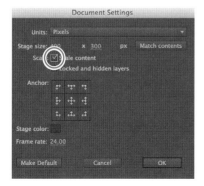

4   Leave the Anchor option as is.

The Anchor option lets you choose the origin from which your content is resized, if the proportions of the new Stage are different.

5   Click OK.

Flash modifies the dimensions of the Stage and automatically resizes all the content. If your new dimensions are not proportional to the original size, Flash will resize everything to maximize the content to fit. This means that if your new Stage size is wider than the original, there'll be extra Stage space to the right. If your new Stage size is taller than the original, there'll be extra Stage space on the bottom.

6   Choose File > Save As > Flash CS6 Document, and name the file **01_workingcopy_resized.fla**.

You now have two Flash files, identical in content but with different Stage dimensions. Close this file and reopen **01_workingcopy.fla** to continue this lesson.

Saving Your Movie

● **Note:** If you have unsaved changes in your open document, Flash adds an asterisk at the end of its filename at the top of the document window as a friendly reminder.

A mantra in multimedia production is "Save early, save often." Applications, operating systems, and hardware crash more often than anyone wants, and at unexpected and inconvenient times. You should always save your movie at regular intervals to ensure that, if a crash does happen, you won't have lost too much of your time.

Flash can help alleviate much of the worry over lost work. The Auto-Recovery feature creates a backup file in case of a crash.

Using Auto-Recovery for a backup

The Auto-Recovery feature is a preference set for the Flash application for all documents.

The Auto-Recovery feature saves a backup file, so that in case of a crash, you have an alternate file to return to.

1   Choose Flash > Preferences.

The Preferences dialog box appears.

2 Choose the General category from the left column.

3 Select the Auto-Recovery option, if it's not already selected, and enter a time (in minutes) for the interval that Flash creates a backup file.

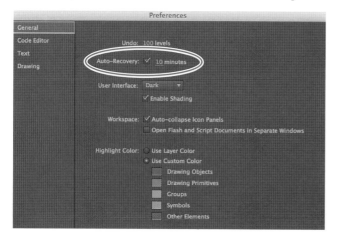

4 Click OK.

Flash creates a new file in the same location as your FLA with **RECOVER_** added to the beginning of the filename. The file remains as long as the document is open. When you close the document or when you quit Flash safely, the file is deleted.

Saving an XFL document

You've already saved your Flash movie as an FLA file, but you can also save your movie in an uncompressed format known as XFL. The XFL format is actually a folder of files rather than a single document. The XFL file format exposes the contents of your Flash movie so that other developers or animators can easily edit your file or manage its assets without having to open the movie in the Flash application. For example, all the imported photos in your Library panel appear in a Library folder within the XFL format. You can edit the library photos or swap them with new photos. Flash will make the substitutions in the movie automatically.

1 Open the 01_workingcopy.fla file. Choose File > Save As.

2 Name the file **01_workingcopy.xfl** and choose Flash Uncompressed Document
(*.xfl). Click Save.

Flash creates a folder named 01_workingcopy, which contains all the files for
your Flash movie.

3 Close the Flash document by choosing File > Close.

Modifying an XFL document

In this exercise, you'll modify the Library folder of the XFL document to make
changes to your Flash movie.

1 Open the LIBRARY folder inside the 01_workingcopy folder.

The folder contains all the photos you imported into your Flash movie.

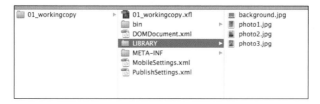

2 Select the photo3.jpg file and delete it.

3 Drag the photo4.jpg file from the 01Start folder and move it to the LIBRARY
folder inside the 01_workingcopy folder. Rename photo4.jpg as **photo3.jpg**.

Swapping out photo3.jpg with a new image in the LIBRARY folder
automatically makes the change in the Flash movie.

4 To open an XFL document, double-click the .xfl file.

The last image in keyframe 24 of your Timeline has been swapped with the photo4.jpg image with which you made the substitution.

Publishing Your Movie

When you're ready to share your movie with others, publish it from Flash. For some projects, that means posting an HTML file and a SWF file to the Web so your audience can view it in a desktop browser. For other projects, it may involve publishing an application file for your audience to download and view on a mobile device. Flash provides options to publish for a variety of platforms. You'll learn more about publishing options in Lesson 11.

For this lesson, you'll create an HTML file and a SWF file. The SWF file is your final Flash movie, and the HTML file tells the Web browser how to display the SWF file. You'll need to upload both files to the same folder on your Web server. Always test your movie after uploading it to be certain that it's working properly.

1 Choose File > Publish Settings, or click the Publish Settings button in the Profile section of the Properties inspector.

The Publish Settings dialog box appears. The output formats appear on the left, and their corresponding settings appear on the right.

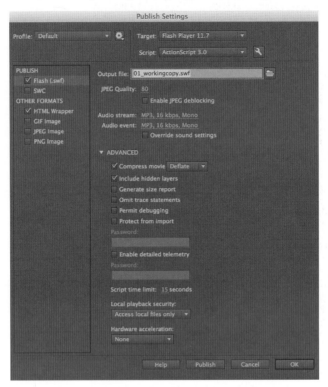

2 Select the Flash and HTML Wrapper check boxes if they are not already checked.

3 Select HTML Wrapper.

The options for the HTML file determine how the SWF file appears in the browser. For this lesson, keep all the default settings.

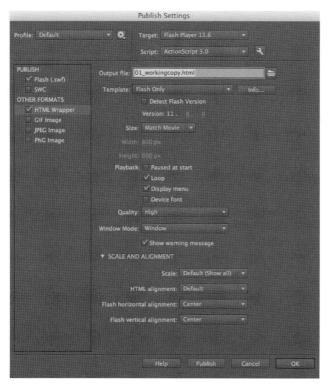

4 Click Publish at the bottom of the Publish Settings dialog box.

5 Click OK to close the dialog box.

6 Navigate to the Lesson01/01Start folder to see the files Flash created.

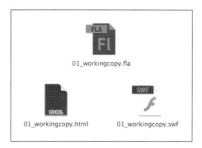

Finding Resources for Using Flash

● **Note:** If Flash detects that you're not connected to the Internet when you start the application, choosing Help > Flash Support Center opens the Help HTML pages installed with Flash. For more up-to-date information, view the Help files online or download the current PDF for reference.

For complete and up-to-date information about using Flash panels, tools, and other application features, visit the Adobe Web site. Choose Help > Flash Support Center.

You'll be connected to the Adobe Flash Professional Help site where you can search for answers in the support documents. There are links to helpful tutorials, forums, product guides, product updates, and more.

Don't be shy about going beyond the Adobe Web site and searching elsewhere on the Web for additional resources. There are numerous worldwide sites, blogs, and forums dedicated to Flash users, from beginner to advanced.

Checking for Updates

● **Note:** To set your preferences for future updates, choose Help > Updates, and then click Preferences in the Adobe Application Manager. Select the applications for which you want Adobe Application Manager to check for updates. Click OK to accept the new settings.

Adobe periodically provides updates to its Creative Cloud applications. You can easily obtain these updates through Adobe Application Manager, as long as you have an active Internet connection.

1 In Flash, choose Help > Updates.

   The Adobe Application Manager automatically checks for updates available for your Adobe software.

2 In the Adobe Application Manager dialog box, select the updates you want to install, and then follow the directions to proceed with the installation.

Review Questions

1 What is the Stage?

2 What's the difference between a frame and a keyframe?

3 What's a hidden tool, and how can you access it?

4 Name two methods to undo steps in Flash and describe them.

5 How can you find answers to questions you have about Flash?

Review Answers

1 The Stage is the rectangular area viewers see when a movie is playing. It contains the text, images, and video that appear on the screen. Objects that you store on the Pasteboard outside of the Stage do not appear in the movie.

2 A frame is used to measure time on the Timeline. A keyframe is represented on the Timeline with a circle and indicates a change in content on the Stage.

3 Because there are too many tools to display at once in the Tools panel, some tools are grouped, and only one tool in the group is displayed. (The tool you most recently used is the one shown.) Small triangles appear on tool icons to indicate that hidden tools are available. To select a hidden tool, click and hold the tool icon for the tool that is shown, and then select the hidden tool from the menu.

4 You can undo steps in Flash using the Undo command or the History panel. To undo a single step at a time, choose Edit > Undo. To undo multiple steps at once, drag the slider up in the History panel.

5 Choose Help > Flash Support Center to browse or search for information about using Flash Professional and ActionScript 3.0. Use the site as the launching-off point for free tutorials, tips, and other resources for Flash users.

2 WORKING WITH GRAPHICS

Lesson Overview

In this lesson, you'll learn how to do the following:

- Draw rectangles, ovals, and other shapes

- Understand the differences between drawing modes

- Modify the shape, color, and size of drawn objects

- Understand fill and stroke settings

- Create and edit curves

- Apply gradients and transparencies

- Group elements and convert art to bitmaps

- Create and edit text

- Add hyperlinks

- Distribute objects on the Stage

 This lesson will take approximately 90 minutes to complete. If needed, remove the previous lesson folder from your hard drive and copy the Lesson02 folder onto it. Download the project files for this lesson from the Lesson & Update Files tab on your Account page at www.peachpit.com and store them on your computer in a convenient location, as described in the Getting Started section of this book. Your Accounts page is also where you'll find any updates to the chapters or to the lesson files. Look on the Lesson & Update Files tab to access the most current content.

You can use rectangles, ovals, and lines to create interesting, complex graphics and illustrations in Flash. Edit their shapes and combine them with gradients, transparencies, text, and filters for even greater possibilities.

Getting Started

● **Note:** If you have not already downloaded the project files for this lesson to your computer from your Account page, make sure to do so now. See "Getting Started" at the beginning of the book.

Start by viewing the finished movie to see the animation you'll be creating in this lesson.

1 Double-click the 02End.html file in the Lesson02/02End folder to view the final project in a browser.

The project is a simple static illustration for a banner ad. This illustration is for Garden Court Cafe, a fictional company that's promoting its store and coffee. In this lesson, you'll draw the shapes, modify them, and learn to combine simple elements to create more complex visuals. You won't create any animation just yet. After all, you must learn to walk before you can run! And learning to create and modify graphics is an important step before doing any Flash animation.

2 In Flash, choose File > New. In the New Document dialog box, choose ActionScript 3.0.

3 On the right-hand side of the dialog box, make the Stage size **700** pixels by **200** pixels and make the color of the Stage a light brown by clicking the icon next to Background color, and then clicking on the **#CC9966** color swatch. Click OK.

4 Choose File > Save. Name the file **02_workingcopy.fla** and save it in the 02Start folder. Saving your file right away is a good working habit (even if you've enabled the Auto-Recovery feature). It ensures that you won't lose your work if the application or your computer crashes.

Understanding Strokes and Fills

Every graphic in Flash starts with a shape. A shape consists of two components: the *fill*, or the insides of the shape; and the *stroke*, or the outlines of the shape. If you always keep these two components in mind, you'll be well on your way to creating beautiful and complicated visuals.

The fill and the stroke function independently of each other, so you can modify or delete either without affecting the other. For example, you can create a rectangle with a blue fill and a red stroke, and then later change the fill to purple and delete the red stroke entirely. You'll be left with a purple rectangle without an outline. You can also move the fill or stroke independently, so if you want to move the entire shape, make sure that you select both its fill and stroke.

Creating Shapes

Flash includes several drawing tools, which work in different drawing modes. Many of your creations will begin with simple shapes such as rectangles and ovals, so it's important that you're comfortable drawing them, modifying their appearance, and applying fills and strokes.

You'll begin by drawing the cup of coffee.

Using the Rectangle tool

The coffee cup is essentially a cylinder, which is a rectangle with an oval at the top and an oval at the bottom. You'll start by drawing the rectangular body. It's useful to break down complicated objects into their component parts to make drawing them easier.

1 In the Tools panel, select the Rectangle tool ( ). Make sure the Object Drawing mode icon ( ) is *not* selected.

2 Choose a stroke color ( ) and a fill color ( ) from the bottom of the Tools panel. Choose #663300 (dark brown) for the stroke and #CC6600 (light brown) for the fill.

Note: Each color has a hexadecimal value in Flash, HTML, and many other applications. The six digits after the # sign represent the red, green, and blue contributions to the color.

3 On the Stage, draw a rectangle that is a little taller than it is wide. You'll specify the exact size and position of the rectangle in step 6.

4 Select the Selection tool ( ).

5 Drag the Selection tool around the entire rectangle to select its stroke and its fill. When a shape is selected, Flash displays it with white dots. You can also double-click a shape, and Flash will select both the stroke and fill of the shape.

6 In the Properties inspector, type **130** for the width and **150** for the height. Press Enter (Windows) or Return (Mac OS) to apply the values.

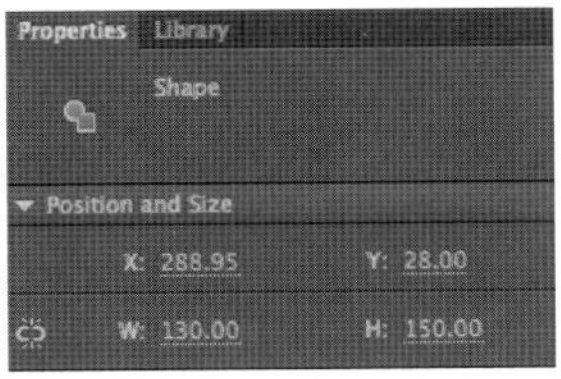

Using the Oval tool

Now you'll create the opening at the top and the rounded bottom.

1 In the Tools panel, choose the Oval tool.

Note: Flash applies the default fill and stroke to the rectangle and oval, which are determined by the last fill and stroke you applied.

2 Make sure the Snap to Objects option ( ) is enabled. This option forces shapes that you draw on the Stage to snap to each other to ensure that lines and corners connect to one another.

3 Click inside the rectangle and drag across it to make an oval inside the rectangle. The Snap to Objects option makes the sides of the oval connect to the sides of the rectangle.

4 Draw another oval near the bottom of the rectangle.

Making Selections

To modify an object, you must first be able to select different parts of it. In Flash, you can make selections using the Selection, Subselection, or Lasso tool. Typically, you use the Selection tool to select an entire object or a section of an object. The Subselection tool lets you select a specific point or line in an object. With the Lasso tool, you can make a freeform selection.

Selecting strokes and fills

Now you'll make the rectangle and ovals look more like a coffee cup. You'll use the Selection tool to delete unwanted strokes and fills.

1 In the Tools panel, select the Selection tool ( ).

2 Click the fill above the top oval to select it.

The shape above the top oval becomes highlighted.

3 Press the Delete key.

The shape is deleted.

4 Select each of the three line segments above the top oval and press the Delete key.

The individual strokes are deleted, leaving the top oval connected to the rectangle.

Note: Hold down the Shift key when making selections to select multiple fills or strokes together.

5 Now select the fill and strokes below the bottom oval, as well as the inside arc at the bottom of the cup, and press the Delete key.

The remaining shape appears as a cylinder.

Editing Shapes

When drawing in Flash, you'll often start with the Rectangle and Oval tools. But to create more complex graphics, you'll use other tools to modify those base shapes. The Free Transform tool, the Copy and Paste commands, and the Selection tool can help transform the plain cylinder into a coffee cup.

Using the Free Transform tool

The coffee cup will look more realistic if you taper the bottom rim. You'll use the Free Transform tool to change its overall shape. With the Free Transform tool, you can change an object's scale, rotation, or skew (the way it is slanted), or distort an object by dragging control points around a bounding box.

1   In the Tools panel, select the Free Transform tool ( ).

2   Drag the Free Transform tool around the cylinder on the Stage to select it.

    Transformation handles appear on the cylinder.

3   Press Ctrl+Shift (Windows)/Command+Shift (Mac OS) as you drag one of the lower corners inward. Holding these keys while dragging lets you move both corners the same distance simultaneously.

4   Click outside the shape to deselect it.

    The bottom of the cylinder is narrow, and the top is wide. It now looks more like a coffee cup.

Note: If you press the Alt or Option key while moving one of the control points, Flash scales the selected object relative to its transformation point, represented by the circle icon. You can move the transformation point anywhere, even outside the object. Press Shift to constrain the object proportions. Press Ctrl (Windows)/Command (Mac OS) to deform the object from a single control point.

Using Copy and Paste

Use Copy and Paste commands to easily duplicate shapes on the Stage. You'll set the surface level of the coffee by copying and pasting the top rim of the coffee cup.

1   Hold down the Shift key and select the top arc and bottom arc of the coffee cup opening.

2   Choose Edit > Copy (Ctrl/Command+C). The top strokes of the oval are copied.

3   Choose Edit > Paste in Center (Ctrl/Command+V).

    A duplicate oval appears on the Stage.

4   In the Tools panel, if necessary, select the Free Transform tool.

    Transformation handles appear on the oval.

5　Press the Shift key and the Alt/Option key as you drag the corners inward. Make the oval about 10 percent smaller. Pressing the Shift key lets you change the shape uniformly so the oval maintains its aspect ratio. Pressing the Alt/Option key changes the shape from its transformation point.

6　Select the Selection tool.

7　Drag the oval over the rim of the coffee cup so it overlaps the front lip.

8　Click outside the selection to deselect the oval.

9　Select the lower part of the smaller oval and delete it.

Your coffee cup now is filled with coffee!

Changing shape contours

With the Selection tool, you can push and pull lines and corners to change the overall contours of any shape. It's a fast and intuitive way of working with shapes.

1　In the Tools panel, select the Selection tool.

2　Move your mouse cursor close to one of the sides of the coffee cup.

A curved line appears near your cursor, indicating that you can change the curvature of the stroke.

3　Click and drag the stroke outward.

The sides of the coffee cup bend, giving the coffee cup a slight bulge.

● **Note:** Hold down the Alt/Option key while dragging the sides of a shape to add a new corner.

4　Click and drag the other side of the coffee cup outward slightly.

The coffee cup now has a more rounded body.

Changing strokes and fills

If you want to change the properties of any stroke or fill, you can use the Ink Bottle tool or the Paint Bucket tool. The Ink Bottle tool changes stroke colors; the Paint Bucket tool changes fill colors.

1 In the Tools panel, select the Paint Bucket tool ( ).

2 In the Properties inspector, choose a darker brown color (#663333).

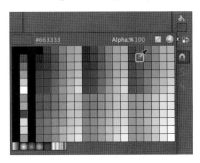

● **Note:** If your Paint Bucket tool changes the fill in surrounding areas, there may be a small gap that allows the fill to spill over. Close the gap, or at the bottom of the Tools panel, choose different gap sizes to close for your Paint Bucket tool.

3 Click the top surface of the coffee that is inside the cup.

   The fill of the top oval changes to the darker brown color.

4 In the Tools panel, select the Ink Bottle tool ( ).

5 In the Properties inspector, choose a darker brown color (#330000).

6 Click the top stroke above the surface of the coffee.

   The stroke around the surface of the coffee changes to a darker brown color.

● **Note:** You can also select a stroke or a fill and change its color in the Properties inspector without using the Paint Bucket or Ink Bottle tool.

Flash Drawing Modes

Flash provides three drawing modes that determine how objects interact with one another on the Stage and how you can edit them. By default, Flash uses Merge Drawing mode, but you can enable Object Drawing mode or use the Rectangle Primitive or Oval Primitive tool to use Primitive Drawing mode.

Merge Drawing mode

In this mode, Flash merges drawn shapes, such as rectangles and ovals, where they overlap, so that multiple shapes appear to be a single shape. If you move or delete a shape that has been merged with another, the overlapping portion is permanently removed.

Object Drawing mode

In this mode, Flash does not merge drawn objects; they remain distinct and separate, even when they overlap. To enable Object Drawing mode, select the tool you want to use, and then click the Object Drawing icon in the options area of the Tools panel.

To convert an object to shapes (Merge Drawing mode), select it and press Ctrl/Command+B. To convert a shape to an object (Object Drawing mode), select it and choose Modify > Combine Objects > Union.

Primitive Drawing mode

When you use the Rectangle Primitive tool or the Oval Primitive tool, Flash draws the shapes as separate objects. Unlike regular objects, however, you can modify the corner radius and start and end angle of rectangle primitives, and adjust the inner radius of oval primitives using the Properties inspector.

Using Gradient and Bitmap Fills

The *fill* is the interior of the drawn object. Currently, you have a solid tan color, but you can also have a gradient or a bitmap image (such as a JPEG file) as a fill, or you can specify that the object has no fill at all.

In a *gradient*, one color gradually changes into another. Flash can create *linear* gradients, which change color horizontally, vertically, or diagonally; or *radial* gradients, which change color moving outward from a central focal point.

For this lesson, you'll use a linear gradient fill to add three-dimensionality to the coffee cup. To give the appearance of a top layer of foaming cream, you'll import a bitmap image to use as the fill. You can import a bitmap file in the Color panel.

Creating gradient transitions

You'll define the colors you want to use in your gradient in the Color panel. By default, a linear gradient moves from one color to a second color, but you can use up to 15 color transitions in a gradient in Flash. A *color pointer* determines where the gradient changes from one color to the next. Add color pointers beneath the gradient definition bar in the Color panel to add color transitions.

You'll create a gradient that moves from tan to white to dark tan on the surface of the coffee cup to give it a rounded appearance.

1 Choose the Selection tool. Select the fill that represents the front surface of the coffee cup.

2 Open the Color panel (Window > Color). In the Color panel, choose the Fill color icon and select Linear gradient.

   The front surface of the coffee cup is filled with a color gradient from left to right.

3 Select the color pointer on the left of the color gradient in the Color panel (the triangle above it turns black when selected), and then type **FFCCCC** in the Hex value field to specify a light tan color. Press Enter/Return to apply the color. You can also choose a color from the color picker or double-click the color pointer to choose a color from the color swatches.

4 Select the far-right color pointer, and then enter **B86241** for a dark tan color. Press Enter/Return to apply the color.

The gradient fill for the coffee cup gradually changes from light tan to dark tan across its surface.

5 Click beneath the gradient definition bar to create a new color pointer.

6 Drag the new color pointer to the middle of the gradient.

7 Select the new color pointer, and then type **FFFFFF** in the Hex value field to specify white for the new color. Press Enter/Return to apply the color.

The gradient fill for the coffee cup gradually changes from light tan to white to dark tan.

8 Deselect the fill on the Stage by clicking elsewhere on the Stage. Choose the Paint Bucket tool and make sure the Lock Fill option (▣) at the bottom of the Tools panel is deselected.

The Lock Fill option locks the current gradient to the first shape to which it was applied so that subsequent shapes extend the gradient. You'll want a new gradient for the back surface of the coffee cup, so the Lock Fill option should be deselected.

9 With the Paint Bucket tool, select the back surface of the coffee cup.

Flash applies the gradient to the back surface.

● **Note:** To delete a color pointer from the gradient definition bar, simply drag it off the bar.

Using the Gradient Transform tool

In addition to choosing colors and positioning the color pointers for a gradient, you can adjust the size, direction, or center of a gradient fill. To squeeze the gradient in the front surface and reverse the gradient in the back surface, you'll use the Gradient Transform tool.

1 Select the Gradient Transform tool. (The Gradient Transform tool is grouped with the Free Transform tool.)

2 Click the front surface of the coffee cup. Transformation handles appear.

3 Drag the square handle on the side of the bounding box inward to squeeze the gradient tighter. Drag the center circle to move the gradient to the left so the white highlight is positioned slightly left of center.

4 Now click the back surface of the coffee cup. Transformation handles appear.

Note: Move the center circle to change the center of the gradient; drag the arrow circle to rotate the gradient; or drag the arrow in the square to stretch the gradient.

5   Drag the round handle on the corner of the bounding box to rotate the gradient 180 degrees so the gradient fades from dark tan to the left to white to light tan on the right.

The coffee cup now looks more realistic because the shadows and highlights make it appear that the front surface is convex and the back surface is concave.

Adding a bitmap fill

You'll make this cup of coffee a little fancier by adding a frothy layer of cream. You'll use a JPEG image of foam as a bitmap fill.

1   Select the top surface of the coffee with the Selection tool.

2   Choose Window > Color to open the Color panel.

3   Select Bitmap fill.

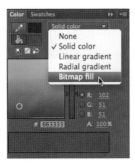

Note: You can also use the Gradient Transform tool to change the way a bitmap fill is applied.

4   In the Import to Library dialog box, navigate to the coffeecream.jpg file in the Lesson02/02Start folder.

5   Select the coffeecream.jpg file and click Open.

The top surface of the coffee fills with the foam image.

The cup of coffee is complete! Rename the layer containing your completed drawing **coffee cup**. All that's left to do is to add some bubbles and hot steam.

Grouping objects

Now that you're finished creating your cup of coffee, you can make it into a single group. A group holds together a collection of shapes and other graphics to preserve their integrity. When the elements that comprise the coffee cup are grouped, you can move them as a unit without worrying that the cup might merge with underlying shapes. Use groups to organize your drawing.

1   Choose the Selection tool.

2   Select all the shapes that make up the cup of coffee.

3   Choose Modify > Group.

The cup of coffee is now a single group. When you select it, a blue outline indicates its bounding box.

4   If you want to change any part of the cup of coffee, double-click the group to edit it.

Notice that all the other elements on the Stage dim, and the Edit bar above the Stage displays Scene 1 Group. This indicates that you are now in a particular group and can edit its contents.

5   Click the Scene 1 icon in the Edit bar at the top of the Stage, or double-click an empty part of the Stage, and return to the main scene.

● **Note:** To change a group back into its component shapes, choose Modify > Ungroup (Shift+Ctrl+G [Windows] or Shift+Command+G [Mac OS]).

Using Custom Line Styles

You can make many different styles of lines for your strokes. In addition to a solid line, you can choose dotted, dashed, or ragged, or even customize your own. In this lesson, you'll use the Pencil tool to create dashed lines to represent the aroma wafting off the coffee.

Adding decorative lines

You'll add some whimsical lines to your coffee illustration to give it some personality.

1   On the Timeline, insert a new layer and name it **coffee aroma**. You'll draw your lines in this layer.

2 In the toolbar, select the Pencil tool (). Choose the Smooth option at the bottom of the toolbar.

3 In the Properties inspector, choose a dark brown color, and for Style, choose Ragged.

Note: If you want more control over the style of your line, you can click the Edit button next to Style to experiment with the options in the Stroke Style dialog box.

Note: Limit the kinds of line styles you use in your Flash project. Custom strokes use more resources to draw and can decrease performance.

4 Draw a few wavy lines above the coffee.

Flash renders a ragged line pattern. Although it appears as though there are gaps in the line, the entire line is a single selectable stroke.

Converting vector art to bitmap art

Vector art, especially art with complex curves and many shapes and different line styles, can be processor-intensive, and can take its toll on mobile devices where performance suffers. An option called Convert to Bitmap provides a way to turn selected artwork on the Stage into a single bitmap, which can be less taxing on the processor.

Once you've converted the object to a bitmap, you can move it without worrying about it merging with underlying shapes. However, the graphics are no longer editable with Flash's editing tools.

1 Choose the Selection tool.

2 Select the wavy coffee aroma lines in the coffee aroma layer, and the coffee group in the coffee cup layer.

3 Choose Modify > Convert to Bitmap.

The cup of coffee and wavy lines become a single bitmap and the bitmap is stored in the Library panel.

Creating Curves

You've used the Selection tool to pull and push on the edges of shapes to intuitively make curves. For more precise control, you can use the Pen tool ( ).

Using the Pen tool

Now you'll create a soothing, wavelike background graphic.

1 Choose Insert > Timeline > Layer, and name the new layer **dark brown wave**.

2 Drag the layer to the bottom of the layer stack.

3 Lock all the other layers.

4 In the Tools panel, select the Pen tool ( ).

5 Set the Stroke color to a dark brown.

6 Begin your shape by clicking on the Stage to establish the first anchor point.

7 Click on another part of the Stage to indicate the next anchor point in your shape. When you want to create a smooth curve, click and drag with the Pen tool.

A handle appears from the anchor point, indicating the curvature of the line.

8 Continue clicking and dragging to build the outline of the wave. Make the wave wider than the Stage.

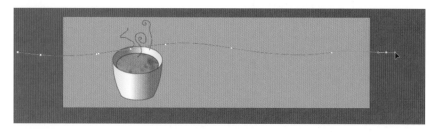

● **Note:** Don't worry about making all the curves perfect. It takes practice to get used to the Pen tool. You'll also have a chance to refine your curves in the next part of the lesson.

9 Close your shape by clicking on the first anchor point.

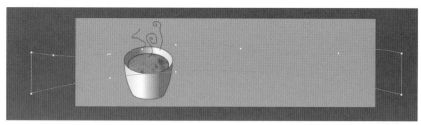

10 Select the Paint Bucket tool.

11 Set the Fill color to a dark brown.

12 Click inside the outline you just created to fill it with color and delete the stroke.

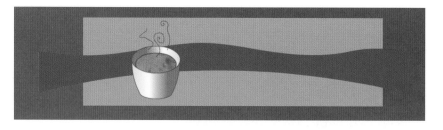

Editing curves with the Selection and Subselection tools

Your first try at creating smooth waves probably won't be very good. Use the Selection tool or the Subselection tool to refine your curves.

1 Choose the Selection tool.

2 Hover over a line segment and look at the curve that appears near your cursor. This indicates that you can edit the curve. If a corner appears near your cursor, this indicates that you can edit the vertex.

3 Drag the curve to edit its shape.

4 In the Tools panel, select the Subselection tool (⬧).

5 Click on the outline of the shape.

6 Drag the anchor points to new locations or move the handles to refine the overall shape.

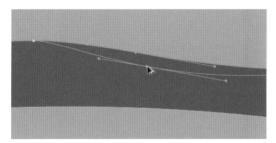

Deleting or adding anchor points

Use the hidden tools under the Pen tool to delete or add anchor points as needed.

1 Press and hold on the Pen tool to access the hidden tools under it.

2 Select the Delete Anchor Point tool (✎).

3 Click on an anchor point on the outline of the shape to delete it.

4 Select the Add Anchor Point tool (✎).

5 Click on the curve to add an anchor point.

Creating Transparencies

Next, you'll create a second wave to overlap the first wave. You'll make the second wave slightly transparent to create more overall depth. Transparency can be applied to either the stroke or the fill. Transparency is measured as a percentage and is referred to as alpha. An alpha of 100% indicates that a color is totally opaque, whereas an alpha of 0% indicates that a color is totally transparent.

Modifying the alpha value of a fill

1 Select the shape in the dark brown wave layer.

2 Choose Edit > Copy.

3 Choose Insert > Timeline > Layer, and name the new layer **light brown wave**.

4 Choose Edit > Paste in Place (Ctrl/Command+Shift+V).

   The Paste in Place command puts the copied item in the exact same position from where it was copied.

5 Choose the Selection tool and move the pasted shape slightly to the left or to the right so the crests of the waves are somewhat offset.

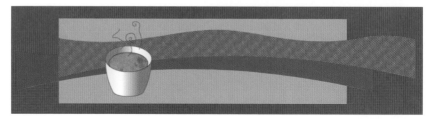

6 Select the fill of the shape in the light brown wave layer.

7 Choose Window > Color to open the Color panel. Set the fill color to a slightly different brown hue (CC6666), and then change the Alpha value to **50%**.

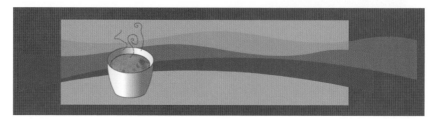

The color swatch in the Color panel previews your newly selected color. Transparencies are indicated by the gray grid that can be seen through the transparent color swatch.

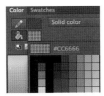

Note: You can also change the transparency of a shape from the Properties inspector by clicking the Fill Color icon and changing the Alpha value in the pop-up color menu.

Adding shadows

Transparent fills are effective for creating shadows, which can provide a sense of depth for your illustration. You'll add a cast shadow for your coffee mug and another decorative shadow at the bottom of the Stage.

1 Choose Insert > Timeline > Layer, and name the new layer **shadow**.

2 Choose Insert > Timeline > Layer again, and name the second new layer **big shadow**.

3 Drag the shadow layer and the big shadow layer to the bottom of the layer stack.

4 Choose the Oval tool.

5 For the Stroke, choose none, and for the Fill, choose a dark brown color (#663300) with a 15% Alpha value.

6 In the shadow layer, draw an oval that sits just under the coffee mug.

7 In the big shadow layer, draw a larger oval where its top edge covers the bottom of the Stage.

The overlapping transparent ovals add a rich, layered appearance to the illustration.

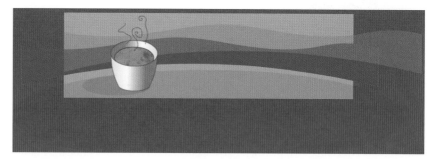

Creating and Editing Text

Now let's add text to complete this illustration. Flash has three text options: Static Text and two more advanced options, Dynamic Text and Input Text. Use Static Text for display. Use Dynamic or Input Text when you want to control the text with ActionScript. We won't cover those advanced functions in this book.

When you create static text on the Stage and publish your project, Flash automatically includes all the necessary fonts to display the text correctly. That means you don't have to worry about your audience having the required fonts to see the text as you intended it.

Using the Text tool

1 Select the top layer.

2 Choose Insert > Timeline > Layer, and name the new layer **text**.

3 Choose the Text tool (![T]).

4 In the Properties inspector, select Static Text.

5 Under the Character options, choose a font, style, size, and color that look appealing to you.

6 Under the Paragraph options, you have additional choices for formatting the text, such as justification or spacing. Choose values there or accept the defaults.

7 Click on the Stage and begin typing. Enter **Garden Court Cafe Taste the Difference**. Alternately, you can click and drag out a text box to define the maximum width of your text.

8 Exit the Text tool by choosing the Selection tool.

9 Add three more pieces of smaller text on the Stage in the same layer: **Coffee**, **Pastries**, and **Free Wi-Fi**.

Matching the color of an existing object

If you want to match a color exactly, you can use the Eyedropper tool ( ) to sample a fill or a stroke. After you click on an object with the Eyedropper tool, Flash automatically provides you with the Paint Bucket tool or the Ink Bottle tool with the selected color and associated properties that you can apply to another object.

You'll use the Eyedropper tool to sample the color of one of the decorative background waves and apply it to the three pieces of smaller text.

1 In the Tools panel, choose the Selection tool.

2 Hold down your Shift key and select all three of the smaller pieces of text; **Coffee**, **Pastries**, and **Free WiFi**.

3 Choose the Eyedropper tool.

4 Click on the fill of the shape in the dark brown wave layer.

The three selected pieces of text change color to match the fill of the dark brown wave layer. Using the same colors help to unify the composition.

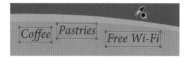 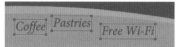

Adding hyperlinks

Adding hyperlinks to text makes your content interactive. Next, you'll add a hyperlink to the tagline in this coffee illustration to take readers to the coffee website.

1 Double-click the tagline and select the text, **Garden Court Cafe Taste the Difference**.

2 In the Properties inspector, expand the Options section, and enter a URL in the Link field. Make sure you begin with **http://** to load a site on the Web.

3 In the Target field, choose **_blank**.

The Target options determine where the URL loads. The URL loads in a blank browser window or tab, if you target **_blank**.

4 Exit the Text tool.

Flash underlines the text to show you that it is hyperlinked. The underline won't show in the final published SWF.

5 Choose Control > Test Movie > in Flash Professional.

Flash exports a SWF file and displays it in a new window.

6 Click on the hyperlinked tagline text.

Your default browser launches with the specified URL.

Aligning and Distributing Objects

Finally, let's tidy up the text so the layout is organized. Although you can use rulers (View > Rulers) and grids (View > Grid > Show Grid) to help position objects, you'll use the Align panel, which is more effective when you're dealing with multiple objects. You'll also rely on the smart guides that appear when you move objects around the Stage.

Aligning objects

The Align panel, as you might guess, aligns any number of selected objects horizontally or vertically. It can also distribute objects evenly.

1 Choose the Selection tool.

2 Select the first small piece of text, **Coffee**.

3 Move the text to the left until smart guides appear. Align the left edge of the selected text with the left edge of the larger text above it.

4 Select the third small piece of text, **Free Wi-Fi**.

5 Move the text to the right until smart guides appear. Align the right edge of the selected text with the right edge of the larger text above it.

6   Select all three small pieces of text.

You might have to lock the lower layers so you don't accidentally select the shapes in the lower layers.

7   Open the Align panel (Window > Align).

8   Deselect the Align to Stage option, if it is already selected. Click on the Align bottom edge button.

The bottom edges of the text become aligned.

 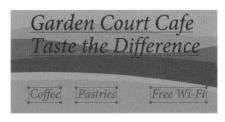

9   Click on the Space evenly horizontally button.

Flash moves the selected text so that the spaces between them become uniform.

Review Questions

1 What are the three drawing modes in Flash, and how do they differ?

2 How can you draw a perfect circle using the Oval tool?

3 When would you use each of the selection tools in Flash?

4 What does the Align panel do?

Review Answers

1 The three drawing modes are Merge Drawing mode, Object Drawing mode, and Primitive Drawing mode.

   • In Merge Drawing mode, shapes drawn on the Stage merge to become a single shape.

   • In Object Drawing mode, each object is distinct and remains separate, even when it overlaps another object.

   • In Primitive Drawing mode, you can modify the angles, radius, or corner radius of an object.

2 To draw a perfect circle, hold down the Shift key as you drag the Oval tool on the Stage.

3 Flash includes three selection tools: the Selection tool, the Subselection tool, and the Lasso tool.

   • Use the Selection tool to select an entire shape or object.

   • Use the Subselection tool to select a specific point or line in an object.

   • Use the Lasso tool to draw a freeform selection area.

4 The Align panel aligns any number of selected elements horizontally or vertically and can distribute elements evenly.

3 CREATING AND EDITING SYMBOLS

Lesson Overview

In this lesson, you'll learn how to do the following:

- Import Illustrator and Photoshop artwork

- Create new symbols

- Edit symbols

- Understand the difference between symbol types

- Understand the difference between symbols and instances

- Use rulers and guides to position objects on the Stage

- Adjust transparency and color, and turn visibility on or off

- Apply blending effects

- Apply special effects with filters

- Position objects in 3D space

 This lesson will take about 90 minutes to complete. If needed, delete the previous lesson folder from your hard drive and copy the Lesson03 folder onto it. Download the project files for this lesson from the Lesson & Update Files tab on your Account page at www.peachpit.com and store them on your computer in a convenient location, as described in the Getting Started section of this book. Your Accounts page is also where you'll find any updates to the chapters or to the lesson files. Look on the Lesson & Update Files tab to access the most current content.

Symbols are reusable assets that are stored in your Library panel. The movie clip, graphic, and button symbols are three types of symbols that you will be creating and using often for special effects, animation, and interactivity.

Getting Started

● **Note:** If you have not already downloaded the project files for this lesson to your computer from your Account page, make sure to do so now. See "Getting Started" at the beginning of the book.

Start by viewing the final project to see what you'll be creating as you learn to work with symbols.

1 Double-click the 03End.html file in the Lesson03/03End folder to view the final project in your browser.

The project is a static illustration of a cartoon frame. In this lesson, you'll use Illustrator graphic files, imported Photoshop files, and symbols to create an attractive static image with interesting effects. Learning how to work with symbols is an essential step to creating any animation or interactivity.

2 Close the 03End.html file.

3 In Flash, choose File > New. In the New Document dialog box, choose ActionScript 3.0.

4 On the right side of the dialog box, change the Stage to **600** pixels wide by **450** pixels high.

5 Choose File > Save. Name the file **03_workingcopy.fla** and save it in the 03Start folder.

Importing Illustrator Files

As you learned in Lesson 2, you can draw objects in Flash using the Rectangle, Oval, and other tools. However, for complex drawings, you may prefer to create the artwork in another application. Adobe Flash Professional supports a variety of graphic formats, including Adobe Illustrator files, so you can create original artwork in that application, and then import it into Flash.

When you import an Illustrator file, you can choose how Flash should import the different layers of the original file and how to import text. You'll import an Illustrator file that contains all the characters for the cartoon frame.

1   Choose File > Import > Import to Stage.

2   Navigate to the Lesson03/03Start folder and select characters.ai.

3   Click Open.

The Import to Stage dialog box appears.

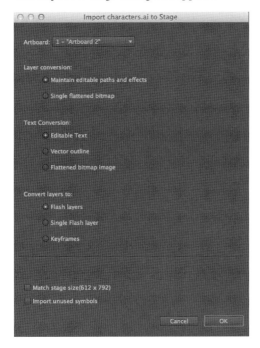

4   For Layer Conversion, choose Maintain editable paths and effects.

Maintaining editable paths and effects lets you continue to edit the vector drawing in Flash. The other option, Single flattened bitmap, imports the Illustrator artwork as a bitmap image.

5 For Text Conversion, choose Editable Text.

The Illustrator file doesn't contain any text, so the settings here don't matter.

6 For Convert layers to, choose Flash layers.

Flash preserves the layers from Illustrator. The Single Flash layer option flattens the Illustrator layers into one Flash layer, and the Keyframes option separates the Illustrator layers into individual Flash keyframes.

7 Click OK.

Flash imports the Illustrator vector graphics, and all the layers from the Illustrator file also appear in the Timeline.

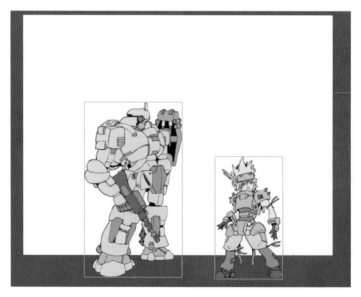

Using Adobe Illustrator with Flash

Flash Professional can import Illustrator files and automatically recognize layers, frames, and symbols. If you're more familiar with Illustrator, you may find it easier to design layouts in Illustrator, and then import them into Flash to add animation and interactivity.

Save your Illustrator artwork in Illustrator AI format, and then choose File > Import > Import To Stage or File > Import > Import To Library to import the artwork into Flash. Alternatively, you can even copy artwork from Illustrator and paste it into a Flash document.

Importing Layers

When an imported Illustrator file contains layers, you can import them in any of the following ways:

* Convert Illustrator layers to Flash layers
* Convert Illustrator layers to Flash keyframes
* Convert all Illustrator graphics to a bitmap
* Convert all Illustrator layers to a single Flash layer

Importing Symbols

Working with symbols in Illustrator is similar to working with them in Flash. In fact, you can use many of the same symbol keyboard shortcuts in both Illustrator and Flash: Press F8 in either application to create a symbol. When you create a symbol in Illustrator, the Symbol Options dialog box lets you name the symbol and set options specific to Flash, including the symbol type (such as movie clip) and registration point location.

If you want to edit a symbol in Illustrator without disturbing anything else, double-click the symbol to edit it in isolation mode. Illustrator dims all other objects on the artboard. When you exit isolation mode, the symbol in the Symbols panel—and all instances of the symbol—are updated accordingly.

Use the Symbols panel or the Control panel in Illustrator to assign names to symbol instances, break links between symbols and instances, swap a symbol instance with another symbol, or create a copy of the symbol.

Copying and Pasting Artwork

When you copy and paste (or drag and drop) artwork between Illustrator and Flash, the Paste dialog box appears. The Paste dialog box provides import settings for the Illustrator file you're copying. You can paste the file as a single bitmap object, or you can paste it using the current preferences for AI files. Just as when you import the file to the Stage or the Library panel, when you paste Illustrator artwork, you can convert Illustrator layers to Flash layers.

About Symbols

A *symbol* is a reusable asset that you can use for special effects, animation, or inter-activity. There are three kinds of symbols that you can create: the **graphic**, **button**, and **movie clip**. Symbols can reduce the file size and download time for many animations because they can be reused. You can use a symbol countless times in a project, but Flash includes its data only once.

Symbols are stored in the Library panel. When you drag a symbol to the Stage, Flash creates an **instance** of the symbol, leaving the original in the Library. An instance is a copy of a symbol located on the Stage. You can think of the symbol as an original photographic negative, and the instances on the Stage as prints of the negative. With just a single negative, you can create multiple prints.

It's also helpful to think of symbols as containers. Symbols are simply containers for your content. A symbol can contain a JPEG image, an imported Illustrator drawing, or a drawing that you created in Flash. At any time, you can go inside your symbol and edit it, which means editing or replacing its contents.

Each of the three kinds of symbols in Flash is used for a specific purpose. You can tell whether a symbol is a graphic (🖼), button (🔘), or movie clip (🎬) by looking at the icon next to it in the Library panel.

Movie clip symbols

Movie clip symbols are one of the most powerful and flexible kinds of symbols. When you create animation, you will typically use movie clip symbols. You can apply filters, color settings, and blending modes to a movie clip instance to enhance its appearance with special effects.

A movie clip symbol also contains its own independent Timeline. You can have an animation inside a movie clip symbol just as easily as you can have an animation on the main Timeline. This makes very complex animations possible; for example, a butterfly flying across the Stage can move from left to right as well as have its wings flapping independently of its movement.

Most important, you can control movie clips with ActionScript to make them respond to the user. For instance, a movie clip can have drag-and-drop behavior.

Button symbols

Button symbols are used for interactivity. They contain four unique keyframes that describe how they appear when the mouse is interacting with them. However, buttons need ActionScript functionality to make them do something.

You can also apply filters, blending modes, and color settings to buttons. You'll learn more about buttons in Lesson 6 when you create a nonlinear navigation scheme to allow the user to choose what to see.

Graphic symbols

Graphic symbols are the most basic kind of symbol. Although you can use them for animation, you'll rely more heavily on movie clip symbols.

Graphic symbols are the least flexible symbols, because they don't support ActionScript and you can't apply filters or blending modes to a graphic symbol. However, in some cases when you want an animation inside a graphic symbol to be synchronized to the main Timeline, you'll find graphic symbols useful.

Creating Symbols

There are two main ways to create a symbol. The first is to have nothing on the Stage selected, and then choose Insert > New Symbol. Flash will bring you to symbol-editing mode where you can begin drawing or importing graphics for your symbol.

The second way is to select existing graphics on the Stage, and then choose Modify > Convert to Symbol (F8). Whatever is selected will automatically be placed inside your new symbol.

Both methods are valid; which one you use depends on your particular workflow preferences. Most designers prefer to use Convert to Symbol (F8) because they can create all their graphics on the Stage and see them together before making the individual components into symbols.

For this lesson, you'll select the different parts of the imported Illustrator graphic, and then convert the various pieces to symbols.

1   On the Stage, select just the cartoon character in the hero layer.

● **Note:** When you use the command Convert to Symbol, you aren't actually "converting" anything; rather, you're placing whatever you've selected inside of a symbol.

2 Choose Modify > Convert to Symbol (F8).

3 Name the symbol **hero** and select Movie Clip for the Type.

4 Leave all other settings as they are. The Registration indicates the center point (x=0, y=0) and transformation point of your symbol. Leave the registration at the top-left corner.

5 Click OK. The hero symbol appears in the Library.

6 Select the other cartoon character in the robot layer and convert it to a movie clip symbol as well. Name it **robot**.

You now have two movie clip symbols in your Library and an instance of each on the Stage as well.

Importing Photoshop Files

You'll import a Photoshop file for the background. The Photoshop file contains two layers with a blending effect. A blending effect can create special color mixes between different layers. You'll see that Flash can import a Photoshop file with all the layers intact and retain all the blending information as well.

1 Select the top layer in your Timeline.

2 From the top menu, choose File > Import > Import to Stage.

3 Navigate to the Lesson03/03Start folder and select background.psd.

4 Click Open.

The Import to Stage dialog box appears.

Note: If you can't select the .psd file, choose All Files from the Enable pull-down menu.

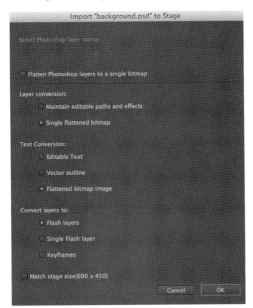

5 For Layer conversion, choose Maintain editable paths and effects.

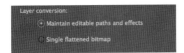

The Lighten blend effect from Photoshop will be preserved.

6 For Text conversion, choose Editable Text.

The Photoshop file doesn't contain any text, so the settings here don't matter.

7 For Convert layers to, choose Flash layers.

Flash preserves the layers from Photoshop. The Single Flash layer option flattens the Photoshop layers into one Flash layer, and the Keyframes option separates the Photoshop layers into individual Flash keyframes.

You also have the option of changing the Flash Stage size to match the Photoshop canvas. However, the current Stage is already set to the correct dimensions (600 pixels x 450 pixels).

8 Click OK. The two Photoshop layers are imported into Flash and placed on separate layers on the Timeline.

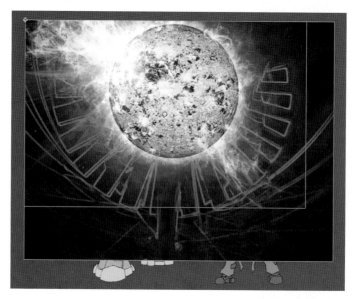

The Photoshop images are automatically converted into movie clip symbols and saved in your Library. The movie clip symbols are contained in the folder called background.psd Asset.

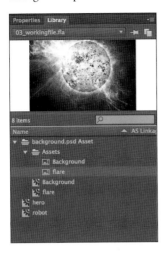

All the blending and transparency information is preserved. If you select the image in the flare layer, you'll see that the Blending option under the Display section in the Properties inspector is set to Lighten.

9   Drag the robot and the hero layers to the top of the Timeline so they overlap the background layers.

● **Note:** If you want to edit your Photoshop files, you don't have to go through the entire import process again. You can edit any image on the Stage or in the Library panel in Adobe Photoshop or any other image-editing application. Right-click/Ctrl-click an image on the Stage or an image in the Library and choose Edit with Adobe Photoshop to edit in Photoshop, or select another Edit with option to choose your preferred application. Flash launches the application, and once you have saved your changes, your image is immediately updated in Flash. Make sure that you right-click/Ctrl-click an image on the Stage or Library, and not the movie clip.

About Image Formats

Flash supports multiple image formats for import. Flash can handle JPEG, GIF, PNG, and PSD (Photoshop) files. Use JPEG files for images that include gradients and subtle variations, such as those that occur in photographs. GIF files are used for images with large solid blocks of color or black and white line drawings. Use PNG files for images that include transparency. Use PSD files if you want to retain all the layer, transparency, and blending information from a Photoshop file.

Converting a Bitmap Image to a Vector Graphic

Sometimes you'll want to convert a bitmap image to a vector graphic. Flash handles bitmap images as a series of colored dots (or pixels); vector graphics are handled as a series of lines and curves. This vector information is rendered on the fly, so that the resolution of vector graphics is not fixed like a bitmap image. That means you can zoom in on a vector graphic and your computer will always display it sharply and smoothly. Converting a bitmap image to a vector often has the effect of making it look "posterized" because subtle gradations are converted to editable, discrete blocks of color, which can be an interesting effect.

To convert a bitmap to a vector, import the bitmap image into Flash. Select the bitmap and choose Modify > Bitmap > Trace Bitmap. The options determine how faithful of a trace the vector image will be to the original bitmap.

In the following figure, the left image is an original bitmap and the right image is a vector graphic.

Exercise caution when using the Trace Bitmap command, because a complicated vector graphic is often more memory- and processor-intensive than the original bitmap image.

Editing and Managing Symbols

You now have multiple movie clip symbols in your Library and several instances on the Stage. You can better manage the symbols in your Library by organizing them in folders. You can also edit any symbol at any time. If you decide you want to change the color of one of the robot's arms, for example, you can easily go into symbol-editing mode and make that change.

Adding folders and organizing the Library

1 In the Library panel, right-click/Ctrl-click in an empty space and select New Folder. Alternatively, you can click the New Folder button (■) at the bottom of the Library panel, or click the panel's upper right and click New Folder.

A new folder is created in your Library.

2 Name the folder **characters**.

3 Drag the hero and the robot movie clip symbols into the characters folder.

4 You can collapse or expand folders to hide or view their contents and keep your Library organized.

Editing a symbol from the Library

1 Double-click the robot movie clip symbol icon in the Library.

Flash takes you to symbol-editing mode. In this mode, you can see the contents of your symbol—in this case, the robot on the Stage. Notice that the Edit Bar at the top of the Stage tells you that you are no longer in Scene 1 but are inside the symbol called robot.

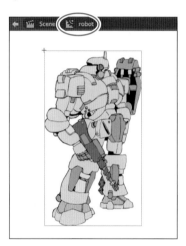

2 Double-click the drawing to edit it. You will need to double-click the drawing groups several times to drill down to the individual shape that you want to edit.

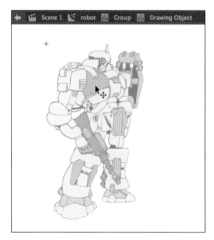

3 Choose the Paint Bucket tool. Select a new fill color and apply it to the shape on the robot drawing.

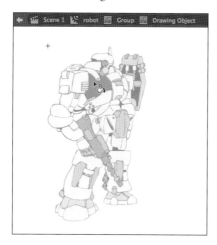

4 Click on Scene 1 on the Edit Bar above the Stage to return to the main Timeline.

The movie clip symbol in the Library reflects the changes you made. The instance on the Stage also reflects the changes you made to the symbol. All instances of the symbol will change if you edit the symbol.

● **Note:** You can quickly and easily duplicate symbols in the Library. Select the Library symbol, right-click/Ctrl-click, and choose Duplicate. Or, from the top-right Options menu in the Library, choose Duplicate. Flash creates an exact copy of the selected symbol in your Library.

Editing a symbol in place

You may want to edit a symbol in context with the other objects on the Stage. You can do so by double-clicking an instance on the Stage. You'll enter symbol-editing mode, but you'll also be able to see the symbol's surroundings. This editing mode is called editing in place.

1 Using the Selection tool, double-click the robot movie clip instance on the Stage.

Flash dims all other objects on the Stage and takes you to symbol-editing mode. Notice on the Edit Bar that you are no longer in Scene 1 but are inside the symbol called robot.

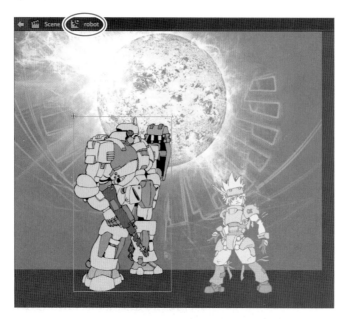

2 Double-click the drawing to edit it. You will need to double-click the drawing groups several times to drill down to the individual shape that you want to edit.

3   Choose the Paint Bucket tool. Select a new fill color and apply it to the shape on the robot drawing.

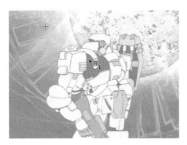

4   Click on Scene 1 on the Edit Bar above the Stage to return to the main Timeline. You can also just double-click any part of the Stage outside the graphic with the Selection tool to return to the next-higher group level.

The movie clip symbol in the Library panel reflects the changes you made. The instance on the Stage also reflects the changes you made to the symbol. All instances of the symbol will change according to the edits you make to the symbol.

Breaking apart a symbol instance

If you no longer want an object on the Stage to be a symbol instance, you can use the Break Apart command to return it to its original form.

1   Select the robot instance on the Stage.

2   Choose Modify > Break Apart.

Flash breaks apart the robot movie clip instance. What's left on the Stage is a group, which you can break apart further to edit.

3 Choose Modify > Break Apart again.

Flash breaks apart the group into its individual components, which are smaller drawing objects.

4 Choose Modify > Break Apart one more time.

Flash breaks apart the drawing objects into shapes.

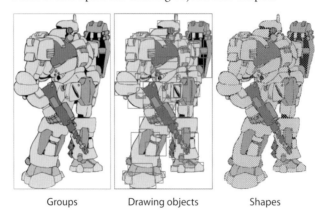

Groups   Drawing objects   Shapes

5 Choose Edit > Undo several times to return your robot to a symbol instance.

Changing the Size and Position of Instances

You can have multiple instances of the same symbol on the Stage. Now you'll add a few more robots to create a small robot army. You'll learn how to change the size and position (and even rotation) of each instance individually.

1 Select the robot layer in the Timeline.

2 Drag another robot symbol from the Library onto the Stage.

A new instance appears.

3   Choose the Free Transform tool.

    Control handles appear around the selected instance.

4   Drag the control handles on the sides of the selection to flip the robot so it is
    facing in the other direction.

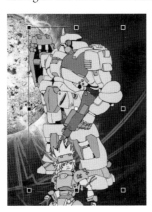

5   Drag the control handles on the corner of the selection while holding down the
    Shift key to reduce the size of the robot.

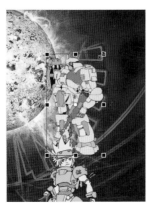

6 Drag a third robot from the Library onto the Stage. With the Free Transform tool, flip the robot, resize it, and make it overlap the second robot. Move the characters in an attractive arrangement.

The robot army is growing! Notice how edits to an instance do not change the Library symbol, and do not change other instances. On the other hand, edits to the Library symbol change all of its instances.

Using rulers and guides

You may want to be more precise in your placement of your symbol instances. In Lesson 1, you learned how to use the X and Y coordinates in the Properties inspector to position individual objects. In Lesson 2, you learned to use the Align panel to align several objects to each other.

Another way to position objects on the Stage is to use rulers and guides. Rulers appear on the top and left edge of the Pasteboard to provide measurement along the horizontal and vertical axes. Guides are vertical or horizontal lines that appear on the Stage but do not appear in the final published movie.

1 Choose View > Rulers (Alt+Shift+R [Windows]/Option+Shift+Command+R [Mac OS]).

Horizontal and vertical rulers measuring in pixels appear along the top and left edges of the Pasteboard. As you move objects on the Stage, tick marks indicate the bounding box positions on the rulers.

2 Click the top horizontal ruler and drag a guide onto the Stage.

A colored line appears on the Stage that you can use as a guide for alignment.

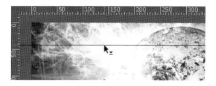

3 Double-click the guide with the Selection tool.

The Move Guide dialog box appears.

4 Enter **435** as the new pixel value of the guide. Click OK.

The guide is repositioned 435 pixels from the top edge of the Stage.

5 Choose View > Snapping > Snap to Guides and make sure Snap to Guides is selected.

Objects will now snap to any guides on the Stage.

6 Drag the robot instance and the hero instance so their bottom edges align with the guide.

Note: Choose View > Guides > Lock Guides to lock your guides. This prevents you from accidentally moving them. Clear all guides by choosing View > Guides > Clear Guides. Change the color of the guides and the snapping accuracy by choosing View > Guides > Edit Guides.

Changing the Color Effect of Instances

The Color Effect option in the Properties inspector allows you to change several properties of any instance. These properties include brightness, tint, or alpha.

Brightness controls how dark or light the instance appears, tint controls the overall coloring, and alpha controls the level of opacity. Decreasing the alpha value decreases the opacity and increases the amount of transparency.

Changing the brightness

1 Using the Selection tool, click the smallest robot on the Stage.

2 In the Properties inspector, choose Brightness from the Color Effect Style menu.

3 Drag the Bright slider to **−40%**.

The robot instance on the Stage becomes darker and appears to recede into the distance.

Changing the transparency

1 Select the glowing orb in the flare layer.

2 In the Properties inspector, choose Alpha from the Color Effect Style menu.

3 Drag the Alpha slider to a value of **50%**.

The orb in the flare layer on the Stage becomes more transparent.

● **Note:** To reset the Color Effect of any instance, choose None from the Style menu.

Understanding Display Options

The Display section in the Properties inspector for movie clips offers options for controlling the instance's visibility, blending, and rendering.

Visible option for movie clips

The visible property makes objects either visible or invisible to the audience. You can directly control the visible property of movie clip instances on the Stage by selecting or deselecting the option in the Properties inspector.

1 Select the Selection tool.

2 Select one of the robot movie clip instances on the Stage.

3 In the Properties inspector, under the Display section, notice that the Visible option is checked by default, meaning that the instance is visible.

4 Deselect the Visible check box.

The selected instance becomes invisible.

The instance is present on the Stage, and you can still move it to a new position, but the audience won't be able to see it. Use the Visible option to turn instances on or off during the course of your movie, rather than deleting them entirely. You can also use the Visible option to position invisible instances on the Stage in order to make them visible later on with ActionScript, the coding language of Flash.

Check the Visible option to make it visible on the Stage again.

Blending effects

Blending refers to how the colors of an instance interact with the colors below it. You saw how the instance in the flare layer had the Lighten option applied to it (carried over from Photoshop), which integrated it more with the instance in the Background layer.

There are many kinds of Blending options. Some have surprising results, depending on the colors in the instance and the colors in the layers below it. Experiment with all the options to understand how they work. The following figure shows some of the Blending options and their effects on the robot instance over a blue-black gradient.

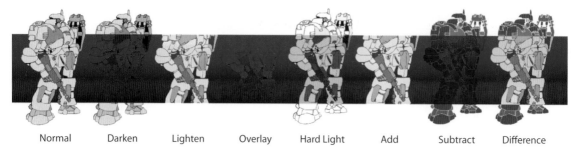

Normal   Darken   Lighten   Overlay   Hard Light   Add   Subtract   Difference

Export as Bitmap

The robots and the hero character in this lesson are movie clip symbols containing complex vector graphics imported from Illustrator. Vector art can be processor-intensive, and can take its toll on performance and playback. A rendering option called Export as Bitmap can help. The Export as Bitmap option renders the vector art as a bitmap, reducing the performance load (but increasing memory use). The movie clip remains as editable vector graphics in the .fla file, however, so you can still modify the artwork.

1 Select the Selection tool.

2 Select the hero movie clip instance on the Stage.

3 In the Properties inspector, choose Export as Bitmap for the Render option.

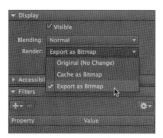

The hero movie clip instance appears as it will be rendered when published. You may see a slight "softening" of the illustration because of the rasterization of the art.

4 In the pulldown menu under the Render options, leave the selection as Transparent.

The Transparent option renders the background in your movie clip symbol as transparent. Alternately, you can choose Opaque and pick a color for the background of your movie clip symbol.

Applying Filters for Special Effects

Filters are special effects that you can apply to movie clip instances. Several filters are available in the Filters section of the Properties inspector. Each filter has different options that can refine the effect.

Applying a blur filter

You'll apply a blur filter to some of the instances to help give the scene a greater sense of depth.

1 Select the glowing orb in the flare layer.

2 In the Properties inspector, expand the Filters section.

3 Click the Add filter button at the top of the Filters section and select Blur.

The Blur filter appears in the Filters window with options for Blur X and Blur Y.

4 If they aren't linked already, click the link icons next to the Blur X and Blur Y options to link the blur effect in both directions.

5 Set the Blur X and Blur Y value to **10** pixels.

The instance on the Stage becomes blurry, helping to give an atmospheric perspective to this scene.

● **Note:** It's best to keep the Quality setting for filters on Low. Higher settings are processor-intensive and can bog down performance, especially if you've applied multiple filters.

More Filter Options

At the top-right corner of the Filters window is a menu of options to help you manage and apply multiple filters.

The Save as preset option lets you save a particular filter and its settings so you can apply it to another instance. The Copy and Paste options let you copy and paste a selected filter or all the filters. The Reset Filter button resets the filter parameters to their default values. The Enable or Disable Filter button (the eyeball icon next to the Filter name) lets you see your instance with or without the filter applied.

Positioning in 3D Space

You also have the ability to position and animate objects in real three-dimensional space. However, objects need to be movie clip symbols to be moved in 3D. Two tools allow you to position objects in 3D: the 3D Rotation tool and the 3D Translation tool. The Transform panel also provides information for position and rotation.

Understanding the 3D coordinate space is essential for successful 3D placement of objects. Flash divides space using three axes: the x, y, and z axes. The x axis runs horizontally across the Stage with $x=0$ at the left edge. The y axis runs vertically with $y=0$ at the top edge. The z axis runs into and out of the plane of the Stage (toward and away from the viewer) with $z=0$ at the plane of the Stage.

Changing the 3D rotation of an object

You'll add some text to your image, but to add a little more interest, you'll tilt it to put it in perspective. Think about the beginning text introduction to the *Star Wars* movies, and see if you can achieve a similar effect.

1   Insert a new layer at the top of the layers stack and rename it **text**.

2   Choose the Text tool from the Tools panel.

3 In the Properties inspector, choose Static Text, and select a large-size font with an interesting color that will add some pizzazz. Your font might look different from what's shown in this lesson, depending on the fonts available on your computer.

4 Click on the Stage in your text layer and begin typing your title.

5 To exit the Text tool, select the Selection tool.

6 With the text still selected, choose Modify > Convert to Symbol (F8).

7 In the Convert to Symbol dialog box, enter **title** for the Name and choose Movie Clip for Type. Click OK.

Your text is put into a movie clip symbol, and an instance remains on the Stage.

8 Choose the 3D Rotation tool ( ).

A circular, multicolored target appears on the instance. This is a guide for the 3D rotation. It's useful to think of the guides as lines on a globe. The red longitudinal line rotates your instance around the x axis. The green line along the equator rotates your instance around the y axis. The circular blue guide rotates your instance around the z axis.

9 Click on one of the guides—red for *x*, green for *y*, or blue for *z*—and drag your mouse in either direction to rotate your instance in 3D space.

You can also click and drag the outer orange circular guide to freely rotate the instance in all three directions.

Changing the 3D position of an object

In addition to changing an object's rotation in 3D space, you can move it to a specific point in 3D space. Use the 3D Translation tool, which is hidden under the 3D Rotation tool.

1 Choose the 3D Translation tool.

2 Click on your text.

A guide appears on the instance. This is a guide for the 3D translation. The red guide represents the *x* axis, the green is the *y* axis, and the blue is the *z* axis.

3 Click on one of the guide axes and drag your mouse in either direction to move your instance in 3D space. Notice that your text stays in perspective as you move it around the Stage.

Global vs. Local Transformations

When you choose the 3D Rotation or 3D Translation tool, be aware of the Global Transform option (it appears as a three-dimensional cube) at the bottom of the Tools panel. When the Global Transform option is depressed (turned on), rotation and positioning are relative to the global, or Stage, coordinate system. The 3D display over the object that you're moving shows the three axes in constant position, no matter how the object is rotated or moved. Notice in the following image how the 3D display is always perpendicular to the Stage.

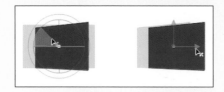

However, when the Global option is turned off (the button is raised), rotation and positioning are relative to the object. The 3D display shows the three axes oriented relative to the object, not the Stage. For example, in the following image, notice that the 3D Translation tool shows the z axis pointing out from the rectangle, not from the Stage.

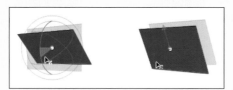

Resetting the transformation

If you've made a mistake in your 3D transformations and want to reset the rotation of your instance, you can use the Transform panel.

1 Choose the Selection tool and select the instance that you want to reset.

2 Choose Window > Transform to open the Transform panel.

The Transform panel shows all the values for the *x*, *y*, and *z* angles and positions.

3   Click the Remove Transform button in the lower-right corner of the
    Transform panel.

The selected instance returns to its original rotation.

Understanding the vanishing point and the perspective angle

Objects in 3D space represented on a 2D surface (such as the computer screen) are rendered with perspective to make them appear as they do in real life. Correct perspective depends on many factors, including the vanishing point and the perspective angle, both of which can be changed in Flash.

The vanishing point determines where on the horizon parallel lines of a perspective drawing converge. Think of railroad tracks and how the parallel tracks converge to a single point as they recede into the distance. The vanishing point is usually at eye level in the center of your field of view, so the default settings are exactly in the middle of the Stage. You can, however, change the vanishing point setting so it appears above or below eye level, or to the right or left.

The perspective angle determines how quickly parallel lines converge to the vanishing point. The greater the angle, the quicker the convergence, and therefore, the more severe and distorted the illustration appears.

1   Select an object on the Stage that has been moved or rotated in 3D space.

2   In the Properties inspector, expand the 3D Position and View section.

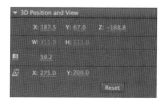

3 Click and drag on the X and Y values of the Vanishing Point to change the vanishing point, which is indicated on the Stage by intersecting gray lines.

4 To reset the Vanishing Point to the default values (to the center of the Stage), click the Reset button.

5 Click and drag on the Perspective Angle value to change the amount of distortion. The greater the angle, the more the distortion.

Review Questions

1 What is a symbol, and how does it differ from an instance?

2 Name two ways you can create a symbol.

3 When you import an Illustrator file, what happens if you choose to convert layers to Flash layers? To keyframes?

4 How can you change the transparency of an instance in Flash?

5 What are the two ways to edit symbols?

Review Answers

1 A *symbol* is a graphic, button, or movie clip that you create once in Flash and can then reuse throughout your document or in other documents. All symbols are stored in your Library panel. An *instance* is a copy of a symbol located on the Stage.

2 You can create a symbol by choosing Insert > New Symbol, or you can select existing objects on the Stage and choose Modify > Convert to Symbol.

3 When you convert layers of an Illustrator file to Flash layers, Flash recognizes the layers in the Illustrator document and adds them as separate layers in the Timeline. When you import layers as keyframes, Flash adds each Illustrator layer to a separate frame in the Timeline and creates keyframes for them.

4 The transparency of an instance is determined by its alpha value. To change the transparency, select Alpha from the Color Effect menu in the Properties inspector, and then change the alpha percentage.

5 To edit a symbol, either double-click the symbol in the Library to enter symbol-editing mode, or double-click the instance on the Stage to edit it in place. Editing a symbol in place lets you see the other objects around the instance.

4 ANIMATING SYMBOLS

Lesson Overview

In this lesson, you'll learn how to do the following:

- Animate the position, scale, and rotation of objects

- Adjust the pacing and timing of your animation

- Animate transparency and special effects

- Change the path of an object's motion

- Create animation inside symbols

- Split a motion tween

- Change the easing of an object's motion

- Animate in 3D space

 This lesson will take approximately 2 hours to complete. If needed, remove the previous lesson folder from your hard drive and copy the Lesson04 folder onto it. Download the project files for this lesson from the Lesson & Update Files tab on your Account page at www.peachpit.com and store them on your computer in a convenient location, as described in the Getting Started section of this book. Your Accounts page is also where you'll find any updates to the chapters or to the lesson files. Look on the Lesson & Update Files tab to access the most current content.

Use Flash Professional to change almost any aspect of an object—position, color, transparency, size, rotation, and more—over time. Motion tweening is the basic technique of creating animation with symbol instances.

Getting Started

● **Note:** If you have not already downloaded the project files for this lesson to your computer from your Account page, make sure to do so now. See "Getting Started" at the beginning of the book.

Start by viewing the finished movie file to see the animated title page that you'll create in this lesson.

1   Double-click the 04End.html file in the Lesson04/04End folder to play the animation in a browser.

The project is an animated splash page for an imaginary soon-to-be-released motion picture. In this lesson, you'll use motion tweens to animate several components on the page: the cityscape, the main actors, several old-fashioned cars, and the main title.

2   Close the 04End.html file.

3   Double-click the 04Start.fla file in the Lesson04/04Start folder to open the initial project file in Flash. This file is partially completed and already contains many of the graphic elements imported into the Library for you to use.

4   From the view options above the Stage, choose Fit in Window, or View > Magnification > Fit in Window so that you can see the entire Stage on your computer screen.

5   Choose File > Save As. Name the file **04_workingcopy.fla**, and save it in the 04Start folder.

Saving a working copy ensures that the original start file will be available if you want to start over.

About Animation

Animation is the movement, or change, of objects through time. Animation can be as simple as moving a box across the Stage from one frame to the next. It can also be much more complex. As you'll see in this lesson, you can animate many different aspects of a single object. You can change an object's position on the Stage, change its color or transparency, change its size or its rotation, and even animate the special filters that you saw in the previous lesson. You also have control over an object's path of motion, and even its easing, which is the way an object accelerates or decelerates.

In Flash, the basic workflow for animation goes like this: Select an object on the Stage, right-click/Ctrl-click, and choose Create Motion Tween. Move the red playhead to a different point in time and move the object to a new position or change one of its properties. Flash takes care of the rest.

Motion tweens create animation for changes in position on the Stage and for changes in size, color, or other attributes. Motion tweens require you to use a symbol instance. If the object you've selected is not a symbol instance, Flash will automatically ask to convert the selection to a symbol.

Flash also automatically separates motion tweens on their own layers, which are called Tween layers. There can be only one motion tween per layer without any other element in the layer. Tween layers allow you to change various attributes of your instance at different key points over time. For example, a spaceship could be on the left side of the Stage at the beginning keyframe and at the far-right side of the Stage at an ending keyframe, and the resulting tween would make the spaceship fly across the Stage.

The term "tween" comes from the world of classic animation. Senior animators would be responsible for drawing the beginning and ending poses for their characters. The beginning and ending poses were the keyframes of the animation. Junior animators would then come in and draw the "in-between" frames, or do the "in-betweening." Hence, "tweening" refers to the smooth transitions between keyframes.

Understanding the Project File

The 04Start.fla file contains a few of the animated elements already or partially completed. Each of the six layers—man, woman, Middle_car, Right_car, footer, and ground—contains an animation. The man and woman layers are in a folder called actors, and the Middle_car and Right_car layers are in a folder called cars.

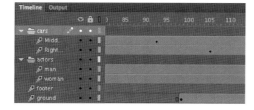

You'll be adding more layers to add an animated cityscape, refining the animation of one of the actors, as well as adding a third car and a 3D title. All the necessary graphic elements have been imported into the Library panel. The Stage is set at a generous 1280 pixels by 787 pixels, and the Stage color is black. You might need to choose a different view option to see the entire Stage. Choose View > Magnification > Fit in Window, or choose Fit in Window from the view options at the top-right corner of the Stage to view the Stage at a magnification percentage that fits your screen.

Animating Position

You'll start this project by animating the cityscape. It will begin slightly lower than the top edge of the Stage, and then rise slowly until its top is aligned with the top of the Stage.

1   Lock all the existing layers so you don't accidentally modify them. Create a new layer above the footer layer and rename it **city**.

2   Drag the bitmap image called cityBG.jpg from the bitmaps folder in the Library panel to the Stage.

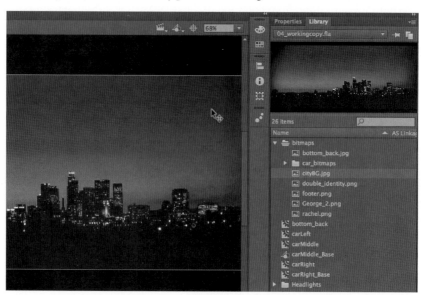

3 In the Properties inspector, set the value of X to **0** and the value of Y to **90**.

This positions the cityscape image just slightly below the top edge of the Stage.

4 Right-click/Ctrl-click on the cityscape image and choose Create Motion Tween. From the top menu, you can also select Insert > Motion Tween.

5 A dialog box appears warning you that your selected object is not a symbol. Motion tweens require symbols. Flash asks if you want to convert the selection to a symbol so it can proceed with the motion tween. Click OK.

Flash automatically converts your selection to a symbol, which is stored in your Library panel. Flash also converts the current layer to a Tween layer so you can begin to animate the instance. Tween layers are distinguished by a special icon in front of the layer name, and the frames are tinted blue. Tween layers are reserved for motion tweens, and hence, no drawing is allowed on a Tween layer.

6 Move the red playhead to the end of the tween span at frame 190.

7 Select the instance of the cityscape on the Stage, and while holding down the Shift key, move the instance up the Stage.

Holding down the Shift key constrains the movement to right angles.

● **Note:** Hide all the other layers to isolate the cityscape and to better see the results of the motion tween.

8 For more precision, set the value of Y to **0** in the Properties inspector.

A small black diamond appears in frame 190 at the end of the tween span. This indicates a keyframe at the end of the tween.

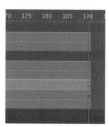

Flash smoothly interpolates the change in position from frame 1 to frame 190 and represents that motion with a motion path.

● **Note:** Remove a motion tween by right-clicking/Ctrl-clicking the motion tween on the Timeline or the Stage and choosing Remove Tween.

9 Drag the red playhead back and forth at the top of the Timeline to see the smooth motion. You can also choose Control > Play (Enter) to make Flash play the animation.

Animating changes in position is simple, because Flash automatically creates keyframes at the points where you move your instance to new positions. If you want to have an object move to many different points, simply move the red playhead to the desired frame, and then move the object to its new position. Flash takes care of the rest.

Using the Controller to preview the animation

The Controller panel allows you to play, rewind, or go step-by-step backward or forward through your Timeline to review your animation in a controlled manner.

Use the playback controls that are integrated at the bottom of the Timeline, or choose the playback commands from the Control menu.

1   Click any of the playback buttons on the controller below the Timeline to go to the first frame, go to the last frame, play, stop, or move forward or backward one frame.

2   Choose the loop option at the bottom of the Timeline and click the play button.

    The playhead loops, allowing you to see the animation over and over for careful analysis.

3   Move the front or rear brackets on the Timeline to define the range of frames that you want to see looped.

    The playhead loops within the bracketed frames. Click on the loop option again to turn it off.

Changing the Pacing and Timing

You can change the duration of the entire tween span or change the timing of the animation by clicking and dragging keyframes on the Timeline.

Changing the animation duration

If you want the animation to proceed at a slower pace (and hence, taking up a much longer period of time), you need to lengthen the entire tween span between the beginning and end keyframes. If you want to shorten the animation, you need to decrease the tween span. Lengthen or shorten a motion tween by dragging the ends on the Timeline.

1 Move your mouse cursor close to the end of the tween span in the city layer.

Your cursor changes to a double-headed arrow, indicating that you can lengthen or shorten the tween span.

2 Click and drag the end of the tween span back toward frame 60.

Your motion tween shortens to 60 frames, so now the cityscape takes a much shorter time to move.

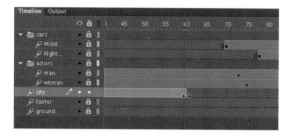

3 Move your mouse cursor close to the beginning of the tween span (at frame 1).

● **Note:** If you have multiple keyframes in a tween, dragging out your tween spans will distribute all your keyframes uniformly. The timing of your entire animation remains the same; only the length changes.

4 Click and drag the beginning of the frame span forward to frame 10.

Your motion tween begins at an earlier time, so it now plays only from frame 10 to frame 60.

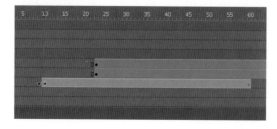

Adding frames

You'll want the last keyframe of your motion tween to hold for the remainder of the animation. Add frames by Shift-dragging the end of a tween span.

1 Move your mouse cursor close to the end of the tween span.

2 Hold down the Shift key, and click and drag the end of the tween span forward to frame 190.

● **Note:** You can also add individual frames by choosing Insert > Timeline > Frame (F5), or remove individual frames by choosing Edit > Timeline > Remove Frames (Shift+F5).

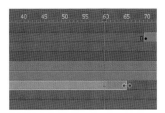

The last keyframe in the motion tween remains at frame 60, but additional frames are added to frame 190.

Moving keyframes

If you want to change the pacing of an animation, you can select individual keyframes, then click and drag the keyframes to new positions.

1 Click on the keyframe at frame 60.

The keyframe at frame 60 is selected. A tiny box appears next to your mouse cursor indicating that you can move the keyframe.

2 Click and drag the keyframe to frame 40.

The last keyframe in the motion tween moves to frame 40, so the motion of the cityscape proceeds quicker.

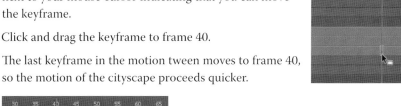

Span-Based vs. Frame-Based Selections

By default, Flash does not use span-based selection, which means you can select individual keyframes within a motion tween. However, if you prefer to click on a motion tween and have the entire span (the beginning and end keyframes, and all the frames in between) be selected, you can enable Span Based Selection from the Options menu on the top-right corner of the Timeline.

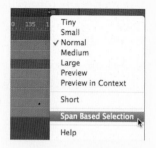

With Span Based Selection enabled, you can click anywhere within the motion tween to select it, and move the whole animation backward or forward along the Timeline as a single unit.

If you want to select individual keyframes while Span Based Selection is enabled, hold down the Ctrl (Windows)/Command (Mac OS) key and click on a keyframe.

Animating Transparency

In the previous lesson, you learned how to change the color effect of any symbol instance to change the transparency, tint, or brightness. You can change the color effect of an instance in one keyframe and change the value of the color effect in another keyframe, and Flash will automatically display a smooth change, just as it does with changes in position.

You'll change the cityscape in the beginning keyframe to be totally transparent but keep the cityscape in the ending keyframe opaque. Flash will create a smooth fade-in effect.

1 Move the red playhead to the first keyframe of the motion tween (frame 10).

2 Select the cityscape instance on the Stage.

3 In the Properties inspector, choose the Alpha option for Color Effect.

4 Set the Alpha value to **0%**.

The cityscape instance on the Stage becomes totally transparent.

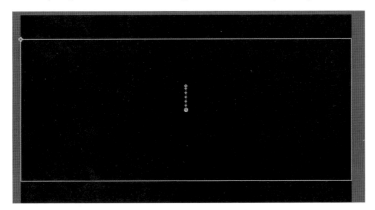

5 Move the red playhead to the last keyframe of the motion tween (frame 40).

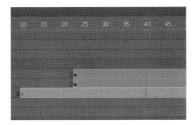

6 Select the cityscape instance on the Stage.

7 In the Properties inspector, under Color Effect, set the Alpha value to **100**%.

The cityscape instance on the Stage becomes totally opaque.

8 Preview the effect by choosing Control > Play (Enter).

Flash interpolates the changes in both position and transparency between the two keyframes.

Animating Filters

Filters, which give instances special effects such as blurs and drop shadows, can also be animated. You'll refine the motion tween of the actors next by applying a blur filter to one of them to make it appear as if the camera changes focus. Animating filters is no different from animating changes in position or changes in color effect. You simply set the values for a filter at one keyframe and set different values for the filter at another keyframe, and Flash creates a smooth transition.

1 Make the actors layer folder on the Timeline visible.

2 Lock all the layers on the Timeline except the woman layer.

3 Move the red playhead to the beginning keyframe of the motion tween in the woman layer—at frame 23.

4   Select the instance of the woman on the Stage. You won't be able to see her because she has an alpha value of 0% (totally transparent), but if you click on the top-right side of the Stage, the transparent instance will be selected.

5   In the Properties inspector, expand the Filters section.

6   Click the Add filter button at the top of the Filters section and select Blur.

    Flash applies the Blur filter to the instance.

7   In the Filters section of the Properties inspector, make sure that the link icons are intact to constrain the blur values to both the x and y directions equally. Set the X and Y Blur values to **20** pixels.

8 Move the red playhead across the entire Timeline to preview the animation.

The 20-pixel Blur filter is applied to the woman instance throughout the motion tween.

9 Right-click/Ctrl-click on the woman layer at frame 140, and choose Insert Keyframe > Filter.

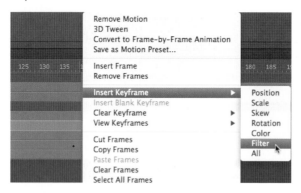

A keyframe for filters is established at frame 140.

10 Move the red playhead to frame 160, and right-click/Ctrl-click on the woman layer and choose Insert Keyframe > Filter.

Another keyframe for filters is established at frame 160.

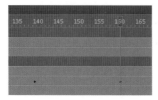

11 Select the instance of the woman on the Stage at frame 160.

12 In the Properties inspector, change the value of the Blur filter to X=**0** and Y=**0**.

The Blur filter changes from the keyframe at frame 140 to the keyframe at 160. Flash creates a smooth transition from a blurry instance to an in-focus instance.

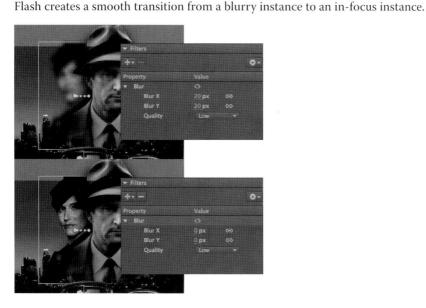

Understanding Property Keyframes

Changes in properties are independent of one another and do not need to be tied to the same keyframes. That is, you can have a keyframe for position, a different keyframe for the color effect, and yet another keyframe for a filter. Managing many different kinds of keyframes can become overwhelming, especially if you want different

properties to change at different times during the motion tween. Fortunately, Flash Professional provides a few helpful tools for keyframe management.

When viewing the tween span, you can choose to view the keyframes of only certain properties. For example, you can choose to view only the Position keyframes to see when your object moves. Or, you can choose to view only the Filter keyframes to see when there is a filter change. Right-click/Ctrl-click on a motion tween in the Timeline, choose View Keyframes, and then select the desired property among the list. You can also choose All or None to see all the properties or none of the properties.

When inserting a keyframe, you can also insert a keyframe specific to the property you want to change. Right-click/Ctrl-click on a motion tween in the Timeline, choose Insert Keyframes, and then select the desired property.

Animating Transformations

Now you'll learn how to animate changes in scale or rotation. These kinds of changes are made with the Free Transform tool or with the Transform panel. You'll add a third car to the project. The car will start small, and then become larger as it appears to move forward toward the viewer.

1 Lock all the layers on the Timeline.

2 Insert a new layer inside the Cars folder and rename it **Left_car**.

3 Select frame 75 and insert a new keyframe (F6).

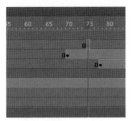

4 Drag the movie clip symbol called carLeft from the Library panel to the Stage at frame 75.

5 Select the Free Transform tool.

The transformation handles appear around the instance on the Stage.

6   While holding down the Shift key, click and drag a corner handle inward to make the car smaller.

7   In the Properties inspector, make sure that the width of the car is about 400 pixels.

8   Alternatively, you can use the Transform panel (Window > Transform) and change the scale of the car to about **29.4**%.

9   Move the car to its starting position at about X=710 and Y=488.

10 In the Properties inspector, select Alpha for the Color Effect.

11 Set the value of the Alpha to **0**%.

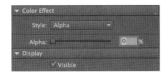

The car becomes totally transparent.

12 Right-click/Ctrl-click on the car on the Stage and select Create Motion Tween.

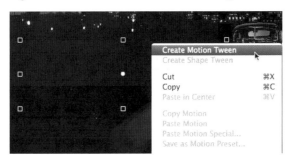

The current layer becomes a Tween layer.

13 Move the red playhead on the Timeline to frame 100.

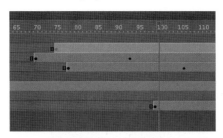

14 Select the transparent instance of the car on the Stage, and in the Properties inspector, change the Alpha value to **100**%.

A new keyframe is automatically inserted at frame 100 to indicate the change in transparency.

15 Select the Free Transform tool.

● **Note:** Hold down the Alt (Windows)/ Option (Mac OS) key while you drag the corner handle of the Transformation tool to change the scale relative to the opposite corner point.

16 While holding down the Shift key, click and drag a corner handle outward to make the car larger. For more precision, use the Properties inspector and set the dimensions of the car to width=**1380** pixels and height=**445.05** pixels.

17 Position the car at X=**607** and Y=**545**.

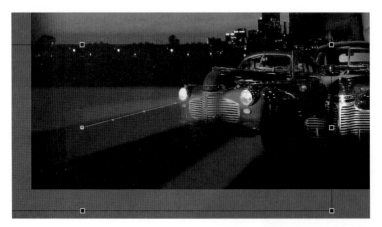

18 Move the Left_car layer in between the Middle_car and Right_car layers so that the car in the center overlaps the cars on the side.

Flash tweens the change in position and the change in scale from frame 75 to frame 100. Flash also tweens the change in transparency from frame 75 to frame 100.

Motion Presets

If your project involves creating identical motion tweens repeatedly, Flash provides a panel called Motion Presets that can help. The Motion Presets panel (Window > Motion Presets) can store any motion tween so you can apply it to different instances on the Stage.

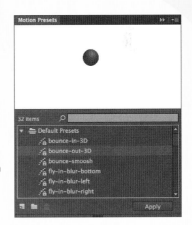

For example, if you want to build a slide show where each image fades out in the same manner, you can save that transition to the Motion Presets panel.

1   Select the first motion tween on the Timeline or the instance on the Stage.

2   In the Motion Presets panel, click the Save selection as preset button at the bottom of the panel.

3   Name your motion preset, and it will be saved in the Motion Presets panel.

4   Select a new instance on the Stage and choose the motion preset.

5   Click Apply, and Flash will apply your saved motion preset to the new instance.

Flash provides a number of motion presets that you can use to quickly build sophisticated animations without much effort.

Changing the Path of the Motion

The motion tween of the left car that you just animated shows a colored line with dots indicating the path of the motion. The path of the motion can be edited easily so that the car travels in a curve, or the path can be moved, scaled, or even rotated just like any other object on the Stage.

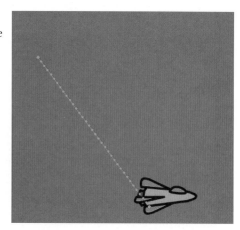

To better demonstrate how you can edit the path of the motion, open the sample file 04MotionPath.fla. The file contains a single Tween layer with a rocket ship moving from the top left of the Stage toward the bottom right.

Moving the path of the motion

You will move the path of the motion so the relative movement of the rocket ship remains the same, but its starting and ending positions change.

1   Choose the Selection tool.

2   Click on the path of the motion to select it.

    The path of the motion becomes highlighted when it is selected.

3   Click and drag the motion path to move it to a different place on the Stage.

    The relative motion and timing of the animation remain the same, but the starting and ending positions are relocated.

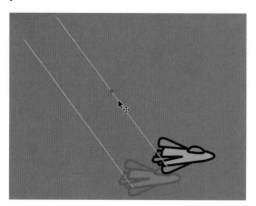

Changing the scale or rotation of the path

You can also manipulate the path of the object's motion using the Free Transform tool.

1   Select the path of the motion.

2   Choose the Free Transform tool.

Transformation handles appear around the path of the motion.

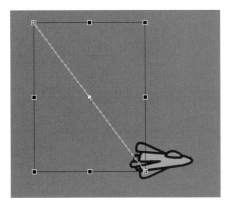

3   Scale or rotate the path of the motion as desired. You can make the path smaller or larger, or rotate the path so the rocket ship starts from the bottom left of the Stage and ends at the top right.

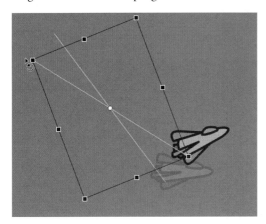

Editing the path of the motion

Making your objects travel on a curved path is a simple matter. You can either edit the path with Bezier precision using anchor point handles, or you can edit the path in a more intuitive manner with the Selection tool.

1 Choose the Convert Anchor Point tool, which is hidden under the Pen tool.

2 Click on the starting point or the ending point of the motion path on the Stage and drag the control handle out from the anchor point.

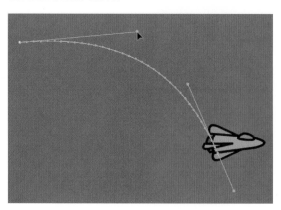

The handle on the anchor point controls the curvature of the path.

3 Choose the Subselection tool.

4 Click and drag the handle to edit the curve of the path. Make the rocket ship travel in a wide curve.

Note: You can also directly manipulate the path of the motion with the Selection tool. Choose the Selection tool and move it close to the path of the motion. A curved icon appears next to your cursor indicating that you can edit the path. Click and drag the path of the motion to change its curvature.

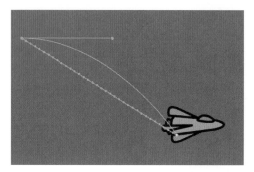

Orienting objects to the path

Sometimes the orientation of the object traveling along the path is important. In the motion picture splash page project, the orientation of the car is constant as it rumbles forward. However, in the rocket ship example, the rocket ship should follow the path with its nose pointed in the direction in which it is heading. The Orient to path option in the Properties inspector gives you this option.

1   Select the motion tween on the Timeline.

2   In the Properties inspector, under Rotation, select the Orient to path option.

Note: To direct the nose of the rocket ship, or any other object, along the path of its motion, you must orient its position so that it is facing in the direction that you want it to travel. Use the Free Transform tool to rotate its initial position so that it is oriented correctly.

Flash inserts keyframes for rotation along the motion tween so that the nose of the rocket ship is oriented to the path of the motion.

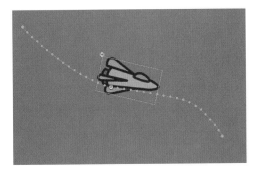

Swapping Tween Targets

The motion tween model in Flash Professional is object-based. This means that an object and its motion are independent of each other, and you can easily swap out the target of a motion tween. If, for example, you'd rather see an alien moving around the

Stage instead of a rocket ship, you can replace the target of the motion tween with an alien symbol from your Library panel and still preserve the animation.

1 Drag the movie clip symbol of the alien from the Library panel onto the rocket ship.

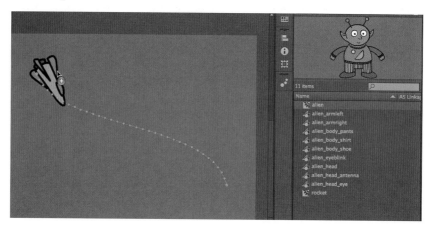

2 Flash asks if you want to replace the existing tween target object with a new object.

3 Click OK.

Flash replaces the rocket ship with the alien. The motion remains the same, but the target of the motion tween has changed.

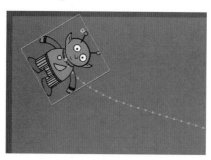

● **Note:** You can also swap instances in the Properties inspector. Select the object that you want to swap on the Stage. In the Properties inspector, click the Swap button. In the dialog box that appears, choose a new symbol and click OK. Flash will swap the target of the motion tween.

Creating Nested Animations

Often, an object that is animated on the Stage will have its own animation. For example, a butterfly moving across the Stage will have an animation of its wings flapping as it moves. Or the alien that you swapped with the rocket ship could be waving his arms. These kinds of animations are called *nested animations*, because they are contained inside the movie clip symbols. Movie clip symbols have their own Timeline that is independent of the main Timeline.

In this example, you'll make the alien wave his arms inside the movie clip symbol, so he'll be waving as he moves across the Stage.

Creating animations inside movie clip symbols

1   In the Library panel, double-click the alien movie clip symbol icon.

You are now in symbol-editing mode for the alien movie clip symbol. The alien appears in the middle of the Stage. In the Timeline, the parts of the alien are separated in layers.

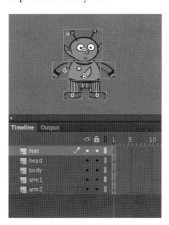

2   Choose the Selection tool.

3   Right-click/Ctrl-click on the alien's left arm and choose Create Motion Tween.

Flash converts the current layer to a Tween layer and inserts 1-second's worth of frames so you can begin to animate the instance.

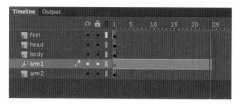

4 Choose the Free Transform tool.

5 Drag the corner rotation control points to rotate the arm upward to the alien's shoulder height.

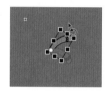

Flash inserts a keyframe at the end of the motion tween. The left arm rotates smoothly from the resting position to the outstretched position.

6 Move the red playhead back to frame 1.

7 Now create a motion tween for the alien's other arm. Right-click/Ctrl-click on his right arm and choose Create Motion Tween.

Flash converts the current layer to a Tween layer and inserts 1-second's worth of frames so you can begin to animate the instance.

8 Choose the Free Transform tool.

9 Drag the corner rotation control points to rotate the arm upward to the alien's shoulder height.

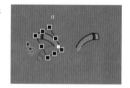

Flash inserts a keyframe at the end of the motion tween. The arm rotates smoothly from the resting position to the outstretched position.

10 Select the last frame in all the other layers and insert frames (F5) so that the head, body, and feet all remain on the Stage for the same amount of time as the moving arms.

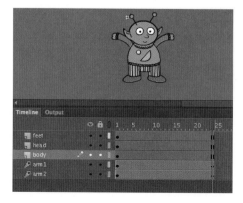

11 Exit symbol-editing mode by clicking the Scene 1 button in the Edit Bar at the top of the Stage.

Your animation of the alien raising his arms is complete. Wherever you use the movie clip symbol, the alien will continue to play its nested animation.

12 Preview the animation by choosing Control > Test Movie > in Flash Professional.

Flash opens a window showing the exported animation. The alien moves along the motion path while the nested animation of his arms moving plays and loops.

● **Note:** Animations inside of movie clip symbols won't play on the main timeline. Choose Control > Test Movie > in Flash Professional to preview nested animations.

● **Note:** Animations inside movie clip symbols will loop automatically. To prevent the looping, you need to add ActionScript to tell the movie clip Timeline to stop on its last frame. You'll learn more about ActionScript in Lesson 6.

Easing

Easing refers to the way in which a motion tween proceeds. You can think of easing as acceleration or deceleration. An object that moves from one side of the Stage to the other side can start off slowly, then build up speed, and then stop suddenly. Or, the object can start off quickly, and then gradually slow to a halt. Your keyframes indicate the beginning and end points of the motion, but the easing determines how your object gets from one keyframe to the next.

You apply easing to a motion tween from the Properties inspector. Easing values range from –100 to 100. A negative value creates a more gradual change from the starting position (known as an ease-in). A positive value creates a gradual slow-down (known as an ease-out).

Splitting a motion tween

Easing affects the entire span of a motion tween. If you want the easing to affect only frames between keyframes of a longer motion tween, you should split the motion tween. For example, return to the 04_workingcopy.fla file of the cinematic animation. The motion tween of the car in the Left_car layer begins at frame 75 and ends at frame 190, at the very end of the Timeline. However, the actual movement of the car starts at frame 75 and ends at frame 100. You'll split the motion tween so you can apply an ease to the tween just from frames 75 to 100.

1   In the Left_car layer, select frame 101, which is the frame just after the second keyframe where the car ends its movement.

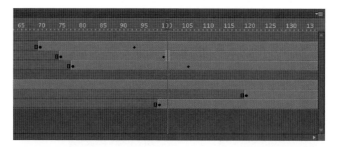

2   Right-click/Ctrl-click on frame 101 and choose Split Motion.

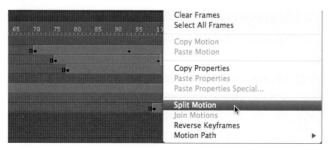

Flash cuts the motion tween into two separate tween spans. The end of the first tween is identical to the beginning of the second tween.

Motion tween split

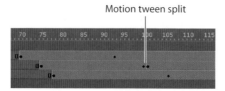

3   In the Middle_car layer, select frame 94, and right-click/Ctrl-click and choose Split Motion.

Flash cuts the motion tween into two separate tween spans.

4   In the Right_car layer, select frame 107, and right-click/Ctrl-click and choose Split Motion.

Flash cuts the motion tween into two separate tween spans. The motion tweens of all three cars are split.

Setting eases of a motion tween

You'll apply an ease-in to the motion tweens of the approaching cars to give them a sense of weight and decelerate as real cars would.

1 In the Middle_car layer, select any frame between the first and second keyframes of the first motion tween (frame 70 to frame 93).

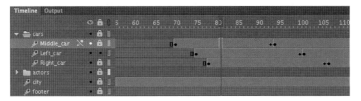

2 In the Properties inspector, enter 100 for the Ease value.

Flash applies an ease-out effect to the motion tween.

3 In the Left_car layer, select any frame between the first and second keyframes of the first motion tween (frame 75 to frame 100).

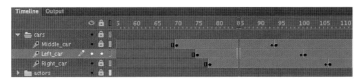

4 In the Properties inspector, enter **100** for the Ease value.

Flash applies an ease-out effect to the motion tween.

5 In the Right_car layer, select any frame between the first and second keyframes of the first motion tween (frame 78 to frame 106).

6 In the Properties inspector, enter **100** for the Ease value.

Flash applies an ease-out effect to the motion tween.

7 Enable the Loop Playback option at the bottom of the Timeline, and move the front and rear markers to bracket frames 60 to 115.

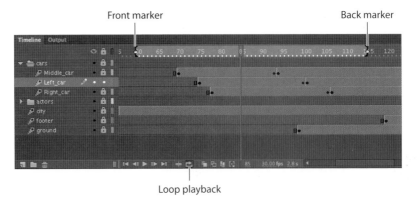

Front marker

Back marker

Loop playback

8 Click Play (Enter/Return).

Flash plays the Timeline in a loop between frames 60 to 115 so you can examine the ease-out motion of the three cars.

Frame-by-Frame Animation

Frame-by-frame animation refers to the illusion of movement created by seeing the incremental changes between every keyframe. It's the closest to traditional hand-drawn cel animation, and it's just as tedious. In Flash, you can change a drawing in every keyframe, and create a frame-by-frame animation.

Frame-by-frame animations increase your file size rapidly because Flash has to store the contents for each keyframe. Use frame-by-frame animation sparingly.

In the next section, you'll insert a frame-by-frame animation inside the carLeft movie clip symbol to make it move up and down in a jittery fashion. When the movie clip loops, the car will rumble slightly to simulate the idle of the motor.

Inserting a new keyframe

The frame-by-frame animations inside the carMiddle and carRight movie clip symbols have already been done. You'll finish the animation for the carLeft symbol.

1 In the Library panel, double-click the carRight movie clip symbol to examine its completed frame-by-frame animation.

Inside the carRight movie clip, three keyframes establish three different positions for the car and its headlights. The keyframes are spaced unevenly to provide the unpredictable up and down motion.

2 In the Library panel, double-click the carLeft move clip symbol.

You enter symbol-editing mode for the carLeft symbol.

3 Select frame 2 in both the lights layer and the smallRumble layer.

4 Right-click/Ctrl-click and choose Insert Keyframe (F6).

Flash inserts a keyframe in frame 2 of the lights layer and the smallRumble layer. The contents of the previous keyframes are copied into the new keyframes.

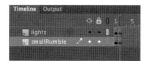

Changing the graphics

In the new keyframe, change the appearance of the contents to create the animation.

1   In frame 2, select all three graphics on Stage (Edit > Select All, or Ctrl/Command+A) and move them down the Stage 1 pixel. You can use the Properties inspector or press the Down Arrow key to nudge the graphics by 1 pixel.

The car and its headlights move down slightly.

2   Next, repeat the process of inserting keyframes and changing the graphics. For a random motion like an idling car, at least three keyframes are ideal.

3   Select frame 4 in both the lights layer and the smallRumble layer.

4   Right-click/Ctrl-click and choose Insert Keyframe (F6).

Flash inserts a keyframe in frame 4 of the lights layer and the smallRumble layer. The contents of the previous keyframes are copied into the new keyframes.

5   Select all three graphics on Stage (Edit > Select All, or Ctrl/Command+A) and move them up the Stage 2 pixels. You can use the Properties inspector or press the Up arrow key twice to nudge the graphics by 2 pixels.

The car and its headlights move up slightly.

6   Test the idling motion by enabling the Loop Playback option at the bottom of the Timeline and click Play (Enter/Return).

Animating 3D Motion

Finally, you'll add a title and animate it in 3D space. Animating in 3D presents the added complication of a third (z) axis. When you choose the 3D Rotation or 3D Translation tool, you need to be aware of the Global Transform option at the bottom of the Tools panel. The Global Transform option toggles between a global option (button depressed) and a local option (button raised). Moving an object with the global option on makes the transformations relative to the global coordinate system, whereas moving an object with the local option on makes the transformations relative to itself.

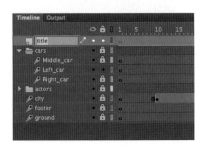

1   Click on Scene 1 in the Edit Bar to return to the main timeline, and insert a new layer at the top of the layer stack and rename it **title**.

2 Lock all the other layers.

3 Insert a new keyframe at frame 120.

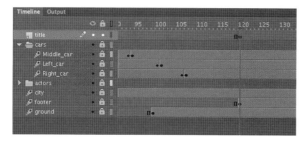

4 Drag the movie clip symbol called movietitle from the Library panel onto the Stage.

The movie title instance appears in your new layer in the keyframe at frame 120.

5 Position the title at x=**180** and y=**90**.

6 Right-click/Ctrl-click on the movie title and choose Create Motion Tween.

Flash converts the current layer to a Tween layer so you can begin to animate the instance.

7 Move the red playhead to frame 140.

8 Select the 3D Rotation tool.

9 Deselect the Global Transform option at the bottom of the Tools panel.

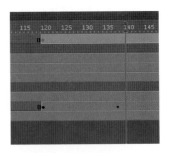

10 Click and drag the title to rotate it around the *y*-axis (green) so that its angle is at about –50 degrees. You can check the rotation values in the Transform panel (Window > Transform).

11 Move the red playhead to the first keyframe at frame 120.

12 Click and drag the title to rotate it around the *y*-axis in the opposite direction so that the instance looks like just a sliver.

Flash motion-tweens the change in the 3D rotation, so the title appears to swing in three dimensions.

Testing Your Movie

You can quickly preview your animation by "scrubbing" the red playhead back and forth on the Timeline or by choosing Control > Play. You can also use the integrated controller at the bottom of the Timeline.

However, to preview your animation as your audience will see it and to preview any nested animations within movie clip symbols, you should test your movie. Choose Control > Test Movie > in Flash Professional.

Flash exports a SWF file and saves it in the same location as your FLA file. The SWF file is the compressed, final Flash media that you would embed in an HTML page to play in a browser. Flash displays the SWF file in a new window with the exact Stage dimensions and plays your animation.

Note: The exported SWF in Test Movie mode will loop automatically. To prevent the looping in Test Movie mode, choose Control > Loop to deselect the loop option.

To exit Test Movie mode, click the Close window button.

You can also preview your animation by choosing Control > Test Movie > in Browser, and Flash will export a SWF file and open it automatically in your default browser.

Note: If you've targeted a different publishing platform in the Publish Settings (such as Adobe AIR), those options will be available for you in the Control > Test Movie menu.

Generating PNG Sequences and Sprite Sheets

While you can create sophisticated animations to play as a SWF file with the Flash Player, you can also use Flash's powerful tools to create your animation and export it as a series of images for use in other environments. For example, animations with HTML5 or on mobile devices often rely on sequential PNG files or a single file that packs all the images organized in rows and columns known as a sprite sheet. The sprite sheet is accompanied by a data file that describes the position of each image, or sprite, in the file.

Generating either PNG sequences or a sprite sheet of your animation is easy. First, your animation must be within a Movie Clip symbol. In the Library panel, right-click/Ctrl-click the symbol and choose Export PNG Sequence.

In the next steps, you select the destination on your hard drive for your images and the dimensions of your images.

For a sprite sheet, right-click/Ctrl-click the symbol and choose Generate sprite sheet. The Generate Sprite Sheet dialog box that appears provides different options such as sizing, background color, and the particular data format.

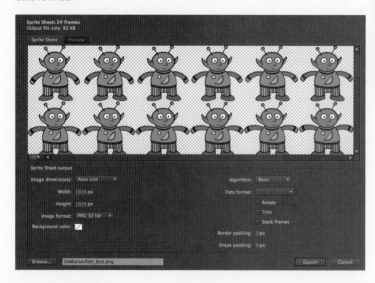

Click Export to output the sprite sheet and data file. The data file determines what kind of development environment you'll use your sprite sheet in. For example, JSON, Starling, and cocos2D are some of the data formats available.

Review Questions

1 What are two requirements of a motion tween?

2 What kinds of properties can a motion tween change?

3 What are property keyframes, and why are they important?

4 How can you edit the path of an object's motion?

5 What does easing do to a motion tween?

Review Answers

1 A motion tween requires a symbol instance on the Stage and its own layer, which is called a Tween layer. No other tween or drawing object can exist on the Tween layer.

2 A motion tween creates smooth transitions between different keyframes of an object's location, scale, rotation, transparency, brightness, tint, filter values, or 3D rotation or translation.

3 A keyframe marks a change in one or more properties of an object. Keyframes are specific to each property, so that a motion tween can have keyframes for position that are different from keyframes for transparency.

4 To edit the path of an object's motion, choose the Selection tool and click and drag directly on the path to bend it. You can also choose the Convert Anchor Point tool and Subselection tool to pull out handles at the anchor points. The handles control the curvature of the path.

5 Easing changes the rate of change in a motion tween. Without easing, a motion tween proceeds linearly, where the same amount of change happens over time. An ease-in makes an object begin its animation slowly, and an ease-out makes an object end its animation slowly.

5 ANIMATING SHAPES AND USING MASKS

Lesson Overview

In this lesson, you'll learn how to do the following:

- Animate shapes with shape tweens
- Use shape hints to refine shape tweens
- Shape tween gradient fills
- View Onion Skin outlines
- Apply easing to shape tweens
- Create and use masks
- Understand mask limitations
- Animate the Mask and Masked layers

 This lesson will take approximately 2½ hours to complete. If needed, remove the previous lesson folder from your hard drive and copy the Lesson05 folder onto it. Download the project files for this lesson from the Lesson & Update Files tab on your Account page at www.peachpit.com and store them on your computer in a convenient location, as described in the Getting Started section of this book. Your Accounts page is also where you'll find any updates to the chapters or to the lesson files. Look on the Lesson & Update Files tab to access the most current content.

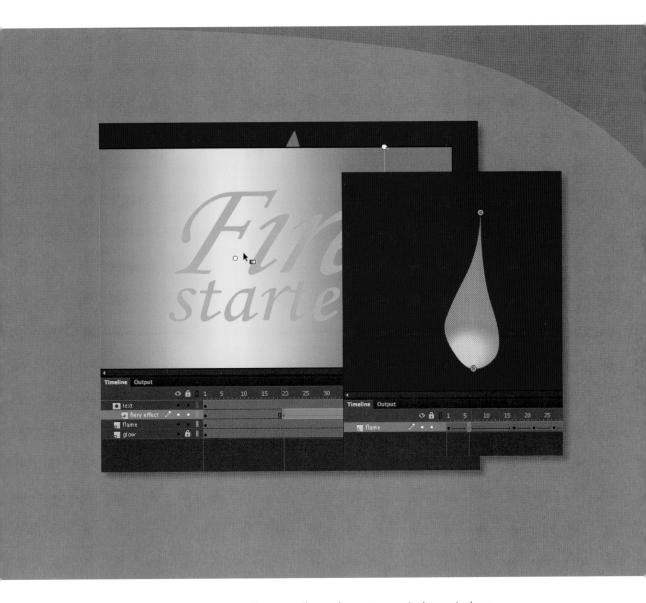

You can easily morph—create organic changes in shape—
with shape tweens. Masks provide a way to selectively
show only parts of a layer. Together, they allow you to add
more sophisticated effects to your animations.

Getting Started

● **Note:** If you have not already downloaded the project files for this lesson to your computer from your Account page, make sure to do so now. See "Getting Started" at the beginning of the book.

You'll start the lesson by viewing the animated logo that you'll create as you learn about shape tweens and masks in Flash.

1 Double-click the 05End.html file in the Lesson05/05End folder to play the animation in a browser.

The project is an animation of a flame flickering atop a fictional company name. The shape of the flame constantly changes as well as the radial gradient fill inside of the flame. A linear gradient sweeps across the letters of the company name from left to right. In this lesson, you'll animate both the flame and the colors that move across the letters.

2 Close your browser. Double-click the 05Start.fla file in the Lesson05/05Start folder to open the initial project file in Flash.

3 Choose File > Save As. Name the file **05_workingcopy.fla**, and save it in the 05Start folder. Saving a working copy ensures that the original start file will be available if you want to start over.

Animating Shapes

In the previous lesson, you learned to create animations with symbol instances. You could animate the motion, scale, rotation, color effect, or the filters applied to symbol instances. However, you couldn't animate the actual contours of a graphic. For example, creating an animation of the undulating surface of the ocean, or the slithering motion of a snake's body is difficult—if not impossible—with motion tweens. To do something more organic, you have to use shape tweening.

Shape tweening is a technique for interpolating the stroke and fill changes between different keyframes. Shape tweens make it possible to smoothly morph one shape into another. Any kind of animation that requires that the stroke or the fill of a shape to change—for example, animation of clouds, water, or fire—is a perfect candidate for shape tweening.

Because shape tweening applies only to shapes, you can't use groups, symbol instances, or bitmap images.

Understanding the Project File

The 05Start.fla file contains most of the graphics already completed and organized in different layers. However, the file is static, and you'll add the animation.

The text layer is at the very top, and contains the company name, "Firestarter." The flame layer contains the flame, and the bottom layer, called glow, contains a radial gradient to provide a soft glow.

There are no assets in the Library.

Creating a Shape Tween

A shape tween requires at least two keyframes on the same layer. The beginning keyframe contains a shape drawn with Flash's drawing tools or imported from Illustrator. The ending keyframe also contains a shape. A shape tween interpolates the smooth changes between the beginning keyframe and the end keyframe.

Establish keyframes containing different shapes

In the following steps, you'll animate the flame that will sit on top of the company name.

1   Select frame 40 for all three layers.

2   Choose Insert > Timeline > Frame (F5).

Flash inserts additional frames to all three layers up to frame 40.

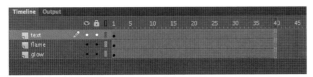

3   Lock the text layer and the glow layer, to prevent you from accidentally selecting or moving the graphics in those layers.

4   Right-click/Ctrl-click on frame 40 in the flame layer and select Insert Keyframe, or choose Insert > Timeline > Keyframe (F6).

Flash inserts a new keyframe at frame 40. The contents of the previous keyframe are copied into the second keyframe.

You now have two keyframes on the Timeline in the flame layer: a beginning keyframe at frame 1, and an end keyframe at frame 40.

5   Move the red playhead to frame 40.

Next, you'll change the shape of the flame in the end keyframe.

6   Choose the Selection tool.

7   Click off the shape to deselect it. Click and drag the contours of the flame to make the flame skinnier.

The beginning keyframe and the end keyframe now contain different shapes—a fat flame in the beginning keyframe, and a skinny flame in the end keyframe.

Apply the shape tween

The next step is to apply a shape tween between the keyframes to create the smooth transitions.

1   Click on any frame between the beginning keyframe and the end keyframe in the flame layer.

2   Right-click/Ctrl-click and select Create Shape Tween. Or, from the top menu choose Insert > Shape Tween.

Flash applies a shape tween between the two keyframes, which is indicated by a black forward-pointing arrow.

3 Watch your animation by choosing Control > Play, or by clicking the Play button at the bottom of the Timeline.

Flash creates a smooth animation between the keyframes in the flame layer, morphing the shape of the first flame into the shape of the second flame.

● **Note:** Don't worry if your flame doesn't morph exactly the way you want it to. Small changes between keyframes work best. Your flame may rotate while going from the first shape to the second. You'll have a chance to refine the shape tweening later in this lesson with shape hints.

Blend Types

In the Properties inspector, you can modify your shape tween by choosing either the Distributive or the Angular option for Blend. These two options determine how Flash makes the interpolations to change the shapes from one keyframe to the next.

The Distributive option is the default, and works well for most cases. It creates animations where the intermediate shapes are smoother.

Use the Angular Blend if your shapes have many points and straight lines. Flash attempts to preserve apparent corners and lines in the intermediate shapes.

Changing the Pace

The keyframes of a shape tween can be easily moved along the Timeline in order to change the timing or pacing of the animation.

Moving a keyframe

The flame slowly transforms from one shape to another over a period of 40 frames. If you want the flame to make the shape change more rapidly, you need to move the keyframes closer together.

1   Select the last keyframe of the shape tween in the flame layer.

2   Click and drag the last keyframe to frame 6.

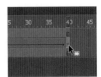

The shape tween shortens.

3   Watch your animation by choosing Control > Play, or by clicking the Play button at the bottom of the Timeline.

The flame flickers quickly, then remains static until frame 40.

Adding More Shape Tweens

You can add shape tweens by creating more keyframes. Each shape tween simply requires two keyframes to define its beginning state and its end state.

Insert additional keyframes

You want the flame to continually change shape, just like a real flame would. You'll add more keyframes and apply shape tweens between all the keyframes.

1   Right-click/Ctrl-click on frame 17 in the flame layer and select Insert Keyframe. Or, choose Insert > Timeline > Keyframe (F6).

Flash inserts a new keyframe at frame 17, and copies the contents of the previous keyframe into the second keyframe.

2 Right-click/Ctrl-click on frame 22 in the flame layer and select Insert Keyframe. Or, choose Insert > Timeline > Keyframe (F6).

Flash inserts a new keyframe at frame 22, and copies the contents of the previous keyframe into the second keyframe.

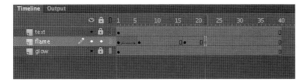

3 Continue inserting keyframes at frame 27, 33, and 40.

Your Timeline now has seven keyframes in the flame layer, with a shape tween between the first and second keyframes.

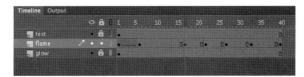

● **Note:** You can quickly make duplicate keyframes by first selecting a keyframe, and then holding down the Option/Alt key, click and drag the keyframe to a new position.

4 Move the red playhead to frame 17.

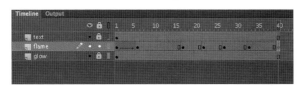

5 Choose the Selection tool.

6 Click off the shape to deselect it. Click and drag the contours of the flame to create another variation in its shape. You can make the base thicker, or change the curvature of the tip to make it lean left or right.

7 Modify the flame shapes in each of the newly inserted keyframes to create subtle variations.

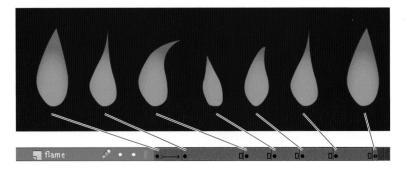

Extending the shape tweens

Your next step is to extend the shape tween so the flame morphs from one shape to the next.

1 Click on any frame between the second and third keyframes.

2 Right-click/Ctrl-click and select Create Shape Tween. Or, from the top menu, choose Insert > Shape Tween.

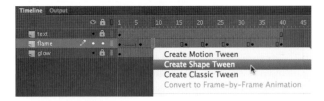

Flash applies a shape tween between the two keyframes, which is indicated by a black forward-pointing arrow.

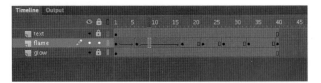

3 Continue to insert shape tweens between all the keyframes.

You should have six shape tweens in the flame layer.

4 Choose Control > Play, or click the Play button at the bottom of the Timeline.

Your flame flickers back and forth for the duration of the animation. Depending on how extensive your modifications to the flame have been, your flame may undergo some weird contortions between keyframes—for example, flipping or rotating unpredictably. Don't worry! You'll have a chance to refine your animation later in the lesson with shape hints.

Broken Tweens

Every shape tween needs a beginning and end keyframe. If the last keyframe of a shape tween is missing, Flash shows the broken tween as a dotted black line (rather than a solid arrow).

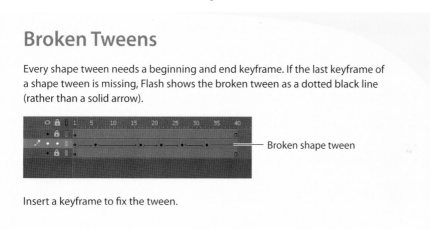

Broken shape tween

Insert a keyframe to fix the tween.

Creating a Looping Animation

Your flame should flicker back and forth continuously, as long as the logo is onscreen. You can create a seamless loop by making the first and last keyframe identical, and by putting the animation inside a movie clip symbol. As you recall from the previous lesson, a movie clip timeline loops continuously, independently of the main Timeline.

Duplicating keyframes

Make the first keyframe identical to the last keyframe by duplicating its contents.

1 Right-click/Ctrl-click the first keyframe on the flame layer and select Copy Frames. Or, from the top menu, choose Edit > Timeline > Copy Frames.

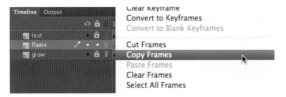

Flash copies the contents of the first keyframe to your clipboard.

● **Note:** You can quickly duplicate keyframes by first selecting a keyframe, and then, holding down the Option/Alt key, clicking and dragging the keyframe to a new position.

2 Right-click/Ctrl-click the last keyframe on the flame layer and select Paste Frames. Or, from the top menu, choose Edit > Timeline > Paste Frames.

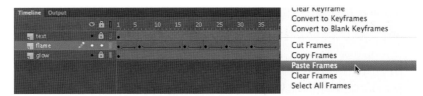

Flash pastes the contents of the first keyframe into the last keyframe. The first and last keyframes now contain identical flame shapes.

Previewing the loop

Use the Loop playback at the bottom of the Timeline to preview your animation.

1 Click the Loop Playback button at the bottom of the Timeline, or choose Control > Loop Playback.

● **Note:** The Loop Playback option loops only in the Flash Professional authoring environment, and not when it is published as a SWF. To create a loop, put your animation in a movie clip symbol, or use a gotoAndPlay() ActionScript command as described in the next lesson on interactivity.

When the Loop Playback option is depressed, the playhead will go back to frame 1 and continue to play when it reaches the end of the Timeline.

2 Extend the Markers to include all the frames on your Timeline (frames 1 through 40), or click on the Modify Markers button and select Marker Range All.

The Markers determine the range of frames that loop during playback.

3   Click the Play button, or choose Control > Play.

The flame animation plays and loops continuosly. Click the Pause button or the Enter/Return key to stop the animation.

Inserting the animation into a Movie Clip

When your animation plays in a movie clip symbol, the animation loops automatically.

1   Select all the frames on the flame layer, and right-click/Ctrl-click and select Cut Frames. Or, choose Edit > Timeline > Cut Frames.

Flash cuts the keyframes and shape tweens from the Timeline.

2   Choose Insert > New Symbol (Command/Ctrl+F8).

The Create New Symbol dialog box appears.

3   Enter **flame** as the name of the symbol, and choose Movie Clip as the Type. Click OK.

Flash creates a new movie clip symbol, and puts you in symbol-editing mode for your new symbol.

4   Right-click/Ctrl-click the first frame on your movie clip timeline and select Paste Frames. Or, choose Edit > Timeline > Paste Frames.

The flame animation from the main Timeline is pasted into your movie clip symbol's timeline.

5   Click on the Scene 1 button on the Edit Bar at the top of the Stage, or choose Edit > Edit Document (Command/Ctrl+E).

You exit symbol-editing mode and return to the main Timeline.

6   Select the flame layer, which is currently empty. Drag your newly created flame movie clip symbol from the Library panel to the Stage.

An instance of the flame movie clip symbol appears on the Stage.

7   Choose Control > Test Movie > In Flash Professional (Command+Return/ Ctrl +Enter).

Flash exports the SWF in a new window, where you can preview the animation. The flame flickers continuously in a seamless loop.

Using Shape Hints

Flash creates the smooth transitions between keyframes of your shape tween, but sometimes the results are unpredictable. Your shapes may go through strange contortions, flips, and rotations to get from one keyframe to another. You may like the effect, but more often than not, you'll want to maintain control of the transformations. Using shape hints can help refine the shape changes.

Shape hints force Flash to map points on the start shape to corresponding points on the end shape. By placing multiple shape hints, you can control more precisely how a shape tween appears.

Adding shape hints

Now you'll add shape hints to the shape of the flame to modify the way it morphs from one shape to the next.

1 Double-click the flame movie clip symbol in the Library to enter symbol-editing mode. Select the first keyframe of the shape tween in the flame layer.

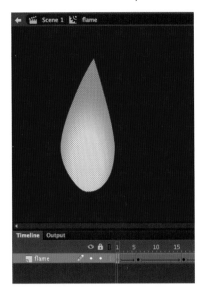

2 Choose Modify > Shape > Add Shape Hint (Command+Shift+H /Ctrl+Shift+H).

   A red circled letter "a" appears on the Stage. The circled letter represents the first shape hint.

3 Choose the Selection tool and make sure that the Snap to Objects option is enabled.

   The magnet icon at the bottom of the Tools panel should be depressed. The Snap to Objects option ensures that objects snap to each other when being moved or modified.

4 Drag the circled letter to the tip of the flame.

● **Note:** Shape hints should be placed on the contours of shapes.

5 Choose Modify > Shape > Add Shape Hint again to create a second shape hint.

A red circled "b" appears on the Stage.

6 Drag the "b" shape hint to the bottom of the flame shape.

You have two shape hints mapped to different points on the shape in the first keyframe.

7 Select the next keyframe of the flame layer (frame 6).

A corresponding red circled "b" appears on the Stage, although an "a" shape hint is directly under it.

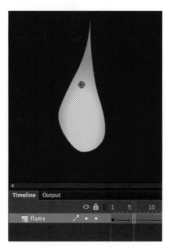

8 Drag the circled letters to corresponding points on the shape in the second keyframe. The "a" hint goes on the top of the flame, the "b" hint goes on the bottom of flame.

The shape hints turn green, indicating that you've correctly placed the shape hint.

9 Select the first keyframe.

Note that the initial shape hints have turned yellow, indicating that they are correctly placed.

10 Scrub the playhead through the first shape tween on the Timeline to see the effects of the shape hints on the shape tween.

The shape hints force the tip of the flame in the first keyframe to map to the tip of the flame in the second keyframe and the bottoms to map to each other. This restricts the transformations.

To demonstrate the value of shape hints, you can deliberately create a mess of your shape tweens. In the end keyframe, put the "b" hint at the top of the flame and the "a" hint at the bottom.

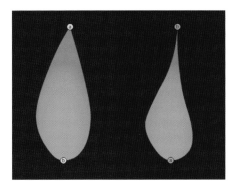

Beginning keyframe   End keyframe

Note: You can add a maximum of 26 shape hints to any shape tween. Be sure to add them in a clockwise or counterclockwise direction for best results.

Note: Commonly, you'll only add shape hints to the first keyframe of a shape tween, and move the corresponding hints in the last keyframe. In this animation, since you have a series of shape tweens placed next to each other, the end keyframe of one shape tween is the beginning keyframe for the next. You can add shape hints for all the keyframes, but you must keep track of which hints correspond to the beginning or end keyframe shapes.

Flash forces the tip of the flame to tween to the bottom of the flame, and vice versa. The result is a strange flipping motion as Flash tries to make the transformation. Put the "a" back at the top and the "b" back at the bottom after your experimentation.

Removing shape hints

If you've added too many shape hints, you can easily delete the unnecessary ones. Removing a shape hint in one keyframe will remove its corresponding shape hint in the other keyframe.

- Drag an individual shape hint entirely off the Stage and Pasteboard.

- Choose Modify > Shape > Remove All Hints to delete all the shape hints.

Only the content in the keyframes of a shape tween are displayed fully rendered. All other frames are shown as outlines. To see all frames fully rendered, click the Onion Skin option.

Previewing the Animation with Onion Skin Outlines

It's sometimes useful to see how your shapes are changing from one keyframe to another on the Stage all at once. Seeing how the shapes gradu-

ally change lets you make smarter adjustments to your animation. You can do so using the Onion Skin Outlines option, available at the bottom of the Timeline.

Onion Skin Outlines show the contents of the frames before and after the currently selected frame.

The term "onion skin" comes from the world of traditional hand-drawn animation, when anima-tors would draw on thin, semi-transparent, trac-ing paper known as onionskin. When creating an action sequence, animators flip back and forth quickly between drawings held between their fingers. This allows them to see how the draw-ings smoothly connect to each other.

To use Onion Skin Outlines, click the Onion Skin Outlines button to enable it. Drag the begin-ning or end marker to select the range of frames around the playhead that you want to show. You can also select the preset marker options in the Modify Markers menu.

Animating Color

Shape tweens interpolate all aspects of a shape, which means both the stroke and fill of a shape can be tweened. So far, you've modified the stroke, or outlines, of the flame. In the next section, you'll modify the fill so that the color gradient can change—perhaps glow brighter and more intense at some points in the animation.

Adjusting the gradient fills

Use the Gradient Transform tool to change the way the color gradient is applied to a shape, and use the Color panel to change the actual colors used in a gradient.

1   If you're not already in symbol-editing mode for your flame symbol, double-click the flame movie clip symbol in the Library to edit it.

    You enter symbol-editing mode.

2   Select the second keyframe on the flame layer (frame 6).

3   Select the Gradient Transform tool, which is grouped with the Free Transform tool in the Tools panel.

    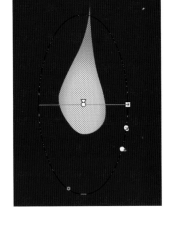

    The control points for the Gradient Transform tool appear on the gradient fill of the flame. The various control points allow you to stretch, rotate, and move the centerpoint of the gradient within the fill.

4   Use the control points to tighten the color gradient into the base of the flame. Make the gradient wider and positioned lower on the flame, and move the centerpoint of the gradient to one side.

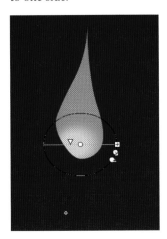

Your flame's orange core appears lower and more intense because the colors are distributed in a smaller area.

5 Move the playhead along the Timeline between the first and second keyframe.

The shape tween automatically animates the colors inside the flame as well as its contours.

6 Select the third keyframe on the flame layer (frame 17). In this frame, you'll adjust the actual color of the gradient.

7 Choose the Selection tool and click on the fill of the flame on the Stage.

8 Open the Color panel (Window > Color).

The Color panel appears, showing you the gradient colors of the selected fill.

9 Click on the inner color marker, which is currently yellow.

10 Change the color to a hot pink (#F019EE).

The center color of the gradient turns pink.

● **Note:** Shape tweens can smoothly animate solid colors or color gradients, but they can't animate between different types of gradients. For example, you can't shape tween a linear gradient into a radial gradient.

11 Move the playhead along the Timeline between the second and third keyframe.

The shape tween automatically animates the center color in the gradient from yellow to pink. Experiment with the other keyframes by modifying the gradient fill and see what kinds of interesting effects you can apply to your flickering flame.

Creating and Using Masks

Masking is a way of selectively hiding and displaying content on a layer. Masking is a way for you to control the content that your audience sees. For example, you can make a circular mask and allow your audience to only see through the circular area, so that you get a keyhole or spotlight effect. In Flash, you put a mask on one layer and the content that is masked in a layer below it.

For the animated logo you're creating in this lesson, you'll add a mask that will make the text a little more visually interesting.

Define the Mask layer

You'll create a mask from the "Fire starter" text that will reveal an image of a fire beneath it.

1   Return to the main Timeline. Unlock the text layer. Double-click the icon in front of the text layer name, or select the text layer and choose Modify > Timeline > Layer Properties.

The Layer Properties dialog box appears.

2   Select Mask and click OK.

The text layer becomes a Mask layer, indicated by the mask icon in front of the layer name. Anything in this layer will act as a mask for a Masked layer below it.

● **Note:** Flash does not recognize different Alpha levels in a mask created on a timeline, so a semitransparent fill in the Mask layer has the same effect as an opaque fill, and edges will always be hard-edged. However, with ActionScript you can dynamically create masks that will allow transparencies.

● **Note:** Masks do not recognize strokes, so use only fills in the Mask layer. Text created from the Text tool also works as a mask.

For this lesson, we're using the text already in place as the mask, but the mask can be any filled shape. The color of the fill doesn't matter. What's important to Flash are the size, location, and contours of the shape. The shape will be the "peephole" through which you'll see the content on the layer below. You can use any of the drawing or text tools to create the fill for your mask.

Create the Masked layer

The Masked layer is always under the Mask layer.

1   Click the New Layer button, or choose Insert > Timeline > Layer.

A new layer appears.

2   Rename the layer **fiery effect**.

● **Note:** You can also double-click a normal layer under a Mask layer, or choose Modify > Timeline > Layer Properties, and choose Masked to modify the layer into a Masked layer.

3   Drag the fiery effect layer under the Mask layer so that it becomes indented.

The fiery effect layer becomes a Masked layer, paired with the Mask layer above it. Any content in the Masked layer will be masked by the layer above it.

4   Choose File > Import > Import to Stage, and select fire.jpg from the 05Start folder.

The bitmap image of fire appears on the Stage, and the words appear over the image.

See the effects of the Mask

To see the effects of the Mask layer on its Masked layer, lock both layers.

1   Click the Lock option for both the text layer and the fiery effect layer.

Both Mask and Masked layers become locked. The shape of the letters in the Mask layer reveals parts of the image in the Masked layer.

2   Choose Control > Test Movie > In Flash Professional.

As the flame flickers above the text, the letters reveal the fiery texture in the layer below it.

● **Note:** You can have multiple Masked layers under a single Mask layer.

Traditional Masks

It might seem counterintuitive that the shapes in the Mask layer reveal, rather than hide, the content in the Masked layer. However, that's exactly how a traditional mask in photography or painting works. When a painter uses a mask, the mask protects the painting from paint splatters. When a photographer uses a mask in the darkroom, the mask protects the photosensitive paper from the light, to prevent those areas from getting any darker. So thinking of a mask as something that protects the lower, Masked, layer is a good way to remember which areas are hidden and which areas are revealed.

Animating the Mask and Masked Layers

The letters of your animated logo have more drama now that you've created a mask with an image of fire behind it. However, the client for this fictional project now demands that it have even more punch. Although she likes the look of the fiery letters, she wants an animated effect.

Fortunately, you can include animations in either the Mask or the Masked layer. You can create an animation in the Mask layer if you want the mask itself to move or expand to show different parts of the Masked layer. Or, you can create an animation in the Masked layer if you want the content to move under a mask, like scenery whizzing by a train window.

Adding a tween to the Masked layer

To make the logo more compelling for your client, you'll add a shape tween to the Masked layer. The shape tween will move a glow from left to right under the letters.

1 Unlock both the text layer and the fiery effect layer.

   The effects of the Mask and Masked layer are no longer visible, but their contents are now editable.

2 Delete the bitmap image of the fire in the fiery effect layer.

3 Select the Rectangle tool and open the Color panel (Window > Color).

4 In the Color panel, choose Linear gradient for the Fill.

5 Create a gradient that starts with red on the left (#FF0000), yellow in the middle (#FFFC00), and red again on the right (#FF0000).

6   Create a rectangle in the fiery effect layer that covers the letters in the text layer.

7   Choose the Gradient Transform tool and click on the fill of your rectangle.

    The control handles for the Gradient Transform tool appear on the fill
    of the rectangle.

8   Move the centerpoint of the gradient so that the yellow color appears on the
    far left side of the Stage.

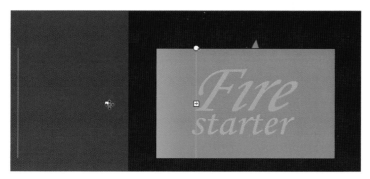

    The yellow glow will begin from the left and move to the right.

9 Right-click/Ctrl-click on frame 20 in the fiery effect layer and select Insert Keyframe. Or, choose Insert > Timeline > Keyframe (F6).

Flash inserts a new keyframe at frame 20, and copies the contents of the previous keyframe into the second keyframe.

10 Right-click/Ctrl-click on the last frame (frame 40) in the fiery effect layer and select Insert Keyframe. Or, choose Insert > Timeline > Keyframe (F6).

Flash inserts a new keyframe at frame 40, and copies the contents of the previous keyframe into the second keyframe. You now have three keyframes in the fiery effect layer.

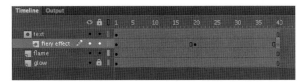

11 Move your playhead to the last frame (frame 40).

12 Click on the rectangle on the Stage and choose the Gradient Transform tool.

The control handles for the Gradient Transform tool appears on the fill of the rectangle.

13 Move the centerpoint of the gradient so that the yellow color appears on the far right side of the Stage.

14 Right-click/Ctrl-click anywhere on the Timeline between the second and third keyframe in the fiery effect layer and select Create Shape Tween. Or, from the top menu, choose Insert > Shape Tween.

Flash applies a shape tween between the two keyframes, indicated by a black forward-pointing arrow. The color gradient is shape-tweened so the yellow glow moves within the fill of the rectangle from left to right.

15 Watch your animation by choosing Control > Test Movie > In Flash Professional.

While the flame burns above the letters, a soft yellow glow flashes across the letters.

Easing a Shape Tween

You've worked with eases in the previous lesson. You can apply eases to a shape tween as easily as you can with a motion tween. Eases help your animation bear a sense of weight by enabling you to add an acceleration or deceleration component to its motion.

You add an ease to a shape tween from the Properties inspector. Ease values range from –100, which indicates an ease-in, to 100, which indicates an ease-out. An ease-in makes the motion start off slowly. An ease-out slows down the motion as it approaches its end keyframe.

Adding an ease-in

You'll make the glow that flashes across the letters of the logo begin slowly, and then pick up speed. The ease-in will help viewers take notice of the animation before it proceeds.

1 Click anywhere inside the shape tween in the fiery effect layer.

2 In the Properties inspector, enter **100** for the Ease value.

Flash applies an ease-in effect to the shape tween.

● **Note:** You can apply either an ease-in or an ease-out to a shape tween, but not both.

3 Choose Control > Test Movie > In Flash Professional to test your movie.

The soft yellow glow flashes across the letters, starting off slowly, adding a little more sophistication to the entire animation.

Review Questions

1   What is a shape tween, and how do you apply it?

2   What are shape hints, and how do you use them?

3   How is a shape tween different from a motion tween?

4   What is a mask, and how do you create one?

5   How do you see the effects of a mask?

Review Answers

1   A shape tween creates smooth transitions between keyframes containing different shapes. To apply a shape tween, create different shapes in an initial keyframe and in a final keyframe. Then, select any frame between the keyframes in the Timeline, right-click/Ctrl-click, and select Create Shape Tween.

2   Shape hints are labeled markers that indicate how one point on the initial shape of a shape tween will map to a corresponding point on the final shape. Shape hints help refine the way the shapes will morph. To use shape hints, first select the initial keyframe of a shape tween. Choose Modify > Shape > Add Shape Hint. Move the first shape hint to the edge of the shape. Move the playhead to the final keyframe, and move the corresponding shape hint to a matching edge of the shape.

3   A shape tween uses shapes while a motion tween uses symbol instances. A shape tween smoothly interpolates the change of stroke or fill of a shape between two keyframes. A motion tween smoothly interpolates the changes in location, scale, rotation, color effect, or filter effect of a symbol instance between two keyframes.

4   Masking is a way of selectively hiding and displaying content on a layer. In Flash, you put a mask on the top Mask layer and the content in the layer below it, which is called the Masked layer. Both the Mask and the Masked layers can be animated.

5   To see the effects of the Mask layer on the Masked layer, you must lock both layers, or test your movie with Control > Test Movie > In Flash Professional.

6 CREATING INTERACTIVE NAVIGATION

Lesson Overview

In this lesson, you'll learn how to do the following:

- Create button symbols

- Add sound effects to buttons

- Duplicate symbols

- Swap symbols and bitmaps

- Name button instances

- Write ActionScript 3.0 to create nonlinear navigation

- Identify code errors with the Compiler Errors panel

- Use the Code Snippets panel to quickly add interactivity

- Create and use frame labels

- Create animated buttons

This lesson will take approximately 3 hours to complete. If needed, remove the previous lesson folder from your hard drive and copy the Lesson06 folder onto it. Download the project files for this lesson from the Lesson & Update Files tab on your Account page at www.peachpit.com and store them on your computer in a convenient location, as described in the Getting Started section of this book. Your Accounts page is also where you'll find any updates to the chapters or to the lesson files. Look on the Lesson & Update Files tab to access the most current content.

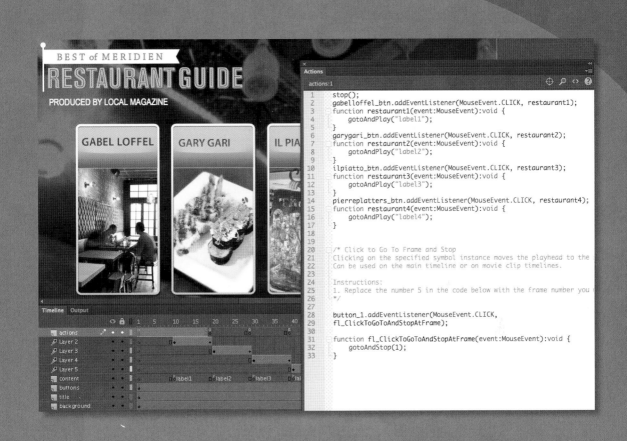

Let your viewers explore your project and become active participants. Button symbols and ActionScript work together to create engaging, user-driven, interactive experiences.

Getting Started

● **Note:** If you have not already downloaded the project files for this lesson to your computer from your Account page, make sure to do so now. See "Getting Started" at the beginning of the book.

To begin, view the interactive restaurant guide that you'll create as you learn to make interactive projects in Flash.

1 Double-click the 06End.html file in the Lesson06/06End folder to play the animation.

The project is an interactive restaurant guide for an imaginary city. Viewers can click any button to see more information about a particular restaurant. In this lesson, you'll create interactive buttons and structure the Timeline properly. You'll learn to write ActionScript to provide instructions for what each button will do.

2 Close the 06End.html file.

● **Note:** Flash warns you if your computer doesn't have the same fonts contained in a FLA file. Choose substitute fonts, or simply click Use Default to have Flash automatically make the substitutions.

3 Double-click the 06Start.fla file in the Lesson06/06Start folder to open the initial project file in Flash. The file includes several assets already in the Library panel, and the Stage has already been sized properly.

4   Choose File > Save As. Name the file **06_workingcopy.fla** and save it in the
    06Start folder. Saving a working copy ensures that the original start file will be
    available if you want to start over.

About Interactive Movies

Interactive movies change based on the viewer's actions. For example, when the
viewer clicks a button, a different graphic with more information is displayed.
Interactivity can be simple, such as a button click, or it can be complex, receiving
inputs from a variety of sources, such as the movements of the mouse, keystrokes
from the keyboard, or even the tilting of a mobile device.

In Flash, you use ActionScript to achieve most interactivity. ActionScript provides
the instructions that tell each button what to do when the user clicks one of them.
In this lesson, you'll learn to create a nonlinear navigation—one in which the
movie doesn't have to play straight from the beginning of the Timeline to the end.
ActionScript can tell the Flash playhead to jump around and go to different frames
of the Timeline based on which button the user clicks. Different frames on the
Timeline contain different content. The user doesn't actually know that the playhead is jumping around the Timeline; the user just sees (or hears) different content
appear as the buttons are clicked on the Stage.

Creating Buttons

A button is a basic visual indicator of something the user can interact with. The
user usually clicks a button, but many other types of interactions are possible. For
example, something can happen when the user rolls the mouse over a button.

Buttons are a kind of symbol that have four special states, or keyframes, that
determine how the button appears. Buttons can look like virtually anything—
an image, graphic, or a bit of text—they don't have to be those typical pill-shaped,
gray rectangles that you see on many Web sites.

Creating a button symbol

In this lesson, you'll create buttons with small thumbnail images and restaurant
names. A button symbol's four special states include the following:

- **Up state.** Shows the button as it appears when the mouse is not interacting
  with it.

- **Over state.** Shows the button as it appears when the mouse is hovering over it.

- **Down state.** Shows the button as it appears when the mouse button is depressed.

- **Hit state.** Indicates the clickable area of the button.

You'll understand the relationship between these states and the button appearance as you work through this exercise.

1 Choose Insert > New Symbol.

2 In the Create New Symbol dialog box, select Button and name the symbol **gabel loffel button**. Click OK.

Flash brings you to symbol-editing mode for your new button.

3 In the Library panel, expand the folder called restaurant thumbnails and drag the graphic symbol gabel loffel thumbnail to the middle of the Stage.

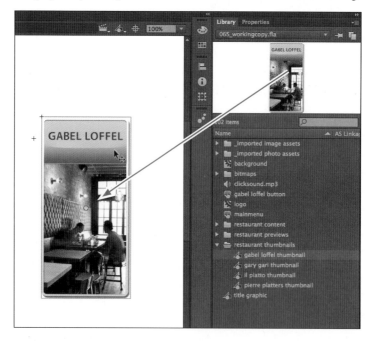

4 In the Properties inspector, set the X value to **0** and the Y value to **0**.

The upper-left corner of the small gabel loffel restaurant image is now aligned to the registration point of the symbol.

5 Select the Hit frame in the Timeline and choose Insert > Timeline > Frame
to extend the Timeline.

The gabel loffel image now extends through the Up, Over, Down, and Hit states.

6 Insert a new layer.

7 Select the Over frame and choose Insert > Timeline > Keyframe.

A new keyframe is inserted in the Over state of the top layer.

8 In the Library panel, expand the folder called restaurant previews, and drag the
movie clip symbol called gabel loffel over info to the Stage.

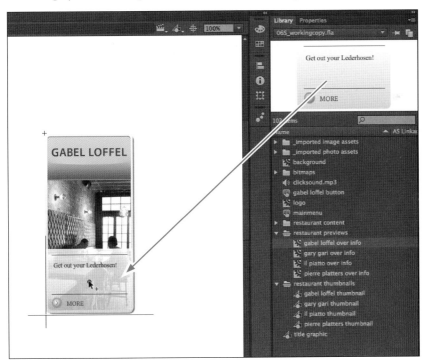

9 In the Properties inspector, set the X value to **0** and the Y value to **215**.

The gray information box will appear over the restaurant image whenever the mouse cursor rolls over the button.

10 Insert a third layer above the first two.

11 Select the Down frame on the new layer and choose Insert > Timeline > Keyframe.

A new keyframe is inserted in the Down state of the new layer.

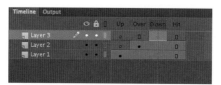

12 Drag the sound file called clicksound.mp3 from the Library panel to the Stage.

The beginning of the sound's waveform appears in the Down keyframe of the top layer of your button symbol.

13 Select the Down keyframe where the waveform appears, and in the Properties inspector, make sure that Sync is set to Event.

● **Note:** You'll learn more about sound in Lesson 7.

A clicking sound will play only when a viewer depresses the button.

14 Click Scene 1 in the Edit bar above the Stage to exit symbol-editing mode and return to the main Timeline. Your first button symbol is complete! Look in your Library panel to see the new button symbol stored there.

Invisible Buttons and the Hit Keyframe

Your button symbol's Hit keyframe indicates the area that is "hot," or clickable by the user. Normally, the Hit keyframe contains a shape that is the same size and location as the shape in your Up keyframe. In most cases, you want the graphics that users see to be the same area where they click. However, in certain advanced applications, you may want the Hit keyframe and the Up keyframe to be different. If your Up keyframe is empty, the resulting button is known as an invisible button.

Users can't see invisible buttons, but because the Hit keyframe still defines a clickable area, invisible buttons remain active. So, you can place invisible buttons over any part of the Stage and use ActionScript to program them to respond to users.

Invisible buttons are useful for creating generic hotspots. For example, placing them on top of different photos can help you make each photo respond to a mouse click without having to make each photo a different button symbol.

Duplicating buttons

Now that you've created one button, you'll be able to create others more easily. You'll duplicate one button here, change the image in the next section, and then continue to duplicate buttons and modify images for the remaining restaurants.

1   In the Library panel, right-click/Ctrl-click the gabel loffel button symbol and select Duplicate. You can also click the options menu at the top-right corner of the Library panel and select Duplicate.

2   In the Duplicate Symbol dialog box, select Button, and name it **gary gari button**. Click OK.

Swapping bitmaps

Bitmaps and symbols are easy to swap on the Stage and can significantly speed up your workflow.

1   In the Library panel, double-click the icon for your newly duplicated symbol (gary gari button) to edit it.

2   Select the restaurant image on the Stage.

3   In the Properties inspector, click Swap.

4   In the Swap Symbol dialog box, select the next thumbnail image, called gary gari thumbnail, and click OK.

The original thumbnail (shown with a black dot next to the symbol name) is swapped for the one you selected. Because they are both the same size, the replacement is seamless.

5   Now select the Over keyframe and click the gray information box on the Stage.

6   In the Properties inspector, click Swap and swap the selected symbol with the symbol called gary gari over info.

The instance in the Over keyframe of your button is replaced with one that is appropriate for the second restaurant. Since the symbol was duplicated, all other elements, such as the sound in the top layer, remain the same.

7   Continue duplicating your buttons and swapping the two instances inside them until you have four different button symbols in your Library panel, each representing a different restaurant. When you're done, it's a good idea to organize all your restaurant buttons in a folder in your Library panel.

Placing the button instances

The buttons need to be put on the Stage and given names in the Properties inspector so that ActionScript can identify them.

1   On the main Timeline, insert a new layer and rename it **buttons**.

2   Drag each of your buttons from the Library panel to the middle of the Stage, placing them in a horizontal row. Don't worry about their exact position because you'll align them nicely in the next few steps.

3   Select the first button, and in the Properties inspector, set the X value to **100**.

4   Select the last button, and in the Properties inspector, set the X value to **680**.

5   Select all four buttons. In the Align panel (Window > Align), deselect the Align to stage option, click the Space Evenly Horizontally button, and then click the Align Top Edge button.

All four buttons are now evenly distributed and aligned horizontally.

6 With all the buttons still selected, in the Properties inspector, enter **170** for the Y value.

All four buttons are positioned on the Stage correctly.

7 You can now test your movie to see how the buttons behave. Choose Control > Test Movie > In Flash Professional. Note how the gray information box in the Over keyframe appears when your mouse hovers over each button, and how the clicking sound is triggered when you depress your mouse over each button. At this point, however, you haven't provided any instructions for the buttons to actually do anything. That part comes after you name the buttons and learn a little about ActionScript.

Naming button instances

Name each button instance so that it can be referenced by ActionScript. This is a crucial step that many beginners forget to do.

1   Click on an empty part of the Stage to deselect all the buttons, and then select just the first button.

2   Type **gabelloffel_btn** in the Instance Name field in the Properties inspector.

3   Name each of the other buttons **garygari_btn**, **ilpiatto_btn**, and **pierreplatters_btn**.

   Make sure that you use all lowercase letters, leave no spaces, and double-check the spelling of each button instance. Flash is very picky, and one typo will prevent your entire project from working correctly!

4   Lock all the layers.

Naming Rules

Naming instances is a critical step in creating interactive Flash projects. The most common mistake made by novices is not to name, or to incorrectly name, a button instance.

Instance names are important because ActionScript uses the names to reference those objects. Instance names are not the same as the symbol names in the Library panel. The names in the Library panel are simply organizational reminders.

Instance naming follows these simple rules:

1   Do not use spaces or special punctuation. Underscores are okay to use.

2   Do not begin a name with a number.

3   Be aware of uppercase and lowercase letters. ActionScript is case-sensitive.

4   End your button name with _btn. Although it is not required, it helps identify those objects as buttons.

5   Do not use any word that is reserved for a Flash ActionScript command.

Understanding ActionScript 3.0

● **Note:** The most recent version of Flash Professional supports only ActionScript 3.0. If you need to program in ActionScript 1.0 or 2.0, you must use an earlier version of Flash Professional.

Adobe Flash Professional uses ActionScript 3.0, a robust scripting language, to extend the functionality of Flash. Although ActionScript 3.0 may seem intimidating to you if you're new to scripting, it can give you great results with some very simple scripts. As with any language, it's best if you take the time to learn the syntax and some basic terminology.

About ActionScript

ActionScript, which is similar to JavaScript, lets you add more interactivity to Flash animations. In this lesson, you'll use ActionScript to attach behaviors to buttons. You'll also learn how to use ActionScript for such simple tasks as stopping an animation.

You don't have to be a scripting expert to use ActionScript. In fact, for common tasks, you may be able to copy script that other Flash users have shared. And you can also use the Code Snippets panel, which provides an easy, visual way to add ActionScript to your project or share ActionScript code among developers.

However, you'll be able to accomplish much more in Flash—and feel more confident using the application—if you understand how ActionScript works.

This lesson isn't designed to make you an ActionScript expert. Instead, it introduces common terms and syntax, walks you through a simple script, and provides an introduction to the ActionScript language.

If you've used scripting languages before, the documentation included in the Flash Help menu may provide additional guidance you need to use ActionScript proficiently. If you're new to scripting and want to learn ActionScript, you may find an ActionScript 3.0 book for beginners helpful.

Understanding scripting terminology

● **Note:** Variable names must be unique, and they are case-sensitive. The variable mypassword is not the same as the variable MyPassword. Variable names can contain only numbers, letters, underscores, and dollar signs (but by convention, $ is not used in ActionScript); they cannot begin with a number. These are the same naming rules that apply to instances. (In fact, variables and instances are conceptually the same.)

Many of the terms used in describing ActionScript are similar to terms used for other scripting languages. The following terms are used frequently in ActionScript documentation.

Variable

A *variable* represents a specific piece of data that helps you keep track of things. For example, you can use variables to keep track of a score in a game, or the number of clicks a user has made with the mouse. When you create, or *declare*, a variable, you also assign a data type, which determines what kind of data the variable can represent. For example, a String variable holds any string of alphanumeric characters, whereas a Number variable must contain a number.

Keyword

In ActionScript, a *keyword* is a reserved word that is used to perform a specific task. For example, *var* is a keyword that is used to create a variable.

You can find a complete list of keywords in Flash Help. Because these words are reserved, you can't use them as variable names or in other ways. ActionScript always uses them to perform their assigned tasks. As you enter ActionScript in the Actions panel, keywords will turn a different color. This is a great way to know if a word is reserved by Flash.

Arguments

Arguments, the values most often seen between parentheses () in a line of code, provide specific details for a particular command. For example, in the code `gotoAndPlay(3);` the argument instructs the script to go to frame 3.

Function

A *function* groups together related lines of code that you can refer to by name. Using a function makes it possible to run the same set of statements without having to type them repeatedly.

Objects

In ActionScript 3.0, you work with objects that help you do certain tasks. A Sound object, for example, helps you control sound, and a Date object can help you manipulate time-related data. The button symbols that you created earlier in this lesson are also objects—they are called SimpleButton objects.

Objects created in the authoring environment (as opposed to those created with ActionScript) can be referenced in ActionScript only if they have a unique instance name. Buttons on the Stage are referred to as instances, and in fact, *instances* and *objects* are synonymous.

Methods

Methods are commands that result in action. Methods are the doers of ActionScript, and each kind of object has its own set of methods. Understanding ActionScript involves learning the methods for each kind of object. For example, two methods associated with a MovieClip object are `stop()` and `gotoAndPlay()`.

Properties

Properties describe an object. For example, the properties of a movie clip include its height and width, *x* and *y* coordinates, and horizontal and vertical scale. Many properties can be changed, whereas other properties can only be "read," meaning they simply describe an object.

Using proper scripting syntax

If you're unfamiliar with program code or scripting, you may find ActionScript code challenging to decipher. Once you understand the basic *syntax*, which is the grammar and punctuation of the language, you'll find it easier to follow a script.

- The *semicolon* at the end of the line tells ActionScript that it has reached the end of the code line.

- As in English, every open *parenthesis* must have a corresponding close parenthesis, and the same is true for *brackets* and *curly brackets*. If you open something, you must close it. Very often, the curly brackets in ActionScript code will be separated on different lines. This makes it easier to read what's inside the curly brackets.

- The *dot* operator (.) provides a way to access the properties and methods of an object. Type the instance name, followed by a dot, and then enter the name of the property or method. Think of the dot as a way to separate objects, methods, and properties.

- Whenever you're entering a string, use *quotation marks.*

- You can add *comments* to remind you or others of what you are accomplishing with different parts of the script. To add a comment for a single line, start it with two slashes (//). To type a multiline comment, start it with /* and end it with */. Comments are ignored by Flash and won't affect your code at all.

Flash provides assistance in the following ways as you write scripts in the Actions panel:

- Words that have specific meanings in ActionScript, such as keywords and statements, appear in blue as you type them in the Actions panel. Words that are not reserved in ActionScript, such as variable names, appear in black. Strings appear in green. Comments, which ActionScript ignores, appear in gray.

- As you work in the Actions panel, Flash detects the action you are entering and displays a code hint. There are two types of code hints: a tooltip that contains the complete syntax for that action and a popup menu that lists possible ActionScript elements.

- As your Actions panel fills up with code, you can collapse groups of code to make reading easier. When you have related blocks of code (grouped by curly braces), click the minus symbol in the code margin to collapse them, and click the plus symbol in the code margin to expand them.

Navigating the Actions panel

The Actions panel is where you write all your code. Open the Actions panel by choosing Window > Actions, or by selecting a keyframe on the Timeline and clicking the ActionScript panel icon on the top right of the Properties inspector.

You can also right-click/Ctrl-click on any keyframe and select Actions.

The Actions panel gives you a flexible environment to enter ActionScript code, as well as different options to help you write, edit, and view your code.

The Actions panel is divided into two parts. On the right of the Actions panel is the Script pane—the blank slate where you can write code. You enter ActionScript in the Script pane just as you would in a text-editing application.

On the left is the Script navigator, which tells you where your code is located. Flash places ActionScript on keyframes on the Timeline, so the Script navigator can be particularly useful if you have lots of code scattered in different keyframes and on different Timelines.

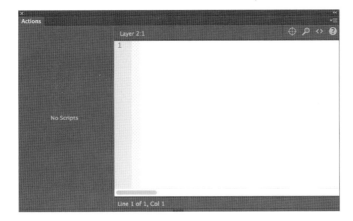

At the bottom of the Actions panel, Flash displays the current line number and column number (or character in the row) of the current selection.

The top-right corner of the Actions panel contains options for finding, replacing, and inserting code.

Preparing the Timeline

Every new Flash project begins with just a single frame. To create room on the Timeline to add more content, you'll have to add more frames to at least one layer.

1 Select a later frame in the top layer. In this example, select frame 50.

2 Choose Insert > Timeline > Frame (F5). You can also right-click/Ctrl-click and choose Insert Frame.

   Flash adds frames in the top layer up to the selected point, frame 50.

3 Select frame 50 in the other two layers and insert frames up to the selected frame.

   All your layers have 50 frames on the Timeline.

Adding a Stop Action

Now that you have frames on the Timeline, your movie will play linearly from frame 1 to frame 50. However, with this interactive restaurant guide, you'll want your viewers to choose a restaurant to see in whichever order they choose. So you'll need to pause the movie at the very first frame to wait for your viewer to click a button. You use a stop action to pause your Flash movie. A stop action simply stops the movie from continuing by halting the playhead.

1   Insert a new layer at the top and rename it **actions**.

2   Select the first keyframe of the actions layer and open the Actions panel (Window > Actions).

3   In the Script pane, type **stop();**.

The code appears in the Script pane and a tiny lowercase "a" appears in the first keyframe of the actions layer to indicate that it contains some ActionScript. The movie will now stop at frame 1.

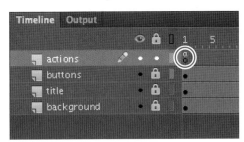

Creating Event Handlers for Buttons

Events are occurrences that happen in the Flash environment that Flash can detect and respond to. For example, a mouse click, a mouse movement, and a key press on the keyboard are all events. A pinch and a swipe gesture on mobile devices are also events. These events are produced by the user, but some events can happen independently of the user, like the successful loading of a piece of data or the completion of a sound. With ActionScript, you can write code that detects events and respond to them with an event handler.

The first step in event handling is to create a listener that will detect the event. A listener looks something like this:

```
wheretolisten.addEventListener(whatevent, responsetoevent);
```

The actual command is addEventListener(). The other words are placeholders for objects and parameters for your situation. *Wheretolisten* is the object where the event occurs (often a button), *whatevent* is the specific kind of event (such as a mouse click), and *responsetoevent* is the name of a function that is triggered when the event happens. So if you want to listen for a mouse click over a button called btn1_btn, and the response is to trigger a function called showimage1, the code would look like this:

```
btn1_btn.addEventListener(MouseEvent.CLICK, showimage1);
```

The next step is to create the function that will respond to the event—in this case, the function called showimage1. A *function* simply groups a bunch of actions together; you can then trigger that function by referencing its name. A function looks something like this:

```
function showimage1 (myEvent:MouseEvent){ };
```

Function names, like button names, are arbitrary. You can name functions whatever makes sense to you. In this particular example, the name of the function is showimage1. It receives one parameter (within the parentheses) called myEvent, the event that invoked the listener. The item following the colon indicates what type of object it is. If an event triggers this function, Flash executes all the actions between the curly brackets.

Adding the event listener and function

You'll add ActionScript code to listen for a mouse click on each button. The response will make Flash go to a particular frame on the Timeline to show different content.

1   Select the first frame of the actions layer.

2   Open the Actions panel.

3 In the Script pane of the Actions panel, beginning on the second line, type

```
gabelloffel_btn.addEventListener(MouseEvent.CLICK,¬
restaurant1);
```

The listener listens for a mouse click over the gabelloffel_btn object on the Stage. If the event happens, it triggers the function called restaurant1.

4 On the next line of the Script pane, type

```
function restaurant1(event:MouseEvent):void {
  gotoAndStop(10);
}
```

● **Note:** The void term refers to the data type that is returned by the function. The term void means that nothing is returned. Sometimes, after functions are executed, they "return" data, such as doing some calculations and returning an answer.

The function called restaurant1 contains instructions to go to frame 10 and stop there. The code for your button called gabelloffel_btn is complete.

Mouse Events

The following list contains the ActionScript codes for common mouse events for the desktop. Use these codes when you create your listener, and make sure that you pay attention to lowercase and uppercase letters. For most users, the first event (MouseEvent.CLICK) will be sufficient for all projects. That event happens when the user presses and releases the mouse button.

* MouseEvent.CLICK
* MouseEvent.MOUSE_MOVE
* MouseEvent.MOUSE_DOWN
* MouseEvent.MOUSE_UP
* MouseEvent.MOUSE_OVER
* MouseEvent.MOUSE_OUT

For a complete list of all the events available for a button, check out the Flash Help files and look for the Events of the SimpleButton class.

Note: Be sure to include the final curly bracket for each function, or the code won't work.

5 On the next line of the Script pane, enter additional code for the remaining three buttons. You can copy and paste lines 2 through 5, and simply change the names of the button, the name of the function (in two places), and the destination frame. The full script should be as follows:

```
stop();
gabelloffel_btn.addEventListener(MouseEvent.CLICK,¬
restaurant1);
function restaurant1(event:MouseEvent):void {
 gotoAndStop(10);
}
garygari_btn.addEventListener(MouseEvent.CLICK, restaurant2);
function restaurant2(event:MouseEvent):void {
 gotoAndStop(20);
}
ilpiatto_btn.addEventListener(MouseEvent.CLICK, restaurant3);
function restaurant3(event:MouseEvent):void {
 gotoAndStop(30);
}
pierreplatters_btn.addEventListener(MouseEvent.CLICK,¬
restaurant4);
function restaurant4(event:MouseEvent):void {
 gotoAndStop(40);
}
```

Note: ActionScript, like other programming languages, is very picky, and a single misplaced period can cause your entire project to grind to a halt. Use the color hinting. Be extra careful with punctuation. Double-check that keywords and identifiers show up in color, and use the Automatic close brace option in Flash > Preferences > Code Editor to have Flash automatically complete curly braces so you don't forget.

ActionScript Commands for Timeline Navigation

The following list contains the ActionScript codes for common navigation commands. Use these codes when you create buttons to stop the playhead, start the playhead, or move the playhead to different frames on the Timeline. The gotoAndStop and gotoAndPlay commands require additional information, or arguments, within their parentheses as indicated.

- `stop();`
- `play();`
- `gotoAndStop(framenumber or "framelabel");`
- `gotoAndPlay(framenumber or "framelabel");`
- `nextFrame();`
- `prevFrame();`

Checking for errors

Debugging is a necessary process, even for veteran coders. Even if you're extra careful, errors will creep into your code. Fortunately, Flash alerts you of syntax errors in the Compiler Errors panel, with information about the nature of the error and its location in the Actions panel.

1 Test your movie by choosing Control > Test Movie > In Flash Professional.

   If there are no code errors, Flash outputs the SWF file in a separate window.

   If Flash catches any code errors, the Compiler Errors panel appears automatically (Window > Compiler Errors) with a description of the error and its location. None of your code will be functional if there is a compiler error in any part of the code.

   For example, in this Compiler Errors window, an extra character was added, which Flash detects in line 18.

2 Double-click the error message in the Compiler Errors panel.

   Flash takes you to the exact location of the error in the Actions panel, where you can fix it.

Creating Destination Keyframes

When the user clicks each button, Flash moves the playhead to a new spot on the Timeline according to the ActionScript instructions you just programmed. However, you haven't yet placed anything different at those particular frames. That's the next step.

Inserting keyframes with different content

You will create four keyframes in a new layer and place information about each of the restaurants in the new keyframes.

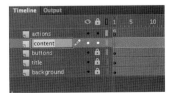

1 Insert a new layer at the top of the layer stack but below the actions layer and rename it **content**.

2 Select frame 10 of the content layer.

3 Insert a new keyframe at frame 10 (Insert > Timeline > Keyframe, or F6).

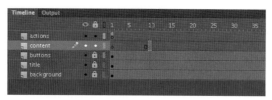

4 Insert new keyframes at frames 20, 30, and 40.

Your Timeline has four empty keyframes in the content layer.

5 Select the keyframe at frame 10.

6 In the Library panel, expand the folder called restaurant content. Drag the symbol called gabel and loffel from the Library panel to the Stage. The symbol named gabel and loffel is a movie clip symbol that contains a photo, graphics, and text about the restaurant.

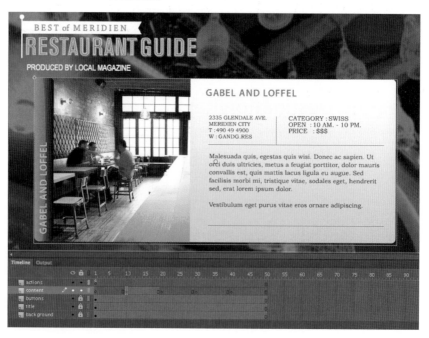

7   In the Properties inspector, set the X value to **60** and the Y value to **150**.

The restaurant information about gabel and loffel is centered on the Stage and covers all the buttons.

8   Select the keyframe at frame 20.

9   Drag the symbol called gary gari from the Library panel to the Stage. The symbol named gary gari is another movie clip symbol that contains a photo, graphics, and text about this restaurant.

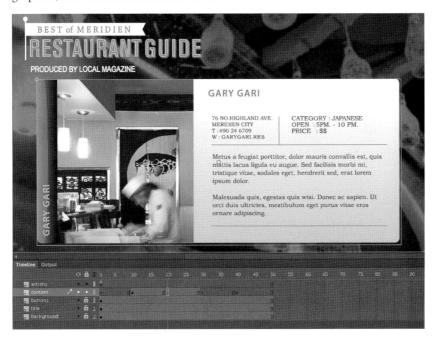

10 In the Properties inspector, set the X value to **60** and the Y value to **150**.

11 Place each of the movie clip symbols from the restaurant content folder in the Library panel to the corresponding keyframes in the content layer.

Each keyframe should contain a different movie clip symbol about a restaurant.

Using labels on keyframes

Your ActionScript code tells Flash to go to a different frame number when the user clicks each of the buttons. However, if you decide to edit your Timeline and add or delete a few frames, you'll need to go back into your ActionScript and change your code so the frame numbers match.

An easy way to avoid this problem is to use frame labels instead of fixed frame numbers. *Frame labels* are names that you give to keyframes. Instead of referring to keyframes by their frame number, you refer to them by their label. So, even if you move your destination keyframes as you edit, the labels remain with their keyframes. To reference frame labels in ActionScript, you must enclose them in quotation marks. The command `gotoAndStop("label1")` makes the playhead go to the keyframe with the label called label1.

1 Select frame 10 on the content layer.

2 In the Properties inspector, enter **label1** in the Label Name field.

A tiny flag icon appears on each of the keyframes that have labels.

3 Select frame 20 on the content layer.

4 In the Properties inspector, enter **label2** in the Label Name field.

5 Select frames 30 and 40, and in the Properties inspector, enter corresponding names in the Label Name field: **label3** and **label4**.

A tiny flag icon appears on each of the keyframes that have labels.

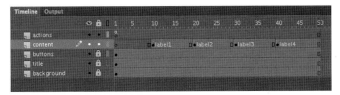

6 Select the first frame of the actions layer and open the Actions panel.

7 In your ActionScript code, change all the fixed frame numbers in each of the `gotoAndStop()` commands to the corresponding frame labels:

- `gotoAndStop(10);` should be changed to `gotoAndStop("label1");`

- `gotoAndStop(20);` should be changed to `gotoAndStop("label2");`

- `gotoAndStop(30);` should be changed to `gotoAndStop("label3");`

- `gotoAndStop(40);` should be changed to `gotoAndStop("label4");`

Note: Be sure that you use straight quotes, and not curly quotes to surround your label name. In ActionScript, straight and curly quotes are treated differently. However, you can use either single or double quotes.

```
actions:1
1    stop();
2    gabelloffel_btn.addEventListener(MouseEvent.CLICK, restaurant1);
3    function restaurant1(event:MouseEvent):void {
4      gotoAndStop("label1");
5    }
6    garygari_btn.addEventListener(MouseEvent.CLICK, restaurant2);
7    function restaurant2(event:MouseEvent):void {
8      gotoAndStop("label2");
9    }
10   ilpiatto_btn.addEventListener(MouseEvent.CLICK, restaurant3);
11   function restaurant3(event:MouseEvent):void {
12     gotoAndStop("label3");
13   }
14   pierreplatters_btn.addEventListener(MouseEvent.CLICK, restaurant4);
15   function restaurant4(event:MouseEvent):void {
16     gotoAndStop("label4");
17   }
18
```

The ActionScript code now directs the playhead to a particular frame label instead of a particular frame number.

8 Test your movie by choosing Control > Test Movie > In Flash Professional.

Each button moves the playhead to a different labeled keyframe on the Timeline, where a different movie clip is displayed. The user can choose to see any restaurant in any order. However, since the restaurant information covers the buttons, you can't see the original menu screen to choose another restaurant. You'll need to provide another button to return to the first frame, which you'll do in the next section.

Creating a Home Button with Code Snippets

A *home button* simply makes the playhead go back to the first frame of the Timeline, or to a keyframe where an original set of choices, or the main menu, are presented to the viewer. Creating a button that goes to frame 1 is the same process as creating the four restaurant buttons. However, in this section, you'll learn to use the Code Snippets panel to add ActionScript to your project.

Adding another button instance

Flash provides a home, or mainmenu, button for you in the Library panel.

1 Select the Buttons layer and unlock it if it is locked.

2 Drag the button called mainmenu from the Library panel to the Stage. Position the button instance at the top-right corner.

3 In the Properties inspector, set the X value to **726** and the Y value to **60**.

Using the Code Snippets panel to add ActionScript

The Code Snippets panel provides common ActionScript code that makes it easy for you to add interactivity to your Flash project, and simplifies the process. If you're unsure of your ability to code your own buttons, you can use the Code Snippets panel to learn how to add interactivity. The Code Snippets panel fills in the Actions panel with all the necessary code and allows you to modify the critical parameters of the code.

You can also save, import, and share code between a team of developers to make the development and production process more efficient.

1   Select the first frame in your Timeline. Select the main menu button on the Stage.

2   Choose Window > Code Snippets, or if your Actions panel is already open, click the Code Snippets button at the top right of the Actions panel.

The Code Snippets panel appears. The code snippets are organized in folders that describe their function.

3   In the Code Snippets panel, expand the folder called Timeline Navigation and double-click Click to Go to Frame and Stop.

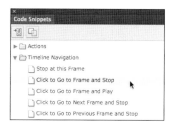

Flash warns you that the selected object (the main menu button) needs to be named in order to work with the code.

4 Click OK.

Flash automatically gives the main menu button an instance name. The Actions panel appears with ActionScript code. There is a commented portion of the code that describes the function of the code and the different parameters.

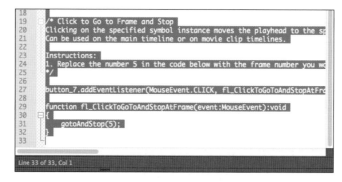

● **Note:** Flash automatically adds code snippets to a new layer called Actions. If your ActionScript is spread out in different layers, it's best to consolidate your code by copying and pasting the code into one keyframe on a single layer.

5 Replace the `gotoAndStop(5)` command with `gotoAndStop(1)`.

Clicking the main menu button will trigger the function that makes Flash move the playhead to frame 1.

Code Snippets Options

Using the Code Snippets panel not only makes adding interactivity quick and learning code easy, but it can help organize frequently used code for yourself and for a team working on the same project. There are additional options in the Code Snippets panel for saving your own code and sharing your code with others.

Creating your own code snippet

If you have your own ActionScript code that you'll use repeatedly, you can store it in the Code Snippets panel and apply it in other projects easily.

1 Open the Code Snippets panel, if it isn't already open.

2 From the Options menu at the upper right of the panel, choose Create New Code Snippet.

The Create New Code Snippet dialog box appears.

3 Enter a title in the Title field and a description in the Description field for your new code snippet. In the Code field, enter the ActionScript you want to save. Use the term **instance_name_here** for any placeholder instance names and be sure to check the option below the Code field.

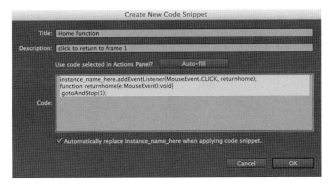

4 Click OK.

Flash saves your code in the Code Snippets panel under a Custom folder. You can now access your code and apply it to future projects.

● **Note:** Choose Auto-fill if you want to use the selected ActionScript code in your Actions panel.

Sharing your code snippet

Soon, you may accumulate a large library of useful code snippets that you want to share with other developers. It's easy to export your custom code snippets and enable other Flash developers to import them into their own Code Snippets panel.

1   Open the Code Snippets panel, if it isn't already open.

2   From the Options menu at the upper right of the panel, choose Export Code Snippets XML.

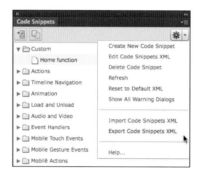

In the Save file dialog box that appears, choose a file name and a destination, and click OK. Flash saves all the code snippets from your Code Snippets panel (the default ones as well as your own custom snippets) in an XML file that can be distributed to other developers on your team.

3   To import custom code snippets, choose Import Code Snippets XML from the Options menu in the Code Snippets panel.

Choose the XML file that contains the custom snippets and click Open. Your Code Snippets panel will now contain all the snippets from the XML file.

Playing Animation at the Destination

So far, this interactive restaurant guide works by using the `gotoAndStop()` command to show information in different keyframes along the Timeline. But how would you play an animation after a user clicks a button? One way is to use the command `gotoAndPlay()`, which moves the playhead to the frame number or frame label specified by its parameter and plays from that point.

Creating transition animations

Next, you'll create a short transition animation for each of the restaurant guides. Then you'll change your ActionScript code to direct Flash to go to each of the beginning keyframes and play the animation.

1   Move the playhead to the label1 frame label.

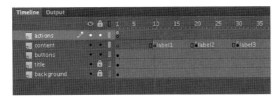

2   Right-click/Ctrl-click on the instance of the restaurant information on the Stage and choose Create Motion Tween.

Flash creates a separate Tween layer for the instance so that it can proceed with the motion tween.

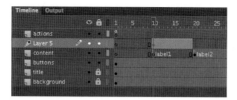

3 In the Properties inspector, select Alpha from the Style pull-down menu in the Color Effect section.

4 Set the Alpha slider to **0**%.

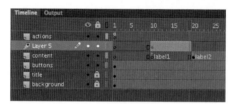

The instance on the Stage becomes totally transparent.

5 Move the playhead to the end of the tween span at frame 19.

6 Select the transparent instance on the Stage.

7 In the Properties inspector, set the Alpha slider to **100**%.

The instance is displayed at a normal opacity level. The motion tween from frame 10 to frame 19 shows a smooth fade-in effect.

8 Create similar motion tweens for the remaining restaurants in the keyframes labeled label2, label3, and label4.

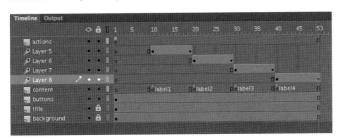

● **Note:** Recall that you can use the Motion Presets panel to save a motion tween and apply it to other objects to save you time and effort. Select the first motion tween on the Timeline and click Save selection as preset. Once saved, you can apply the same motion tween to another instance.

Using the gotoAndPlay command

The gotoAndPlay command makes the Flash playhead move to a specific frame on the Timeline and begin playing from that point.

1 Select the first frame of the actions layer and open the Actions panel.

Note: A fast and easy way of doing multiple replacements is to use the Find and Replace command in the Actions panel. From the options menu in the upper-right corner, select Find, and then choose Find and Replace from the drop-down menu.

2 In your ActionScript code, change all the first four gotoAndStop() commands to gotoAndPlay() commands. Leave the parameter unchanged:

- gotoAndStop("label1"); should be changed to gotoAndPlay("label1");

- gotoAndStop("label2"); should be changed to gotoAndPlay("label2");

- gotoAndStop("label3"); should be changed to gotoAndPlay("label3");

- gotoAndStop("label4"); should be changed to gotoAndPlay("label4");

```
actions:1
1   stop();
2   gabelloffel_btn.addEventListener(MouseEvent.CLICK, restaurant1);
3   function restaurant1(event:MouseEvent):void {
4     gotoAndPlay("label1");
5   }
6   garygari_btn.addEventListener(MouseEvent.CLICK, restaurant2);
7   function restaurant2(event:MouseEvent):void {
8     gotoAndPlay("label2");
9   }
10  ilpiatto_btn.addEventListener(MouseEvent.CLICK, restaurant3);
11  function restaurant3(event:MouseEvent):void {
12    gotoAndPlay("label3");
13  }
14  pierreplatters_btn.addEventListener(MouseEvent.CLICK, restaurant4);
15  function restaurant4(event:MouseEvent):void {
16    gotoAndPlay("label4");
17  }
18
```

For each of the restaurant buttons, the ActionScript code now directs the playhead to a particular frame label and begins playing at that point.

Make sure you keep the function for your Home button unchanged. You'll want that function to remain a gotoAndStop() command.

Stopping the animations

If you test your movie now (Control > Test Movie > In Flash Professional), you'll see that each button goes to its corresponding frame label and plays from that point, but it keeps playing, showing all the remaining animations in the Timeline. The next step is to tell Flash when to stop.

1 Select frame 19 of the actions layer, the frame just before the label2 keyframe on the content layer.

2 Right-click/Ctrl-click and choose Insert Keyframe.

A new keyframe is inserted in frame 19 of the actions layer.

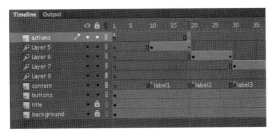

3 Open the Actions panel.

The Script pane in the Actions panel is blank. Don't panic! Your code has not disappeared. Your code for the event listeners is on the first keyframe of the actions layer. You have selected a new keyframe in which you will add a stop command.

4 In the Script pane, enter **stop();**.

Note: If you wish, you could also use the Code Snippets panel to add the *stop* command.

Flash will stop playing when it reaches frame 19.

5 Insert keyframes at frames 29, 39, and 50.

6 In each of those keyframes, add a stop command in the Actions panel.

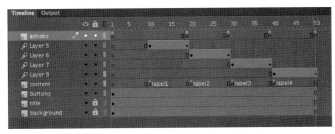

Note: If you want a quick and easy way to duplicate the keyframe containing the stop command, hold down the Alt/Option key while you move it to a new location on the Timeline.

7 Test your movie by choosing Control > Test Movie > In Flash Professional.

Each button takes you to a different keyframe and plays a short fade-in animation. At the end of the animation, the movie stops and waits for the viewer to click the Home button.

Animated Buttons

Currently, when you hover your mouse cursor over one of the restaurant buttons, the gray additional information box suddenly appears. But imagine if that gray information box were animated. It would give more life and sophistication to the interaction between the user and the button.

Animated buttons display an animation in the Up, Over, or Down keyframes. The key to creating an animated button is to create an animation inside a movie clip symbol, and then place that movie clip symbol inside the Up, Over, or Down keyframes of a button symbol. When one of those button keyframes is displayed, the animation in the movie clip plays.

Creating the animation in a movie clip symbol

Your button symbols in this interactive restaurant guide already contain a movie clip symbol of a gray information box in their Over states. You will edit each movie clip symbol to add an animation inside it.

1   In the Library panel, expand the restaurant previews folder. Double-click the movie clip symbol icon for gabel loffel over info.

    Flash puts you in symbol-editing mode for the movie clip symbol called gabel loffel over info.

2   Select all the visual elements on the Stage (Ctrl/Command+A).

3   Right-click/Ctrl-click and choose Create Motion Tween.

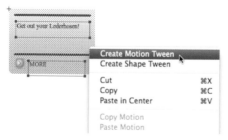

4 In the dialog box that appears asking for confirmation to convert the selection to a symbol, click OK.

Flash creates a Tween layer and adds 1 second's worth of frames to the movie clip Timeline.

5 Drag the end of the tween span back so the Timeline only has 10 frames.

6 Move the playhead to frame 1 and select the instance on the Stage.

7 In the Properties inspector, select Alpha from the Style pull-down menu in the Color Effect section and set the Alpha slider to **0**%.

The instance on the Stage becomes totally transparent.

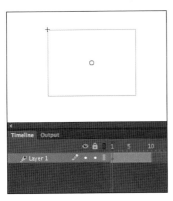

8 Move the playhead to the end of the tween span at frame 10.

9 Select the transparent instance on the Stage.

10 In the Properties inspector, set the Alpha slider to **100**%.

Flash creates a smooth transition between the transparent and opaque instance in the 10 frame tween span.

11 Insert a new layer and rename it **actions**.

12 Insert a new keyframe in the last frame (frame 10) of the actions layer.

13 Open the Actions panel (Window > Actions) and enter **stop();** in the Script pane.

Adding the stop action in the last frame ensures that the fade-in effect plays only once.

14 Exit symbol-editing mode by clicking the Scene 1 button in the Edit bar above the Stage.

● **Note:** If you want an animated button to repeat its animation, leave out the stop command at the end of the movie clip's Timeline.

15 Choose Control > Test Movie > In Flash Professional.

When your mouse cursor hovers over the first restaurant button, the gray information box fades in. The motion tween inside the movie clip symbol plays the fade-in effect, and the movie clip symbol is placed in the Over state of the button symbol.

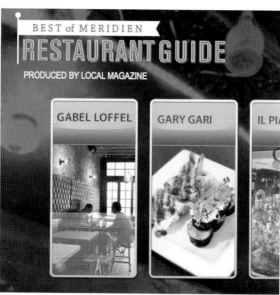

16 Create identical motion tweens for the other gray information box movie clips so that Flash will animate all of the restaurant buttons.

Review Questions

1 How and where do you add ActionScript code?

2 How do you name an instance, and why is it necessary?

3 How can you label frames, and when is it useful?

4 What is a function?

5 What is an event? What is an event listener?

6 How do you create an animated button?

Review Answers

1 ActionScript code can be attached to keyframes of the Timeline. Keyframes that contain ActionScript are indicated by a small lowercase "a." You add ActionScript in the Actions panel. Choose Window > Actions, or select a keyframe and click the ActionScript panel icon in the Properties inspector, or right-click/Ctrl-click and select Actions. You enter code directly in the Script pane in the Actions panel, or you can add ActionScript through the Code Snippets panel.

2 To name an instance, select it on the Stage, and then type in the Instance Name field in the Properties inspector. You need to name an instance so that ActionScript can identify it with code.

3 To label a frame, select a keyframe on the Timeline, and then type a name in the Frame Label box in the Properties inspector. You can label frames in Flash to make it easier to reference frames in ActionScript and to give you more flexibility.

4 A function is a group of statements that you can refer to by name. Using a function makes it possible to run the same set of statements without having to type them repeatedly into the same script. When an event is detected, a function is executed in response.

5 An event is an occurrence that is initiated by a button click, a keystroke, or any number of inputs that Flash can detect and respond to. An event listener, also called an event handler, is a function that is executed in response to specific events.

6 Animated buttons display an animation in the Up, Over, or Down keyframes. To create an animated button, make an animation inside a movie clip symbol, and then place that movie clip symbol inside the Up, Over, or Down keyframes of a button symbol. When one of those button keyframes is displayed, the animation in the movie clip plays.

7 WORKING WITH SOUND AND VIDEO

Lesson Overview

In this lesson, you'll learn how to do the following:

- Import sound files

- Edit sound files

- Use Adobe Media Encoder

- Understand video and audio encoding options

- Play external video from your Flash project

- Customize options on the video playback component

- Work with video that contains alpha channels

- Embed video in your Flash project

- Export video from Flash

 This lesson will take approximately 3 hours to complete. If needed, remove the previous lesson folder from your hard drive and copy the Lesson07 folder onto it. Download the project files for this lesson from the Lesson & Update Files tab on your Account page at www.peachpit.com and store them on your computer in a convenient location, as described in the Getting Started section of this book. Your Accounts page is also where you'll find any updates to the chapters or to the lesson files. Look on the Lesson & Update Files tab to access the most current content.

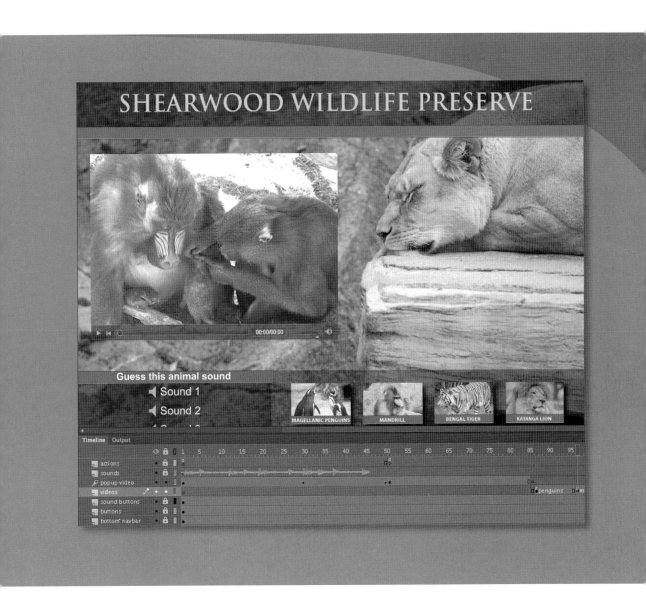

Sound and video add new dimensions to your projects. Import sound files and edit them directly in Flash, and use Adobe Media Encoder to compress and convert video files to use in Flash, or to export Flash animations as video.

Getting Started

● **Note:** If you have not already downloaded the project files for this lesson to your computer from your Account page, make sure to do so now. See "Getting Started" at the beginning of the book.

Start the lesson by viewing the finished animated zoo kiosk. You'll create the kiosk by adding sound and video files to a project in Flash.

1 Double-click the **07End.html** file in the Lesson07/07End folder to play the animation.

View the movie of the polar bear with a short soundtrack of an African beat. A zoo director pops up and introduces himself.

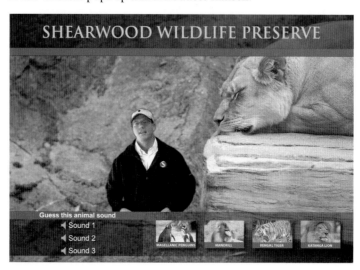

2 Click a sound button to hear an animal sound.

3 Click a thumbnail button to view a short movie about the animal. Use the interface controls below the movie to pause, continue, or lower the volume.

In this lesson, you'll import audio files and put them on the Timeline to provide the short introductory audio flourish. You'll also learn how to embed sounds in each button. You'll use Adobe Media Encoder to compress and convert the video files to the appropriate format for Flash. You'll learn how to work with transparent backgrounds in video to create the silhouetted zoo director video. Using a project you completed in an earlier lesson, you'll also learn to export Flash content to high-quality video.

1   Double-click the **07Start.fla** file in the Lesson07/07Start folder to open the initial project file in Flash.

2   Choose File > Save As. Name the file **07_workingcopy.fla**, and save it in the 07Start folder. Saving a working copy ensures that the original start file will be available if you want to start over.

Understanding the Project File

The initial setup of the project has been completed except for the audio and video portions and some of the ActionScript code. The Stage is 1000 x 700 pixels. A row of buttons of colorful animals is on the bottom row, another set of buttons on the left, a title at the top, and a background image of a resting lion.

The Timeline contains several layers that separate the different content.

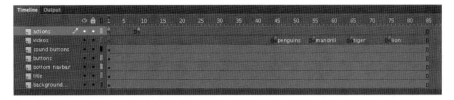

The bottom three layers, called background photo, title, and bottom navbar, contain design elements, text, and images. The next two layers above, called buttons and sound buttons, contain instances of button symbols. The videos layer and the highlights layer contain several labeled keyframes, and the actions layer contains ActionScript that provides the event handlers for the bottom row of buttons.

If you've completed Lesson 6, you should be familiar with the structure of this Timeline. The individual buttons on the bottom row are already coded so that when the user clicks a button, the playhead moves to a corresponding labeled keyframe in the videos layer. You'll be inserting content into each of those keyframes. But first you'll learn to work with sound.

Using Sounds

You can import several types of sound files into Flash. Flash supports MP3 and WAV files, which are two common sound formats. When you import sound files into Flash, they are stored in your Library panel. You can then drag the sound files from the Library panel onto the Stage at different points along the Timeline to synchronize those sounds to whatever may be happening on the Stage.

Importing sound files

You'll import several sound files to the Library panel, which you'll use throughout this lesson.

1 Choose File > Import > Import To Library.

2 Select the Monkey.wav file in the Lesson07/07Start/Sounds folder, and click Open.

   The Monkey.wav file appears in your Library panel. The sound file is indicated by a unique icon, and the preview window shows a waveform—a series of peaks and valleys that represent the sound.

3 Click the Play button on the far upper-right corner of the Library preview window.

The sound plays.

4 Double-click the sound icon in front of your Monkey.wav file.

The Sound Properties dialog box appears, providing information on your sound file, including its original location, size, and other technical properties.

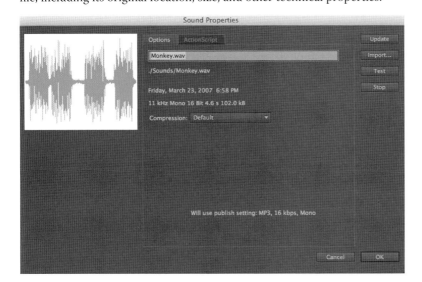

5 Choose File > Import > Import To Library and select the other sound files to import into your Flash project. Import Elephant.wav, Lion.wav, Africanbeat.mp3, and Afrolatinbeat.mp3.

Your Library panel should contain all the sound files.

6 Create a folder in your Library panel and place all the sound files in it to organize your Library panel. Name the folder **sounds**.

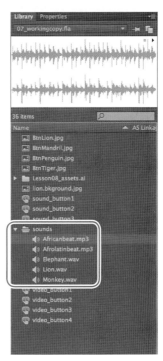

Note: Hold down the Shift key to select multiple files to import all at once.

Placing sounds on the Timeline

You can place a sound at any keyframe along the Timeline, and Flash will play that sound when the playhead reaches the keyframe. You'll place a sound on the very first keyframe to play as the movie starts to provide a pleasant audio introduction and set the mood.

1   Select the videos layer on the Timeline.

2   Insert a new layer and rename it **sounds**.

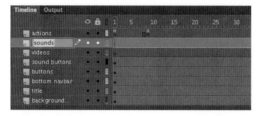

3   Select the first keyframe of the sounds layer.

4   Drag the Afrolatinbeat.mp3 file from the sounds folder in your Library panel onto the Stage.

The waveform of your sound appears on the Timeline.

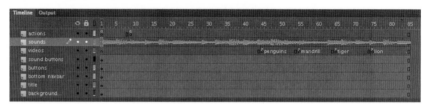

5   Select the first keyframe of the sounds layer.

In the Properties inspector, note that your sound file is now listed on the pull-down menu under the Sound section.

6 Select Stream for the Sync option.

The Sync options determine how the sound plays on the Timeline. Use Stream sync for long passages of music or narration when you want to time the sound with the Timeline.

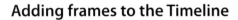

7 Move the playhead back and forth on the Timeline.

The sound plays as you scrub the Timeline.

8 Choose Control > Test Movie > In Flash Professional.

The sound plays only for a short while before getting cut off. Because the sound is set to Stream, it plays only when the playhead moves along the Timeline, and if there are sufficient frames to play. There is a stop action at frame 9 that stops the playhead, and hence, stops the sound.

Adding frames to the Timeline

The next step is to extend the Timeline so that the entire sound (or at least the portions that you desire) plays before the stop action halts the playhead.

1 Click on the Stage to deselect the Timeline, and then place the playhead between frames 1 and 9 by clicking on the top frame numbers.

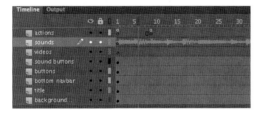

2 Choose Insert > Timeline > Frame, or press F5, to insert frames in all the layers between frames 1 and 9.

3 Insert enough frames so that there are about 50 frames to play the sound before the stop action in the second keyframe of the actions layer.

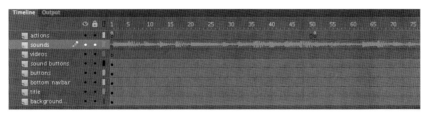

4 Choose Control > Test Movie > In Flash Professional.

The sound lasts longer because it has more frames to play before the playhead stops.

Clipping the end of a sound

The sound clip you imported is a bit longer than you need. You'll shorten the sound file by using the Edit Envelope dialog box. Then you'll apply a fade so the sound gradually decreases as it ends.

1 Select the first keyframe of the sounds layer.

2 In the Properties inspector, click the Pencil button.

The Edit Envelope dialog box appears, showing you the sound's waveform.

The top and the bottom waveform are the left and right channels of the sound (stereo). A timeline is between the waveforms, a pull-down menu of preset effects at the left corner, and view options at the bottom.

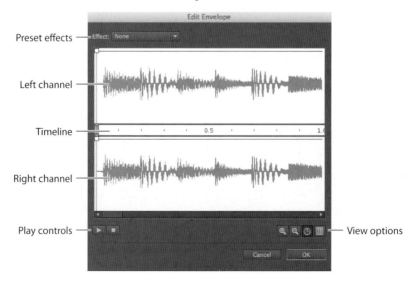

3 In the Edit Envelope dialog box, click the Seconds icon, if it isn't already selected.

The timeline changes units to show seconds instead of frames. Click the Frames icon to switch back. You can switch back and forth, depending on how you want to view your sound.

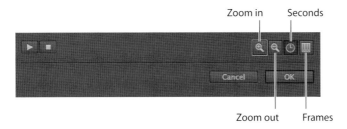

4 Click the Zoom Out icon until you can see the entire waveform.

The waveform appears to end at around 240 frames, or about 10 seconds.

5 Drag the right end of the time slider inward to about frame 45.

The sound shortens by being clipped from the end. The sound now plays for about 45 frames.

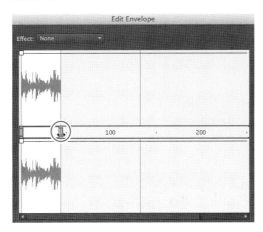

6 Click OK to accept the changes you've made.

The waveform on the main Timeline indicates the shortened sound.

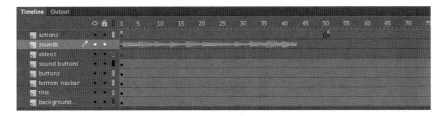

Changing the volume of a sound

The sound will be more elegant if it slowly fades out instead of being abruptly cut off. You can change the volume levels through time in the Edit Envelope dialog box. Use it to fade in, fade out, or modulate the volume of the left and right channels separately.

1 Select the first keyframe of the sounds layer.

2 In the Properties inspector, click the Pencil button.

   The Edit Envelope dialog box appears.

3 Select the Frames viewing option, and zoom in on the waveform to see its end near frame 45.

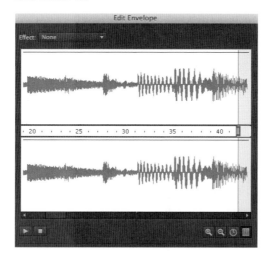

4 Click on the top horizontal line of the top waveform above frame 20.

   A box appears on the line, indicating a keyframe for the sound volume.

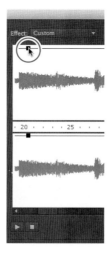

5   Click on the top horizontal line of the upper waveform above frame 45 and drag it down to the bottom of the window.

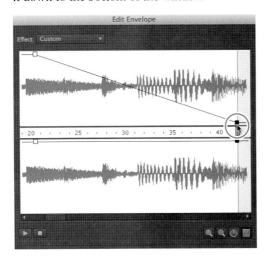

The downward diagonal line indicates the drop in volume from 100% to 0%.

6   Click on the corresponding keyframe on the lower waveform and drag it down to the bottom of the window.

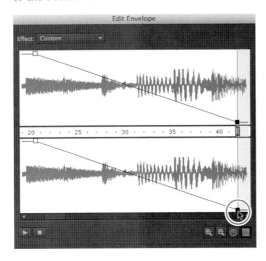

● **Note:** You can choose and apply some of the preset effects from the pull-down menu in the Edit Envelope dialog box. Common effects like a fade-in or a fade-out are provided for your convenience.

The volume levels for both the left and right channels slowly decrease starting at frame 20. By frame 45, the volume level is at 0%.

7   Test the effects of your sound edits by clicking the Play button on the lower-left side of the dialog box. Click OK to accept the changes.

Deleting or changing the sound file

If you don't want the sound on your Timeline, or you want to change to a different sound, you can make those changes in the Properties inspector.

1 Select the first keyframe of the sounds layer.

2 In the Properties inspector, select None in the Name pull-down menu.

The sound is removed from the Timeline.

3 Now let's add a different sound. Select Africanbeat.mp3 for Name.

The Africanbeat.mp3 sound is added to the Timeline. The settings in the Edit Envelope dialog box that clip the sound and fade it out are reset (since you selected None to remove the Afrolatinbeat.mp3 sound). Return to the Edit Envelope dialog box to customize the Africanbeat.mp3 sound in the same way as the previous sound.

Setting the quality of the sounds

You can control how much or how little your sounds are compressed in the final SWF file. With less compression, your sounds will be better quality. However, your final SWF size will be much larger. With more compression, you'll have poor-quality sounds but a smaller file size. You must determine the balance of quality and file size based on your needs. Set the sound quality and compression in the Publish Settings options.

1 Choose File > Publish Settings.

The Publish Settings dialog box appears.

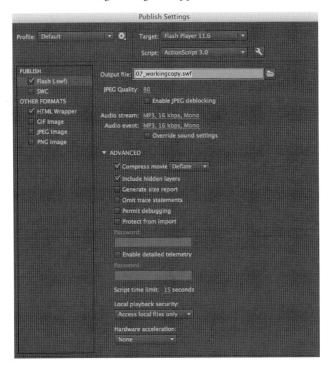

2 Select the Flash (.swf) check box on the left if it's not checked already to see the Audio stream and Audio event settings.

3 Click the Audio Stream settings to open the Sound Settings dialog box. Change the Bit rate to 64 kbps and deselect the Convert stereo to mono check box. Click OK to accept the settings.

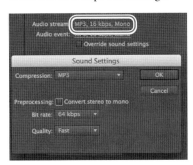

4 Click the Audio Event settings.

The Sound Settings dialog box appears.

5 Change the Bit rate to 64 kbps and deselect the Convert stereo to mono check box. Click OK to accept the settings.

Now both the Audio Stream and Audio Event settings should be at 64 kbps with stereo sounds preserved.

The Africanbeat.mp3 file in particular relies on stereo effects, so keeping both the left and right channels is important.

The Bit rate is measured in kilobits per second, and it determines the quality of the sound in your final, exported Flash movie. The higher the bit rate, the better the quality. However, the higher the bit rate, the larger your file becomes. For this lesson, change the bit rate to 64 kbps.

6 Select Override sound settings, and click OK to save the settings.

The sound settings in the Publish Settings will determine how all your sounds are exported.

7 Choose Control > Test Movie > In Flash Professional.

The stereo effect of the sound is preserved, and the quality is determined by your settings in the Publish Settings dialog box.

Adding sounds to buttons

In the kiosk, the buttons appear on your stage on the left. You'll add sounds to the buttons so that they play whenever the user clicks them.

1 In the Library panel, double-click the icon of the button symbol called sound_button1.

You enter symbol-editing mode for that button symbol.

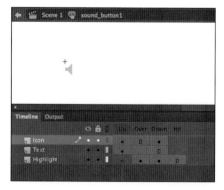

2 The three layers in the button symbol help organize the content for the Up, Over, Down, and Hit states.

3 Insert a new layer and rename it **sounds**.

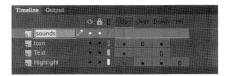

4 Select the Down frame in your sounds layer and insert a keyframe.

A new keyframe appears in the Down state of your button.

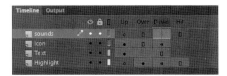

5 Drag the Monkey.wav file from the sounds folder in your Library panel to the Stage.

A waveform for the Monkey.wav file appears in the Down keyframe of the sounds layer.

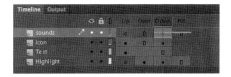

6 Select the Down keyframe in the sounds layer.

7 In the Properties inspector, choose Start for the Sync option.

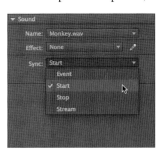

● **Note:** You can also add sound to the Over state of a button symbol, and the sound will play whenever the mouse cursor just hovers over the button.

A Start sync option triggers the sound whenever the playhead enters that particular keyframe.

8 Choose Control > Test Movie > In Flash Professional. Test the first button to hear the monkey, and then close the preview window.

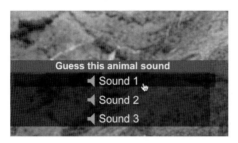

9 Edit the sound_button2 and the sound_button3 to add the Lion.wav and the Elephant.wav sounds to their Down states.

Understanding Sound Sync Options

Sound sync refers to the way a sound is triggered and played. There are several options: Event, Start, Stop, and Stream. Stream ties the sound to the Timeline so you can easily synchronize animated elements to the sound. Event and Start are used to trigger a sound (usually a short sound) to a specific event, like a button click. Event and Start are similar except that the Start sync does not trigger the sound if it is already playing (so there are no overlapping sounds possible with Start sync). The Stop option is used to stop a sound, although you'll use it rarely, if ever. If you want to stop a sound with a Stream sync, simply insert a blank keyframe.

Understanding Flash Video

● **Note:** Flash can actually play back any video encoded in H.264, so your video file doesn't have to have the .f4v extension. For example, a video with a .mov extension encoded by QuickTime Pro with H.264 is compatible with Flash, as are .mp4 files.

Flash makes it very easy to deliver video over the Web. Combining video, interactivity, and animation can create a very rich and immersive multimedia experience for your viewers.

There are two options to display video in Flash. The first option is to keep the video separate from your Flash file and use a playback component from Flash to play the video. If you have a very short video clip, you can use the second option, which is to embed the video in your Flash file.

Both methods require that the video be formatted correctly first. The appropriate video format for Flash is Flash Video, which uses the extension .flv or the extension .f4v. F4V supports the H.264 standard, a video codec that delivers high quality with very efficient compression. A codec (*compression-deco*mpression) is a method computers use to compress a video file to save space, and then decompress it to play it back. FLV is the standard format for previous versions of Flash and uses the older codecs Sorenson Spark or On2 VP6.

Using Adobe Media Encoder

You can convert your video files to the proper FLV or F4V format using Adobe Media Encoder, a stand alone application that comes with Flash Professional. Adobe Media Encoder can convert single files or multiple files (known as batch processing) to make your workflow easier.

● **Note:** Windows users should download the free QuickTime from Apple (http://www.apple.com/quicktime/download/) to work with the provided .mov files in this lesson.

Adding a video file to Adobe Media Encoder

The first step to convert your video file to a compatible Flash format is to add the video to Adobe Media Encoder for encoding.

1 Launch Adobe Media Encoder, which comes installed with Adobe Flash Professional.

Queue   Preset browser

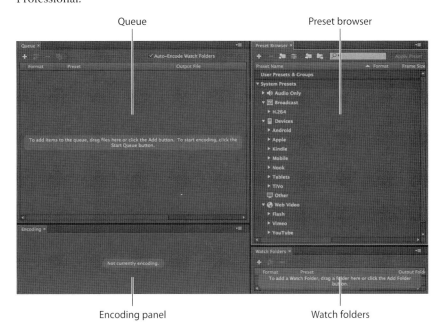

Encoding panel   Watch folders

The opening screen displays the Queue in the upper left, which shows any current video files that have been added for processing. The Queue panel should be empty. The other panels are the Encoding panel, which shows any video currently being processed; the Watch Folders, which shows folders that have been identified for batch processing; and the Preset Browser, which provides common predefined settings.

2 Choose File > Add Source, or click the Plus button in the Queue panel.

A dialog box opens for you to select a video file.

● Note: You can also drag the file directly to the Queue from your desktop.

● Note: In Adobe Media Encoder, the default setting is not to start the Queue automatically when the program is idle. You can change the setting by choosing Adobe Media Encoder > Preferences > General, and check the Start queue automatically option.

3 Navigate to the Lesson07/07Start folder, select the Penguins.mov file, and click Open.

The Penguins.mov file is added to the Queue and is ready for conversion to your choice of a video format.

Converting video files to Flash Video

Converting your video files is easy, and the length of time it takes depends on how large your original video file is, and your computer's processing speed.

1 In the first column under Format, select the F4V format.

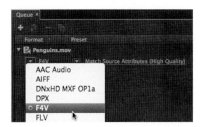

F4V is the latest video format that encodes video using high-quality, low-bit rate H.264 format for Flash. FLV is a lower quality, but still valid, format.

2 Under the Preset options, choose Web – 320x240, 4x3, Project Framerate, 500 kbps.

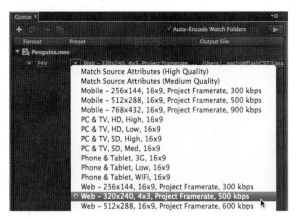

You can choose one of many standard preset options from the menu. The options determine the dimensions of the video and the quality of the video. The Web – 320x240 option converts your original video to a relatively small-sized video so that you can incorporate it into your zoo kiosk project in Flash.

3 Click the Output File.

The Save As dialog box appears. You can choose to save the converted file in a different location on your computer and choose a different filename. Your original video will not be deleted or altered in any way.

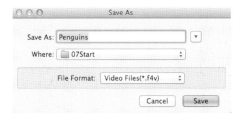

4 Click the Start queue button (triangular icon) in the upper-right corner.

Adobe Media Encoder begins the encoding process. Media Encoder displays the settings for the encoded video and shows the progress and a preview of the video in the Encoding panel.

Note: You can change the status of individual files in the Queue by selecting the file in the display list and choosing Edit > Reset Status or Edit > Skip Selection. Reset Status removes the green check from a completed file so it can be encoded again, whereas Skip Selection makes Flash skip that particular file when you have multiple files in the Queue.

When the encoding process finishes, a "Done" label and a green check appear in the Status column of the Queue panel. A sound indicates that the file has been converted successfully.

You now have the Penguins.f4v file in your Lesson07/07Start folder along with the original Penguins.mov file.

Using Watch Folders and the Preset Browser Settings

The Watch Folders panel can be helpful in processing multiple videos, while the Preset Browser stores predefined settings for specific target devices.

Adding a folder to the Watch Folders panel adds all of its contents to the queue, where they are automatically encoded. You can also add a different Output setting to the same folder, which will result in multiple formats for the same set of videos. To add a new Output setting, select a watch folder, and then click the Add Output button at the top of the Watch Folders panel.

Add Watch folder

Add output

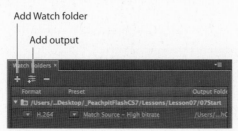

A duplicate selection appears in the list. Choose a new format and/or new preset options. If you want to apply a particular setting from the Preset Browser, choose the setting and simply drag and drop it on top of your selection in the Watch Folders panel.

This is useful when you need different video formats for high-bandwidth and low-bandwidth viewers, or for different devices such as tablets and mobile phones.

Understanding Encoding Options

You can customize many settings when converting your original video. You can crop and resize your video to specific dimensions, just convert a snippet of the video, adjust the type of compression and the compression levels, and even apply filters to the video. To display the encoding options, choose Edit > Reset Status to reset the Penguins.mov file, and then click the Format or the Preset selection in the display list or choose Edit > Export Settings. The Export Settings dialog box appears.

Cropping options

Preset options

Trimming options

Summary of export settings

Cue points

Advanced video and audio encoding

Cropping your video

If you want to show only a portion of your video, you can crop it. If you haven't done so already, choose Edit > Reset Status to reset the Penguins.mov file, and then choose Edit > Export Settings so you can experiment with the cropping settings.

1   Select the Source tab in the upper-left corner of the Export Settings dialog box, and then click the Crop button.

The cropping box appears over the video preview window.

2 Drag the sides inward to crop from the top, bottom, left, or right.

The grayed-out portions outside the box will be discarded. Flash displays the new dimensions next to your cursor. You can also use the Left, Top, Right, and Bottom settings above the preview window to enter exact pixel values.

3 If you want to keep the crop in a standard proportion, click the Crop Proportions menu and choose a desired ratio.

The cropping box will be constrained to the selected proportions.

4 To see the effects of the crop, click the Output tab in the upper-left corner of the preview window.

The preview window shows how your final video will appear.

5 The Source Scaling pull-down menu contains options for setting how the crop will appear in the final output file:

If the video has the selected crop shown here, then the Crop Setting options will affect the outputted file as follows:

- **Scale To Fit** adjusts the dimensions of the crop and adds black borders to fit the output file.

- **Scale To Fill** adjusts the dimensions of the crop to fill the size of the output file.

- **Stretch To Fill** adjusts the dimensions of the crop by distorting the image, if necessary, to fill the size of the output file.

- **Scale To Fit With Black Borders** adds black bands on any of the sides to fit the crop in the dimensions of the output file.

- **Change Output Size to Match Source** changes the dimensions of the output file to match the crop dimensions.

6 Exit the cropping mode without making the crop by clicking the Crop button again under the Source tab to deselect it. You will not need to crop the Penguins.mov video for this lesson.

Adjusting video length

Your video may have unwanted segments at the beginning or the end. You can shave off footage from either end to adjust the overall length of your video.

1 Click and drag the playhead (top yellow marker) to scrub through your video to preview the footage. Place the playhead at the desired beginning point of your video.

Time markers indicate the number of seconds that have elapsed.

2 Click the Set In Point icon.

The In point moves to the current position of the playhead.

3　Drag the playhead to the desired ending point of your video.

4　Click the Set Out Point icon.

The Out point moves to the current position of the playhead.

5　You can also simply drag the In and Out point markers to bracket the desired video segment.

The highlighted portion of your video between the In and Out point markers will be the only segment of your original video that will be encoded.

● **Note:** You can use the Left or Right Arrow keys on your keyboard to move back or ahead frame by frame for finer control.

6　Drag the In and Out points back to their original positions, or choose Entire Clip from the Source Range pull-down menu, because you do not need to adjust the video length for this lesson.

Cue Points

At the bottom left of the Export Settings dialog box is an area where you can set cue points for your video.

Cue points are special markers at various points along the video. With ActionScript, you can program Flash to recognize when those cue points are encountered, or you can navigate to specific cue points. Cue points can transform an ordinary, linear video into a true interactive, immersive video experience. Learn more about how you can add event listeners for cue points in the Adobe ActionScript reference from Help > Flash Help.

Setting advanced video and audio options

The right side of the Export Settings dialog box contains information about the original video and summarizes the export settings.

You can choose one of the preset options from the top Preset menu. At the bottom, you can navigate to advanced video and audio encoding options using the tabs. At the very bottom, Flash displays the estimated final output size.

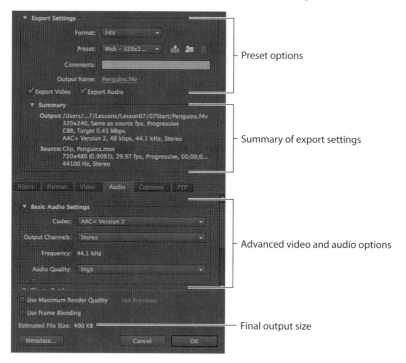

Preset options

Summary of export settings

Advanced video and audio options

Final output size

You will export the Penguins.mov file again but at a larger size.

1   Make sure the Export Video and Export Audio boxes are selected.

2   Click the Format tab and note that you're exporting the file to the F4V format.

3   Click the Video tab.

4   Make sure that Resize Video and the Constrain option (chain link icon) are
    selected. Enter **480** for the Width and click outside the field to accept the change.

    The Height automatically changes to keep the proportions of the video.

5   Click OK.

    Flash closes the Export Settings dialog box and saves your advanced video and
    audio settings.

6   Click Start Queue to begin the encoding process with your custom resize settings.

    Flash creates another F4V file of Penguins.mov. Delete the first one you created
    and rename the second one **Penguins.f4v**.

Saving advanced video and audio options

If you want to process many videos similarly, it makes sense to save your advanced
video and audio options. You can do that in Adobe Media Encoder. Once saved,
you can easily apply your settings to other videos in the queue.

1   Choose Edit > Reset Status to reset the status of your penguin video in the
    queue, then choose Edit > Export Settings.

2   In the Export Settings dialog box, click the Save Preset button.

3 In the dialog box that opens, provide a descriptive name for the video and audio options. Click OK.

4 Return to the queue of videos. You can apply your custom settings to additional videos by simply choosing the preset from the Preset pull-down menu or from the Preset browser panel on the right.

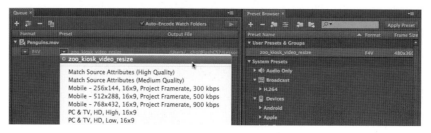

Playback of External Video

Now that you have successfully converted your video to the correct Flash-compatible format, you can use it in your Flash zoo kiosk project. You will have Flash play each of the animal videos at the different labeled keyframes on the Timeline.

You will keep your videos external to the Flash project. By keeping videos external, your Flash project remains small, the videos can be edited separately, and the videos can maintain different frame rates from your Flash project.

1 Open your 07_workingcopy.fla project in Flash Professional.

2 Select the keyframe labeled penguins in the videos layer.

3 Choose File > Import > Import Video.

The Import Video wizard appears. The Import Video wizard guides you step by step through the process of adding video to Flash.

4 In the Import Video wizard, select On Your Computer and click Browse.

5 In the dialog box, select Penguins.f4v from the Lesson07/07Start folder and click Open.

The path to the video file appears.

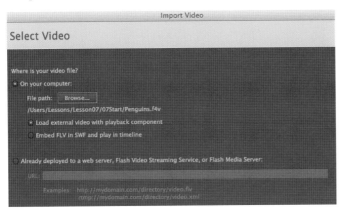

6 Select the Load external video with playback component option. Click Next or Continue.

7 In the next screen of the Import Video wizard, you select the skin, or the interface controls for the video. From the Skin menu, select the third option from the top, MinimaFlatCustomColorPlayBackSeekCounterVolMute.swf, if it's not already selected.

● **Note:** The skin is a small SWF file that determines the functionality and appearance of the video's controls. You can use one of the skins provided with Flash, or you can choose None from the top of the menu.

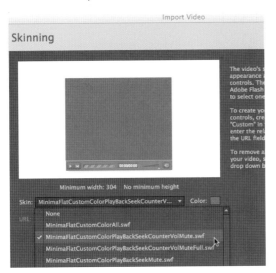

The skins fall in three broad categories. The skins that begin with "Minima" are the latest designs and include options with a numeric counter. The skins that begin with "SkinUnder" are controls that appear below the video. The skins that begin with "SkinOver" are controls that overlap the bottom edge of the video. A preview of the skin and its controls appear in the preview window.

8 Select color #333333 with a 75% Alpha. Click Next or Continue.

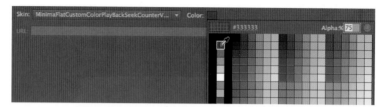

9 On the next screen of the Import Video wizard, review the information for the video file, and then click Finish to place the video.

● **Note:** The FLV or F4V files, the 07_workingcopy.swf file, and the skin file are all required for your zoo kiosk project to work. The skin file is published in the same folder as your swf file.

10 Your video with the selected skin appears on the Stage. Place the video on the left side of the Stage.

An FLVPlayback component also appears in your Library panel. The component is a special widget that is used on the Stage to play your external video.

11 Choose Control > Test Movie > In Flash Professional. After the musical introduction, click the Magellanic Penguins button.

The FLVPlayback component plays the external penguin video with the skin you chose in the Import Video wizard. Close the preview window.

● Note: You can't preview your video in Flash. You must test your movie (Control > Test Movie > In Flash Professional) to see your video play within the video component.

12 The other animal videos have already been encoded (in FLV format) and provided in the 07Start folder. Import the Mandrill.flv, Tiger.flv, and Lion.flv videos in each of their corresponding keyframes. Choose the same skin as the Penguin.f4v video.

Controlling the video playback

The FLVPlayback component lets you control which video plays, whether the video plays automatically, and other aspects of playback. The options for playback can be accessed in the Properties inspector. Select the FLVPlayback component on the Stage and expand the Component Parameters section in the Properties inspector.

Individual properties are listed in the left column, and their corresponding values are listed in the right column. Select one of the videos on the Stage, and then choose from among the following options:

- To change the autoPlay option, deselect the check box. When the check box is selected, the video plays automatically. When the check box is deselected, the video is paused on the first frame.

- To hide the controller and only display it when users roll their mouse cursor over the video, select the check box for the skinAutoHide option.

- To choose a new controller (the skin), click the name of your skin file and select a new skin in the dialog box that appears.

- To change the transparency of the skin, enter a decimal value from 0 (totally transparent) to 1 (totally opaque) for the skinBackgroundAlpha.

- To change the color of the skin, click on the color chip and choose a new color for the skinBackgroundColor.

- To change the video file or the location of the video file that Flash seeks to play, click the source option.

  In the Content Path dialog box that appears, enter a new filename or click the Folder icon to choose a new file to play. The path is relative to the location of your Flash file.

Working with Video and Transparency

For the various animal videos, you want to show the entire frame with the animals in the foreground and the lush environment in the background. But sometimes you want to use a video file that doesn't include a background. For this project, the zoo director was filmed in front of a green screen, which was removed using Adobe After Effects. When you use the video in Flash, the zoo director appears to be in front of the Flash background. A similar effect is used for news weatherpersons, where the background of the video is totally transparent and can show weather graphics behind the person.

Transparencies in video (called alpha channels) are supported only in the FLV format using the On2 VP6 codec. When encoding a video with an alpha channel from Adobe Media Encoder, be sure to choose Edit > Export Settings, click the Video tab, and then select the Encode Alpha Channel option.

You'll import the video file, which is already in FLV format, into Flash for display with the playback component.

Importing the video clip

Now you'll use the Import Video wizard to import the Popup.flv file, which has already been encoded with an alpha channel.

1   Insert a new layer called **popup video**.

2   Insert a keyframe at frame 50 and insert another keyframe at frame 86.

You'll place the video of the zoo director at the end of the musical introduction at the same time the stop action appears (frame 50). The keyframe at frame 86 ensures that the video of the zoo director disappears from the Stage when the animal videos appear.

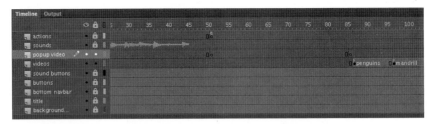

3   Select the keyframe at frame 50.

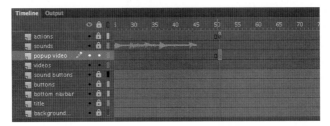

4   Choose File > Import > Import Video.

5   In the Import Video wizard, select On Your Computer and click Browse. Select the Popup.flv file in the Lesson07/07Start folder and click Open.

6   Select Load external video with playback component. Click Next or Continue.

7   Select None for the skin. Click Next or Continue.

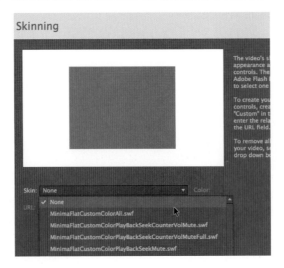

8 Click Finish to place the video.

The video of the zoo director with a transparent background appears on the Stage. Move the video so its bottom edge lines up with the top edge of the navigation bar. Make x=**260** in the Properties inspector.

9 Choose Control > Test Movie > In Flash Professional.

After the musical introduction, the zoo director appears and gives a brief talk. If you click on one of the animal video buttons, the popup video is removed from the Timeline.

● **Note:** If you don't stop one video before navigating to another keyframe containing a second video, the audio can overlap. One way to prevent overlapping sounds is to use the command SoundMixer.stopAll() to stop all sounds before starting a new video. The ActionScript in the first keyframe of the actions layer in your 07_workingcopy.fla file contains the correct code to stop all sounds before navigating to a new animal video.

Embedding Flash Video

In the previous section, you used the FLVPlayback component to play an external video that's in FLV or F4V format. Another way to integrate video in Flash is to use embedded video. Embedded video requires the FLV format and is best for only very short clips. The FLV file is saved in the Library panel of your Flash file, where you can place it on the Timeline. The video plays as long as there are sufficient frames on your Timeline.

Embedding video in Flash is supported by Flash Player versions 6 and later. Keep in mind the following limitations of embedded video: Flash cannot maintain audio synchronization in embedded video that runs over 120 seconds. The maximum length of embedded movies is the maximum length of any timeline, which is 16,000 frames. Another drawback of embedding your video is the increase in the size of your Flash project, which makes testing the movie (Control > Test Movie > In Flash Professional) a longer process and the authoring sessions more tedious.

Because the embedded FLV plays within your Flash project, it is critically important that your FLV have the same frame rate as your Flash file. If not, your embedded video will not play at its intended speed. To make sure your FLV has the same frame rate as your FLA, be sure to set the correct frame rate in the Video tab of Adobe Media Encoder.

Encoding the FLV for embedding

You'll embed a short video of a polar bear in the beginning of your zoo kiosk project.

1　Open the Adobe Media Encoder.

2　Choose File > Add Source, or click the Plus button in the Queue panel and choose the polarbear.mov file in the Lesson07/07Start folder.

The polarbear.mov file is added to the Queue.

3   In the options under Format, select the FLV format.

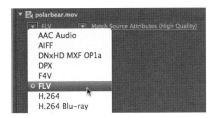

4   Click the Preset settings, or choose Edit > Export Settings to open the Edit Export options.

5   Click the Video tab and set Frame Rate to 24. Make sure that the Resize Video check box is deselected.

The Flash file 07_workingcopy.fla is set at 24 frames per second, so you want your FLV to also be at 24 frames per second.

6   Deselect Export Audio at the top of the dialog box. Click OK.

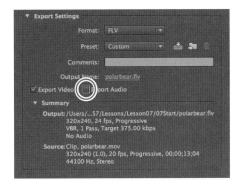

7   Click the Start Queue button (triangular icon) in the upper-right corner to encode your video.

Flash creates the polarbear.flv file.

Embedding an FLV on the Timeline

Now that you have an FLV, you can import it into Flash and embed it on the Timeline.

1 Open the file 07_workingcopy.fla.

2 Select the first frame of the popup video layer.

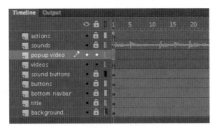

3 Choose File > Import > Import Video. In the Import Video wizard, select On Your Computer and click Browse. Select the polarbear.flv file in the Lesson07/07Start folder and click Open.

4 In the Import Video wizard, select Embed FLV in SWF and play in timeline. Click Next or Continue.

5 Deselect Expand timeline if needed and deselect Include audio. Click Next or Continue.

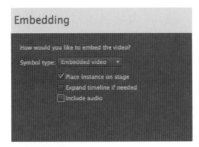

6 Click Finish to import the video.

The video of the polar bear appears on the Stage. Use the Selection tool to move it to the left side of the Stage.

● **Note:** This video of the polar bear does not have audio. If you do have a video that contains audio, you will not be able to hear audio in the authoring environment for embedded videos. To hear the audio, you must choose Control > Test Movie > In Flash Professional.

The FLV also appears in your Library panel.

7 Choose Control > Test Movie > In Flash Professional to see the embedded video file play from frame 1 to frame 49.

Using embedded video

It's useful to think of embedded video as a multiframe symbol, very much like a symbol with a nested animation. You can convert an embedded video to a movie clip symbol, and then apply a motion tween to it to create interesting effects.

Next, you'll apply a motion tween to the embedded video so it elegantly fades out just before the zoo director pops up and speaks.

1   Select the embedded video of the polar bear on the Stage, right-click/Ctrl-click it, and select Create Motion Tween.

2   Flash asks to convert the embedded video to a symbol so it can apply a motion tween. Click OK.

3   Flash asks to add enough frames inside the movie clip symbol so that the entire video can play. Click Yes.

Flash creates a motion tween on the layer.

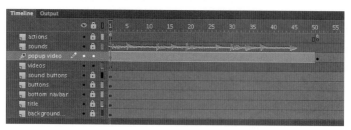

4 Right-click/Ctrl-click on frame 30 of the popup video layer and choose Insert Keyframe > All (F6).

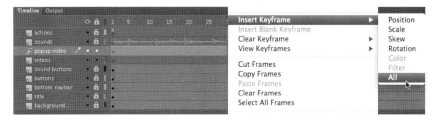

Flash inserts a new keyframe at frame 30.

5 While your playhead is still at frame 30, select the movie clip containing the embedded video on the Stage, and in the Properties inspector, choose Alpha for Style and 100% for the Alpha value.

Flash establishes the initial Alpha value at frame 30 at 100%.

6 Move the playhead on the Timeline to frame 49.

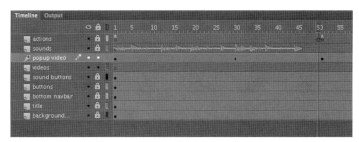

7 Select the movie clip containing the embedded video on the Stage, and in the Properties inspector, choose Alpha for Style and 0% for the Alpha value.

Flash inserts a new keyframe at frame 49 with the Alpha value for your selected movie clip at 0%. The instance fades out from frame 30 to frame 49.

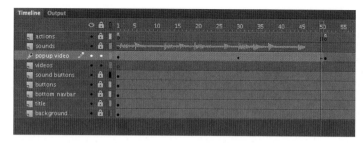

8 Choose Control > Test Movie > In Flash Professional to see the embedded video play and fade out.

Your interactive zoo kiosk is complete!

Exporting Video from Flash

So far, you've been using Adobe Media Encoder to prepare video to integrate within Flash. However, you can also use Media Encoder to export your Flash content to video.

For example, use the powerful drawing and animation tools within Flash to create animation, and then export it as an HD broadcast-quality video, or for playback on a variety of platforms such as an iPhone, Nook, Kindle, or Android device.

Exporting video

For this part of the lesson, you'll use the animation you created in Lesson 4. In that lesson, you created the cinematic splash screen for the fictional motion picture *Double Identity*.

As part of the promotion for the motion picture, the client requests that the animation run on multiple platforms. You'll export the animation and encode the video to be compatible for a variety of devices.

1 Open the 04_workingcopy.fla file from Lesson 4, or if you haven't completed that lesson, open the 04End.fla file in the Lesson04/04End folder.

2 Choose File > Export > Export Video.

The Export Video dialog box appears. Uncheck ignore stage color, check Convert video in Adobe Media Encoder, and choose When last frame is reached for the Stop exporting option.

Choose Browse if you want to export the video in a different location. The default location is in the same folder as the 04End.fla file.

● **Note:** Windows
users need to download
and install QuickTime,
free from Apple at
http://www.apple.com/
quicktime/download/
to work with the video
examples in this lesson.

3 Click Export.

Flash exports and saves a .mov file and automatically opens the Adobe Media
Encoder with the file added to the Queue.

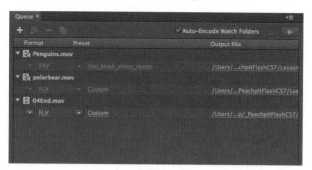

Choosing a target device for encoding

Now you can export the video to several target devices. You'll export the video
to files compatible with the iPhone, Nook, Kindle, and Android devices.

1 In Adobe Media Encoder, change the Format of the 04End.mov selection to H.264
and the Preset to Amazon Kindle Fire Native Resolution – 1024x580 29.97.

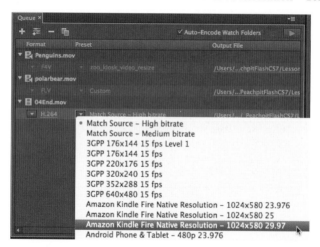

Adobe Media Encoder configures all the export options so the exported file is
compatible with the Amazon Kindle Fire. The resolution is set at 1024 pixels by
580 pixels and the frame rate at 29.97 frames per second.

2 Select 04End.mov or the output. In the Preset Browser panel, choose Android Phone – 320x240 29.97 and click Apply Preset at the top-right corner of the panel.

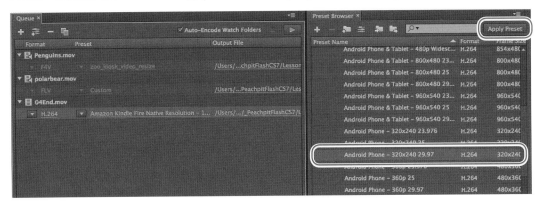

Adobe Media Encoder adds a second output, configured for the Android phone.

3 Select the output and apply additional presets from the Preset Browser panel. Choose Apple iPhone, iPod – 320x240 29.97 and Barnes and Noble Nook Color – 854x480 29.97.

Your Queue contains four outputs for the 04End.mov selection.

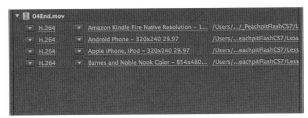

4 Click the Start Queue button at the top of the Queue panel.

Adobe Media Encoder begins encoding the 04End.mov file into the four specified formats, and saves the files in the path specified in the Output File column.

The videos are ready and compatible with the specified devices.

Review Questions

1 How can you edit the length of a sound clip?

2 What is a skin for a video?

3 What are the limitations for embedded video clips?

4 How do you export a Flash animation into a video that's compatible with a specific device?

Review Answers

1 To edit the length of a sound clip, select the keyframe that contains it and click the Pencil button in the Properties inspector. Then move the time slider in the Edit Envelope dialog box to clip the sound from the front or from the end.

2 The skin is the combination of functionality and appearance of video controls, such as Play, Fast Forward, and Pause buttons. You can choose from a wide array of combinations with the buttons in different positions, and you can customize the skin with a different color or level of transparency. If you don't want viewers to be able to control the video, apply None from the Skin menu.

3 When you embed a video clip, it becomes part of the Flash document and is included in the Timeline. Because embedded video clips significantly increase the size of the document and produce audio synchronization issues, it's best to embed video only if it is very brief and contains no audio track.

4 In Flash Professional, you can export an animation as a video by choosing File > Export > Export Video. The video is added automatically to the Adobe Media Encoder Queue, where you can configure encoding options or choose Preset options that target various platforms, such as the Amazon Kindle, Barnes and Noble Nook, Apple iPhone, Android, and other devices.

8 LOADING AND DISPLAYING EXTERNAL CONTENT

Lesson Overview

In this lesson, you'll learn how to do the following:

- Load and display an external SWF file

- Position a loaded SWF file

- Manage how loaded SWF files overlap each other

- Remove a loaded SWF file

- Control a movie clip's Timeline

This lesson will take about 60 minutes to complete. If needed, remove the previous lesson folder from your hard drive and copy the Lesson08 folder onto it. Download the project files for this lesson from the Lesson & Update Files tab on your Account page at www.peachpit.com and store them on your computer in a convenient location, as described in the Getting Started section of this book. Your Accounts page is also where you'll find any updates to the chapters or to the lesson files. Look on the Lesson & Update Files tab to access the most current content.

Use ActionScript to load external Flash content.
By keeping Flash content modular, you'll make your
projects more manageable and easier to edit.

Getting Started

● **Note:** If you have not already downloaded the project files for this lesson to your computer from your Account page, make sure to do so now. See "Getting Started" at the beginning of the book.

You'll start the lesson by viewing the finished movie.

1 Double-click the 08End.html file in the Lesson08/08End folder to view the final movie.

The project is a fictional online lifestyle magazine called *Check*. A jazzy animation appears on the front page showing four main sections of the magazine. Each section on the front page is a movie clip with a nested animation.

The first section is an article on the star of the upcoming movie *Double Identity* (whose Web site you created in Lesson 4), the second section describes a new car, the third section presents some facts and figures, and the fourth section is a self-improvement article.

You can click on each section on the front page to access the content. The inside content is not complete, but you can imagine that each section could contain more information. Click again to return to the front page.

2 Double-click the page1.swf, page2.swf, page3.swf, and page4.swf files in the Lesson08/08End folder.

Each of the four sections is a separate Flash file. Note that the front page, 08End.swf, loads each SWF file as needed.

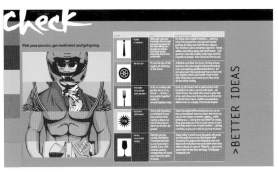

3 Close all the SWF files and open the **08Start.fla** file in the Lesson08/08Start folder.

Many of the images, graphic elements, and animations have already been completed in this file. You will add the necessary ActionScript to make the Flash file load the external Flash content.

4 Choose File > Save As. Name the file **08_workingcopy.fla** and save it in the 08Start folder. Saving a working copy ensures that the original start file will be available if you want to start over.

● **Note:** Flash warns you if your computer doesn't have the same fonts contained in a FLA file. Choose substitute fonts, or simply click Use Default to have Flash automatically make the substitutions.

Loading External Content

You'll use ActionScript to load each of the external SWFs into your main Flash movie. Loading external content keeps your overall project in separate modules and prevents the project from becoming too bloated and difficult to download. It also makes it easier for you to edit, because you can edit individual sections instead of one, large, unwieldy file.

For example, if you wanted to change the article on the new car in the second section, you would simply open and edit the Flash file page2.fla, which contains that content.

To load the external files, you'll use two ActionScript objects: one called a **ProLoader** and another called a **URLRequest**.

Note: The ProLoader object is an ActionScript object introduced in Flash Professional CS5.5. Older versions of Flash rely on a similar object called the Loader object. The ProLoader and the Loader objects are identical, except that the ProLoader handles the loading of external libraries for more reliable and consistent performance.

1 Insert a new layer at the top and rename it **actionscript**.

2 Press F9 (Windows) or Option+F9 (Mac OS) to open the Actions panel.

3 Type the following two lines exactly as they appear here:

```
import fl.display.ProLoader;
var myProLoader:ProLoader=new ProLoader();
```

This code first imports the necessary code for the ProLoader class, and then creates a ProLoader object and names it myProLoader.

Note: To compare punctuation, spacing, spelling, or any other aspects of the ActionScript, view the Actions panel in the 08End.fla file.

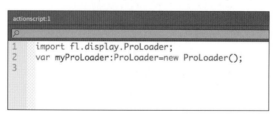

4 On the next line, type the following lines exactly as they appear here:

```
page1_mc.addEventListener(MouseEvent.CLICK, page1content);
function page1content(e:MouseEvent):void {
 var myURL:URLRequest=new URLRequest("page1.swf");
 myProLoader.load(myURL);
 addChild(myProLoader);
}
```

```
actionscript:1

1    import fl.display.ProLoader;
2    var myProLoader:ProLoader=new ProLoader();
3    page1_mc.addEventListener(MouseEvent.CLICK, page1content);
4    function page1content(e:MouseEvent):void {
5        var myURL:URLRequest=new URLRequest("page1.swf");
6        myProLoader.load(myURL);
7        addChild(myProLoader);
8    }
9
```

You've seen this syntax before in Lesson 6. On line 3, you create a listener that detects a mouse click on the object called page1_mc. This is a movie clip on the Stage. In response, Flash executes the function called page1content.

The function called page1content does several things: First, it creates a URLRequest object referencing the name of the file you want to load. Second, it passes the URLRequest object to the ProLoader object's load method. Third, it adds the ProLoader object to the Stage so you can see it.

5 Select the movie clip on the left side of the Stage with the movie star.

6 In the Properties inspector, name it **page1_mc**.

The ActionScript you entered refers to the object called page1_mc, so you need to apply the name to one of the movie clips on the Stage.

● **Note:** You can also use the ProLoader and URLRequest objects to dynamically load image files. The syntax is identical. Simply replace the SWF filename with a JPEG, GIF, or PNG filename, and Flash loads the specified image.

● **Note:** Adding event listeners to movie clips can make them respond to mouse clicks, but your cursor doesn't automatically change to a hand icon to indicate that it is clickable. In the Actions panel, set the property buttonMode to true for each movie clip instance to enable the hand cursor. For example, page1_mc.buttonMode=true makes the hand cursor appear when you move your mouse over that movie clip on the Stage.

7 Choose Control > Test Movie > In Flash Professional to see your movie so far.

The front page plays its animation and stops. When you click on the movie star, the file called page1.swf loads and is displayed.

8 Close the test movie window called 08_workingcopy.swf.

9 Select the first frame of the actionscript layer and open the Actions panel.

10 Copy and paste the event listener and the function so you have four distinct listeners for each of the four movie clips on the Stage. The four listeners should appear as follows:

```
page1_mc.addEventListener(MouseEvent.CLICK, page1content);
function page1content(e:MouseEvent):void {
  var myURL:URLRequest=new URLRequest("page1.swf");
  myProLoader.load(myURL);
  addChild(myProLoader);
}
```

```
page2_mc.addEventListener(MouseEvent.CLICK, page2content);
function page2content(e:MouseEvent):void {
 var myURL:URLRequest=new URLRequest("page2.swf");
 myProLoader.load(myURL);
 addChild(myProLoader);
}
page3_mc.addEventListener(MouseEvent.CLICK, page3content);
function page3content(e:MouseEvent):void {
 var myURL:URLRequest=new URLRequest("page3.swf");
 myProLoader.load(myURL);
 addChild(myProLoader);
}
page4_mc.addEventListener(MouseEvent.CLICK, page4content);
function page4content(e:MouseEvent):void {
 var myURL:URLRequest=new URLRequest("page4.swf");
 myProLoader.load(myURL);
 addChild(myProLoader);
}
```

```
actionscript:1

1    import fl.display.ProLoader;
2    var myProLoader:ProLoader=new ProLoader();
3    page1_mc.addEventListener(MouseEvent.CLICK, page1content);
4    function page1content(e:MouseEvent):void {
5        var myURL:URLRequest=new URLRequest("page1.swf");
6        myProLoader.load(myURL);
7        addChild(myProLoader);
8    }
9    page2_mc.addEventListener(MouseEvent.CLICK, page2content);
10   function page2content(e:MouseEvent):void {
11       var myURL:URLRequest=new URLRequest("page2.swf");
12       myProLoader.load(myURL);
13       addChild(myProLoader);
14   }
15   page3_mc.addEventListener(MouseEvent.CLICK, page3content);
16   function page3content(e:MouseEvent):void {
17       var myURL:URLRequest=new URLRequest("page3.swf");
18       myProLoader.load(myURL);
19       addChild(myProLoader);
20   }
21   page4_mc.addEventListener(MouseEvent.CLICK, page4content);
22   function page4content(e:MouseEvent):void {
23       var myURL:URLRequest=new URLRequest("page4.swf");
24       myProLoader.load(myURL);
25       addChild(myProLoader);
26   }
27
```

11 Click on each of the remaining three movie clips on the Stage and name them
   in the Properties inspector. Name the yellow car **page2_mc**, name the data
   section **page3_mc**, and name the self-improvement section on the lower right
   page4_mc.

Using the Code Snippets panel

You can also use the Code Snippets panel to add code to load external SWF or image files. Using the Code Snippets panel can save you time and effort, but writing your own code by hand is the only way to understand how the code works and will help you begin building your own more sophisticated, customized projects.

Follow these alternate steps if you wish to rely on the Code Snippets panel. However, the remainder of this lesson will refer to the code presented in the previous section.

1   Choose Window > Code Snippets, or if your Actions panel is already open, click the Code Snippets button at the top right of the Actions panel.

The Code Snippets panel appears. The code snippets are organized in folders that describe their function.

2   In the Code Snippets panel, expand the folder called Load and Unload.

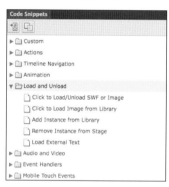

3   Select the movie clip on the Stage that you wish to trigger the loading function.

4   Select the snippet, Click to Load/Unload SWF or Image, and click the Add to current frame button, or simply double-click the snippet.

Add to current frame

If you hadn't given a name to your instance on the Stage, a dialog box appears to allow you to name the instance. Name the instance **page1_mc**.

Flash adds the code snippet to the current keyframe on the Timeline.

5 Open the Actions panel to view the code.

```
Actions:1

1
2    /* Click to Load/Unload SWF or Image from a URL.
3    Clicking on the symbol instance loads and displays the specified SWF or image URL. Clicking on the
4
5    Instructions:
6    1. Replace "http://www.helpexamples.com/flash/images/image1.jpg" below with the desired URL address
7    2. Files from internet domains separate from the domain where the calling SWF resides cannot be loa
8    */
9
10   page1_mc.addEventListener(MouseEvent.CLICK, fl_ClickToLoadUnloadSWF_3);
11
12   import fl.display.ProLoader;
13   var fl_ProLoader_3:ProLoader;
14
15   //This variable keeps track of whether you want to load or unload the SWF
16   var fl_ToLoad_3:Boolean = true;
17
18   function fl_ClickToLoadUnloadSWF_3(event:MouseEvent):void
19   {
20       if(fl_ToLoad_3)
21       {
22           fl_ProLoader_3 = new ProLoader();
23           fl_ProLoader_3.load(new URLRequest("http://www.helpexamples.com/flash/images/image1.jpg"));
24           addChild(fl_ProLoader_3);
25       }
26       else
27       {
28           fl_ProLoader_3.unload();
29           removeChild(fl_ProLoader_3);
30           fl_ProLoader_3 = null;
31       }
32       // Toggle whether you want to load or unload the SWF
33       fl_ToLoad_3 = !fl_ToLoad_3;
34   }
35
```

Examine the code. The code is a little more complex than the code presented in the previous section. The code includes a reference to a sample JPG image (online) and a toggling functionality, so the user can click once to load the SWF, and then click again to unload the SWF. However, because the external SWF that loads covers the entire Stage, the original movie clip is hidden and inaccessible to click on. Use this code snippet if your layout allows the button or movie clip that triggers the loading function to remain visible on the Stage.

Delete the code and return to the code you entered manually.

Positioning of the Loaded Content

Loaded content is aligned with the Stage (or whatever it is loaded into). The registration point of the ProLoader object is at its top-left corner, so the top-left corner of the external SWFs aligns with the top-left corner of the Stage (where x=0 and y=0). Since the four external Flash files (page1.swf, page2.swf, page3.swf, and page4.swf) all have the same Stage size as the Flash file that loads them, the Stage is completely covered.

However, you can position the ProLoader object wherever you want. If you want to place the ProLoader object in a different horizontal position, you can set a new x value for the ProLoader object with ActionScript. If you want to place the ProLoader in a different vertical position, you can set a new y value for the ProLoader. Here's how: In the Actions panel, enter the name of the ProLoader object, followed by a period, the property x or y, and then the equals symbol and a new value.

```
27
28    myProLoader.x = 200;
29    myProLoader.y = 100;
```

In the following example, the ProLoader object called myProLoader is repositioned 200 pixels from the left edge and 100 pixels from the top edge.

When the external SWF content loads, it shows up exactly 200 pixels to the right and 100 pixels down.

Removing External Content

Once an external SWF file is loaded, how do you unload it to return to the main Flash movie? One way is to unload the SWF content from the ProLoader object, so the audience can no longer see it. You will use the command unload() to do this.

1 Select the first frame of the actionscript layer and open the Actions panel.

2 Add the following lines to your code in the Script pane:

```
myProLoader.addEventListener(MouseEvent.CLICK, unloadcontent);
function unloadcontent(e:MouseEvent):void {
  myProLoader.unload();
}
```

Note: If you want to remove the ProLoader object from the Stage entirely, you can use the removeChild() command. The code removeChild (myProLoader) removes the ProLoader object called myProLoader so that it is no longer displayed on the Stage.

Note: If your loaded content contains open streams (such as video or sounds), those sounds may continue even after you've unloaded the SWF from the ProLoader object. Use the unloadAndStop() command to extinguish the sounds as well as unload the SWF content.

```
actionscript:1
 1   import fl.display.ProLoader;
 2   var myProLoader:ProLoader=new ProLoader();
 3   page1_mc.addEventListener(MouseEvent.CLICK, page1content);
 4   function page1content(e:MouseEvent):void {
 5       var myURL:URLRequest=new URLRequest("page1.swf");
 6       myProLoader.load(myURL);
 7       addChild(myProLoader);
 8   }
 9   page2_mc.addEventListener(MouseEvent.CLICK, page2content);
10   function page2content(e:MouseEvent):void {
11       var myURL:URLRequest=new URLRequest("page2.swf");
12       myProLoader.load(myURL);
13       addChild(myProLoader);
14   }
15   page3_mc.addEventListener(MouseEvent.CLICK, page3content);
16   function page3content(e:MouseEvent):void {
17       var myURL:URLRequest=new URLRequest("page3.swf");
18       myProLoader.load(myURL);
19       addChild(myProLoader);
20   }
21   page4_mc.addEventListener(MouseEvent.CLICK, page4content);
22   function page4content(e:MouseEvent):void {
23       var myURL:URLRequest=new URLRequest("page4.swf");
24       myProLoader.load(myURL);
25       addChild(myProLoader);
26   }
27   myProLoader.addEventListener(MouseEvent.CLICK, unloadcontent);
28   function unloadcontent(e:MouseEvent):void {
29       myProLoader.unload();
30   }
```

This code adds an event listener to the ProLoader object called myProLoader. When you click on the ProLoader object, the function called unloadcontent is executed.

The function performs just one action: It removes any loaded content from the ProLoader object.

3 Choose Control > Test Movie > In Flash Professional to preview the movie. Click on any of the four sections, and then click on the loaded content to return to the main movie.

Controlling Movie Clips

When you return to the front page, you'll see the four sections, so you can click another movie clip to load a different section. But wouldn't it be nice to replay the initial animation? The initial animations are nested inside each movie clip, and you can control the four movie clips that are on the Stage. You can use the basic navigation commands that you already learned in Lesson 6 (gotoAndStop, gotoAndPlay, stop, play) to navigate the Timelines of these movie clips. Simply precede the command with the name of the movie clip and separate them with a dot. Flash targets that particular movie clip and moves its Timeline accordingly.

1 Select the first frame of the actionscript layer and open the Actions panel.

2 Add to the commands in the function called unloadcontent so the entire function appears as follows:

```
function unloadcontent(e:MouseEvent):void {
myProLoader.unload();
page1_mc.gotoAndPlay(1);
page2_mc.gotoAndPlay(1);
page3_mc.gotoAndPlay(1);
page4_mc.gotoAndPlay(1);
}
```

```
actionscript:1

1   import fl.display.ProLoader;
2   var myProLoader:ProLoader=new ProLoader();
3   page1_mc.addEventListener(MouseEvent.CLICK, page1content);
4   function page1content(e:MouseEvent):void {
5       var myURL:URLRequest=new URLRequest("page1.swf");
6       myProLoader.load(myURL);
7       addChild(myProLoader);
8   }
9   page2_mc.addEventListener(MouseEvent.CLICK, page2content);
10  function page2content(e:MouseEvent):void {
11      var myURL:URLRequest=new URLRequest("page2.swf");
12      myProLoader.load(myURL);
13      addChild(myProLoader);
14  }
15  page3_mc.addEventListener(MouseEvent.CLICK, page3content);
16  function page3content(e:MouseEvent):void {
17      var myURL:URLRequest=new URLRequest("page3.swf");
18      myProLoader.load(myURL);
19      addChild(myProLoader);
20  }
21  page4_mc.addEventListener(MouseEvent.CLICK, page4content);
22  function page4content(e:MouseEvent):void {
23      var myURL:URLRequest=new URLRequest("page4.swf");
24      myProLoader.load(myURL);
25      addChild(myProLoader);
26  }
27  myProLoader.addEventListener(MouseEvent.CLICK, unloadcontent);
28  function unloadcontent(e:MouseEvent):void {
29      myProLoader.unload();
30      page1_mc.gotoAndPlay(1);
31      page2_mc.gotoAndPlay(1);
32      page3_mc.gotoAndPlay(1);
33      page4_mc.gotoAndPlay(1);
34  }
```

In this function, which is executed when the user clicks the ProLoader object, the ProLoader object is removed from the Stage, and then the playhead of each movie clip on the Stage moves to the first frame and begins playing.

3 Choose Control > Test Movie > In Flash Professional to preview the movie. Click on any of the four sections, and then click on the loaded content to return to the main movie.

When you return to the main movie, all four movie clips play their nested animations.

Managing Overlapping Content

In this lesson, there is only one ProLoader object that loads and displays a single external SWF at a time that covers the whole Stage. However, when you use multiple ProLoader objects to load several different external files or images at time, you often have to manage overlapping content.

Juggling how different pieces of content overlap each other depends on their depth level in the Display List, which is a list that organizes all the visible content. The Display List manages the order of visible items with a simple number, called an index, starting at 0. Items that are higher on the list appear above objects that are lower on the list.

For example, consider the following example, where you have two ProLoader objects that each load a different JPG image:

```
import fl.display.ProLoader;
var myProLoader1:ProLoader=new ProLoader();
var myProLoader2:ProLoader=new ProLoader();
var myURL1:URLRequest=new URLRequest("dog.jpg");
var myURL2:URLRequest=new URLRequest("cat.jpg");
myProLoader1.load(myURL1);
myProLoader2.load(myURL2);
addChild(myProLoader1);
addChild(myProLoader2);
```

Flash adds myProLoader1 before myProLoader2, so the loaded content of myProLoader2 appears above the content of myProLoader1. The cat.jpg image overlaps the dog.jpg image. The index of myProLoader1 is 0 and the index of myProLoader2 is 1.

If you want to swap the overlapping order of the two ProLoader objects, you can do so several different ways. You can use the command, addChildAt(), which takes two arguments inside of its parentheses. The first argument is the object you want to place, and the second is the index in the Display List. So you can write the following statement to put the cat image under of the dog image:

```
addChildAt(myProLoader2, 0);
```

This statement adds the myProLoader2 object (which shows the cat) at index=0, which is the bottom-most level of the Display List. The myProLoader1 object gets bumped up to index=1 to accommodate the myProLoader2 object. If the object is already on the Display List, you can just use the command, setChildIndex(myProLoader2, 0);

Another approach is to swap the depth levels of two objects using swapChildren(). Provide two objects as the arguments and Flash switches their order in the Display List. For example, swapChildren(myProLoader1, myProLoader2) swaps the overlapping order of the dog and cat images.

Refer to the online Adobe ActionScript 3 Reference for the object DisplayObjectContainer to see additional methods to help you manage overlapping objects in the Display List.

Review Questions

1 How do you load external Flash content?

2 What are the advantages of loading external Flash content?

3 How do you control the Timeline of a movie clip instance?

4 How do you manage the overlapping order of objects that are added to the Stage?

Review Answers

1 You use ActionScript to load external Flash content. You create two objects: a ProLoader and a URLRequest object. The URLRequest object specifies the filename and file location of the SWF file that you want to load. To load the file, use the `load()` command to load the URLRequest object into the ProLoader object. Then display the ProLoader object on the Stage with the `addChild()` command.

2 Loading external content keeps your overall project in separate modules and prevents the project from becoming too bloated and difficult to download. It also makes it easier for you to edit, because you can edit individual sections instead of one, large, unwieldy file.

3 You can control the Timeline of movie clips with ActionScript by first targeting them by their instance name. After the name, type a dot (period), and then the command that you desire. You can use the same commands for navigation that you learned in Lesson 6 (`gotoAndStop`, `gotoAndPlay`, `stop`, `play`). Flash targets that particular movie clip and moves its Timeline accordingly.

4 You manage the overlapping order of objects on the Stage with their index number in the Display List. Objects are automatically assigned index numbers as they are added to the Stage with `addChild()`. Objects with a greater index in the Display List appear above objects with a smaller index. You can change any object's index in the Display List with the method `setChildIndex()` or `addChildAt()`, or use `swapChildren()` to switch the index of two objects.

9 USING VARIABLES AND CONTROLLING VISUAL PROPERTIES

Lesson Overview

In this lesson, you'll learn how to do the following:

- Change the appearance of movie clip instances with ActionScript
- Understand an object's registration point and the coordinate system
- Work with advanced mouse events
- Create and use variables to store information
- Understand data types
- Display information in the Output panel
- Track the position of the mouse cursor
- Hide the mouse cursor
- Replace the mouse cursor with a custom icon

This lesson will take approximately 90 minutes to complete. If needed, remove the previous lesson folder from your hard drive and copy the Lesson09 folder onto it. Download the project files for this lesson from the Lesson & Update Files tab on your Account page at www.peachpit.com and store them on your computer in a convenient location, as described in the Getting Started section of this book. Your Accounts page is also where you'll find any updates to the chapters or to the lesson files. Look on the Lesson & Update Files tab to access the most current content.

Use ActionScript to control your graphics on the Stage while your movie is playing. Combine complex mouse interactions with variables to create interfaces that respond dynamically to your user for more immersive environments.

Getting Started

● **Note:** If you have not already downloaded the project files for this lesson to your computer from your Account page, make sure to do so now. See "Getting Started" at the beginning of the book.

Start the lesson by viewing the finished interactive project. You'll create a feature that shows a more detailed image of a smaller thumbnail, much like the interfaces on retail product sites like Amazon.com.

1   Double-click the **09End.html** file in the Lesson09/09End folder to run the Flash project.

Read the overview of this fictional digital single lens reflex camera, and look at the accompanying small thumbnail image on the left.

2   Move your mouse over the camera image.

A larger image appears on the Stage. As you move your mouse cursor over the thumbnail image, you see details of different parts of the camera.

Your cursor changes to an icon of a magnifying glass.

3   Move your mouse cursor off of the camera image.

The larger image disappears and the default arrow mouse cursor returns.

In this lesson, you'll add the ActionScript to create the interactivity. All the content—the images, text, and accompanying graphics—are already included in the Library panel and ready for you to use.

In previous lessons, you've learned to create event listeners to detect mouse clicks. In this lesson, you'll learn about more complex mouse interactions—when the mouse cursor moves over an object, when the mouse cursor moves off of an object, and when the mouse cursor simply moves. You'll tie these events to changes in the appearance of graphics on the Stage, so the visual feedback is immediate.

1   Close the 09.html file.

2   Double-click the **09Start.fla** file in the Lesson09/09Start folder to open the initial project file in Flash.

3   Choose File > Save As. Name the file **09_workingcopy.fla**, and save it in the 09Start folder. Saving a working copy ensures that the original start file will be available if you want to start over.

Understanding the Project File

The initial setup of the project has been partially completed. The Stage is 800x600 pixels, and the Stage color is white. The top banner and text are positioned on the Stage in a layer called banner.

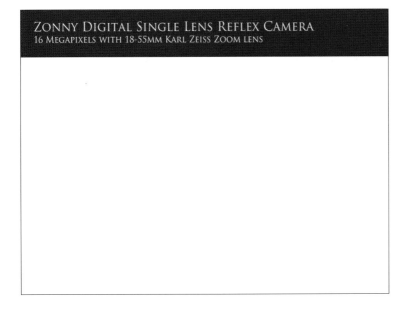

All the text and image files have already been imported into the Library, and the content has been converted to movie clip symbols.

Setting up the text and graphics

You'll place the small thumbnail of the camera and the summary information on the left. The more detailed text information appears in the center of the Stage.

1 Create a new layer and name it **thumbnail**.

2 Drag the movie clip symbol called **image_thumbnail** from the Library panel to the Stage.

An instance of the movie clip appears on the Stage.

3 In the Properties inspector, position the instance at x=25, y=115 to position the instance at the top-left corner, just below the banner graphic.

4 Create a new layer called **text summary** and drag the movie clip symbol called **text_summary** from the Library panel to the Stage.

An instance of the movie clip appears on the Stage.

5 In the Properties inspector, position the instance at x=25, y=290, just below the thumbnail image of the camera.

6 Create a new layer called **text detail** and drag the movie clip symbol called **text_detail** from the Library panel to the Stage.

An instance of the movie clip appears on the Stage.

7 In the Properties inspector, position the instance at x=225, y=115, to the right of the thumbnail image of the camera.

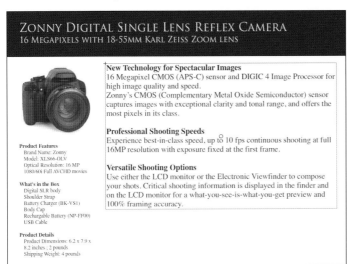

You now have four layers, each containing a separate movie clip.

Creating the mask for the camera detail

The large image of the camera that shows the close-up details is under a mask, so only a rectangular portion of the larger image appears.

1 Create a new layer and name it **mask**.

2 Select the Rectangle tool, and choose any color for its fill and choose no color for its stroke.

3 Create a rectangle on the Stage in the mask layer.

4 In the Properties inspector, modify the rectangle so it is 550 pixels wide, 450 pixels high, and positioned at x=225, y=115.

The rectangular area will be the portion that reveals the larger image of the camera.

5 Double-click the icon next to the layer name, or select the mask layer, and choose Modify > Timeline > Layer properties.

The Layer Properties dialog box appears.

6 Choose Mask for Type, and click OK.

The mask layer becomes a Mask layer.

7 Create a new layer and name it **large image**.

8 Drag the large image layer under the mask layer.

The large image layer becomes a Masked layer. Any content in this layer is masked by the rectangular shape in the Mask layer above it.

9 Drag the **image_big** movie clip symbol from the Library onto the Stage in the large image layer.

10 In the Properties inspector, position the image_big movie clip instance at x=225, y=115, at the same coordinates as the rectangle in the Mask layer.

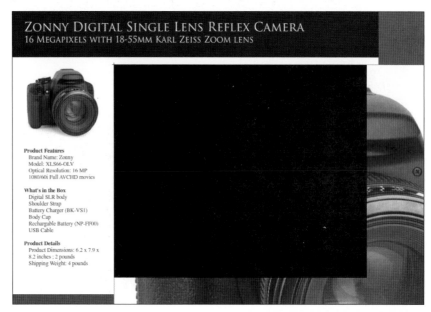

11 Lock the Mask and Masked layer pair to see the effects of the mask.

Flash masks the large camera image with the rectangle.

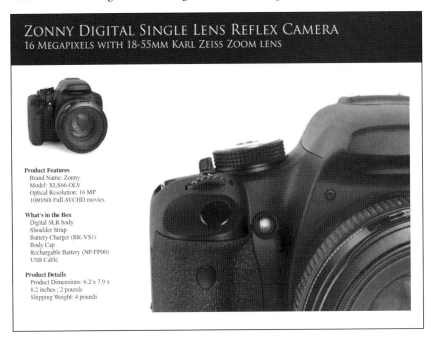

12 Reorder your layers, if needed, so that the text_detail layer that contains the text in the main part of the Stage is under the Mask-Masked layer pair.

The masked camera covers the text. In this lesson, you'll dynamically make the masked image visible or not visible, depending on the user's mouse interactions with the small thumbnail image.

Visual Properties of Movie Clips

In previous lessons, you learned that you can change the appearance of movie clip instances without changing the actual movie clip symbol in your Library. For example, you use the Free Transform tool or Transform panel to make rotations, or to change an object's width or height. You can also use the Color Effect options in the Properties inspector to change the transparency of an object.

You can make the same kinds of modifications to a movie clip purely with ActionScript. You can change an object's rotation, width, height, transparency, and many other visual properties just with code. This allows you to change the appearance of movie clip instances to respond dynamically so you can make more sophisticated and more interactive environments.

To change the appearance of a movie clip instance with ActionScript, first you enter the name of the object you want to target, then type a period (a dot), the property name, and then an equal sign. To the right of the equal sign, enter a value. The equal sign assigns the value to the property. For example:

```
thumbnail.rotation=45;
```

In this statement, the object named **thumbnail** is targeted, and its **rotation** property is assigned a value of 45. As a result, Flash rotates the thumbnail object 45 degrees clockwise. As you build your vocabulary in ActionScript, you learn the properties for each kind of object as well as the data type for those values. Some properties take Number data for degrees, while others may use Number data for pixels. Some properties take String values (characters) for names, and others use Boolean values (true or false).

The following is an essential list of movie clip properties, and their data types that you should know:

BASIC PROPERTIES OF THE MOVIE CLIP

x	Horizontal position, in pixels (Number data)
y	Vertical position, in pixels (Number data)
rotation	Angle, in degrees clockwise from the vertical (Number data)
alpha	Transparency, from 0 (transparent) to 1 (opaque) (Number data)
width	Width, in pixels (Number data)
height	Height, in pixels (Number data)
scaleX	Percentage of horizontal scale of original movie clip, 1=100% (Number data)
scaleY	Percentage of vertical scale of original movie clip, 1=100% (Number data)
visible	Visibility, false=invisible, true=visible (Boolean data)
name	Instance name (String data)

● **Note:** Some properties are "read-only," which means you can only find out their value, but can't assign new values. For example, the movie clip property currentFrame is a read-only property. It tells you the current frame number of the movie clip's playhead, but you can't assign a new value to the property. To change the value of currentFrame use the method, gotoAndStop() to move the playhead to a new position on the timeline.

Name the movie clip instance

Before you can change the appearance of a movie clip instance with code, you must provide an instance name.

1 Unlock the Masked layer (but keep the Mask layer locked), and select the large camera image on the Stage.

2 In the Properties inspector, name the instance **largeimage**.

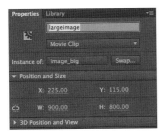

Flash can now reference the large camera image by its instance name and change the value of one or more of its properties.

Making the large image invisible

The first thing you'll want to do is to hide the large camera image when this project first launches. The detail of the camera will only appear when the user rolls the mouse over the thumbnail.

In order to hide the large camera image, you'll change its *visible* property. The visible property determines whether the object can be seen. Assigning a value of false makes the object invisible, and a value of true makes the object visible.

1 Create a new layer and name it **actions**.

2 Select the first keyframe of the actions layer and open the Actions panel.

3 Enter the following statement:

```
largeimage.visible=false;
```

Flash makes the object called largeimage invisible.

> **Note:** A visible value of false is not the same as an alpha value of 0, although the end effect may appear identical. If an object's visible property is false, the user can't interact with the object using the mouse. If an object's alpha property is 0, then it is simply transparent, but the user can still interact with the object using the mouse.

4 Test the movie by choosing Control > Test Movie > In Flash Professional.

The large image of the camera under the mask, which is visible in the Flash authoring environment, is invisible in the SWF file.

Beyond the Mouse-Click

Previously, you've learned to add event listeners to detect mouse clicks over buttons. But many complex interactions involve multiple events, with each event triggering a different function.

In this section, you'll add event listeners for a mouseover event and a mouseout event. A mouseover event happens when the mouse cursor moves over the object. A mouseout event happens when the mouse cursor moves off of the object.

Adding event listeners for mouseover and mouseout

Add a mouseover event on the thumbnail image to show the larger camera image, and add a mouseout event on the thumbnail image to hide the larger camera image.

1 Select the thumbnail image of the camera on the Stage, and in the Properties inspector, enter **thumbnail** for the instance name.

2 Select the first keyframe of the actions layer, and open the Actions panel.

3 On the next available line, enter:

```
thumbnail.addEventListener(MouseEvent.MOUSE_OVER, showlarge);
```

`MouseEvent.MOUSE_OVER` is the keyword for the mouseover event. When a mouseover event is detected, Flash executes the function called showlarge (which you haven't written yet).

```
actions:1
1    largeimage.visible=false;
2    thumbnail.addEventListener(MouseEvent.MOUSE_OVER, showlarge);
```

4 On the next available line, enter:

```
thumbnail.addEventListener(MouseEvent.MOUSE_OUT, hidelarge);
```

```
actions:1
1    largeimage.visible=false;
2    thumbnail.addEventListener(MouseEvent.MOUSE_OVER, showlarge);
3    thumbnail.addEventListener(MouseEvent.MOUSE_OUT, hidelarge);
```

`MouseEvent.MOUSE_OUT` is the keyword for the mouseout event. When a mouseout event is detected, Flash executes the function called hidelarge (which you haven't written yet).

Showing and hiding the large image

Now you'll add the showlarge and hidelarge functions.

1 On the next available line of the Actions panel, enter:

```
function showlarge(e:MouseEvent):void{
  largeimage.visible=true;
}
```

```
actions:1
1    largeimage.visible=false;
2    thumbnail.addEventListener(MouseEvent.MOUSE_OVER, showlarge);
3    thumbnail.addEventListener(MouseEvent.MOUSE_OUT, hidelarge);
4    function showlarge(e:MouseEvent):void{
5        largeimage.visible=true;
6    }
7
```

The showlarge function does one thing: it makes the object called largeimage visible.

2 On the next available line, enter the code for the other function:

```
function hidelarge(e:MouseEvent):void{
  largeimage.visible=false;
}
```

```
actions:1
1    largeimage.visible=false;
2    thumbnail.addEventListener(MouseEvent.MOUSE_OVER, showlarge);
3    thumbnail.addEventListener(MouseEvent.MOUSE_OUT, hidelarge);
4    function showlarge(e:MouseEvent):void{
5        largeimage.visible=true;
6    }
7    function hidelarge(e:MouseEvent):void{
8        largeimage.visible=false;
9    }
10
```

The hidelarge function also does one thing: it makes the object called largeimage invisible.

3 Test the movie by choosing Control > Test Movie > In Flash Professional.

When you move your mouse cursor over the thumbnail image, the large camera image appears. Move your mouse cursor off of the thumbnail image, and the large image disappears, revealing the informational text behind it.

Mapping Mouse Movements to Visual Changes

So far, you've programmed Flash to show the large image when you move your cursor over the thumbnail, and to hide the large image when you move your cursor off of the thumbnail. But you can only see the top-left corner of the large image. In the final project, the large image moves relative to the mouse cursor's position over the thumbnail. You'll code that interactivity next.

The essential idea for the interactivity is to map one set of values—the position of the mouse cursor—to another set of values—the position of the large image. This is a useful approach that you see in many different interfaces. For example, a basic volume controller maps the position of a knob on a slider to the volume level of sound. A scroll bar maps the position of the scroll button to the position of text on a Web page. Google Maps correlates the position of the zoom slider to the scale factor of the map.

For this project, you first want to identify the position of the mouse cursor over the thumbnail. Use the properties, `mouseX` and `mouseY` to get the x and y position of the mouse cursor.

Once you have the mouse cursor position, you'll make calculations to translate one range of values (the position of the mouse cursor) to the other range of values (the position of the large image). To make those calculations easier, it's helpful to use variables to store information. Let's turn our attention to variables.

Using Variables to Store Information

Variables are objects that you create to help you store, modify, and test information. A variable is simply a container that has a name, and is where you put a specific kind of data.

Creating a variable

To create, or "declare," a variable, you use the keyword `var`. You'll use variables to store information about the positions of the cursor and the large image on the Stage.

1   Select the first keyframe of the actions layer and open the Actions panel.

2 Make room to add code on the first line of the Actions panel. Add the following two statements:

```
var xpos:Number
var ypos:Number
```

```
actions:1
1     var xpos:Number
2     var ypos:Number
3
4
5     largeimage.visible=false;
6     thumbnail.addEventListener(MouseEvent.MOUSE_OVER, showlarge);
7     thumbnail.addEventListener(MouseEvent.MOUSE_OUT, hidelarge);
8     function showlarge(e:MouseEvent):void{
9         largeimage.visible=true;
10    }
11    function hidelarge(e:MouseEvent):void{
12        largeimage.visible=false;
13    }
14
```

Note: In ActionScript, you must declare your variables before you start using them. For that reason, it's customary to declare all your variables at the beginning of your block of code.

The first statement creates a variable called **xpos**. The colon after the variable name is required. The term after the colon identifies the data type that the variable can hold. In this example, xpos holds Number data.

The second statement creates another variable called **ypos**, which also holds Number data.

Data types

When you declare a variable, ActionScript 3.0 requires that your variables be "strictly typed." That means ActionScript needs you to tell it what kind of data the variable stores. You can't mix data types. For example, if you create a variable for Number data, you can't assign characters (String data) to the variable.

There are many different kinds of data types. The basic data types are Number, String, and Boolean.

- Number data includes any kind of number such as a negative number, positive number, or decimals. There are also more specific data types for numbers, such as int (for integers) and uint (for unsigned integers).

- String data includes any sequence of characters, such as a password, or Web address. String data are enclosed in quotation marks.

- Boolean data is either true or false, and you do not use quotation marks around those terms.

Assigning a value to a variable

Use the equals sign (=) to assign a value to a variable. This just means you're putting information in a variable to store for later retrieval. You'll use the xpos and ypos variables to store information about the position of the mouse cursor over the thumbnail image.

Recall that the position of the mouse cursor is in the properties mouseX and mouseY. Since you want to capture the most recent position of the mouse cursor, you must grab that information whenever your reader moves the mouse. Use the event MOUSE_MOVE to detect whenever the mouse cursor moves.

1 Just after your other event listener statements, enter the following event listener:

```
thumbnail.addEventListener(MouseEvent.MOUSE_MOVE, showbigger);
```

```
actions:1
1    var xpos:Number
2    var ypos:Number
3
4
5    largeimage.visible=false;
6
7    thumbnail.addEventListener(MouseEvent.MOUSE_OVER, showlarge);
8    thumbnail.addEventListener(MouseEvent.MOUSE_OUT, hidelarge);
9    thumbnail.addEventListener(MouseEvent.MOUSE_MOVE, showbigger);
10
11   function showlarge(e:MouseEvent):void{
12       largeimage.visible=true;
13   }
```

The statement listens for any movement of the mouse cursor over the thumbnail image of the camera. Whenever the mouse moves, Flash triggers the function called showbigger.

You'll write the code for that function next.

2 On the next available line, enter this function:

```
function showbigger(e:MouseEvent):void{
 xpos=(mouseX-thumbnail.x)/thumbnail.width;
 ypos=(mouseY-thumbnail.y)/thumbnail.height;
}
```

```
actions:1
1    var xpos:Number
2    var ypos:Number
3
4
5    largeimage.visible=false;
6
7    thumbnail.addEventListener(MouseEvent.MOUSE_OVER, showlarge);
8    thumbnail.addEventListener(MouseEvent.MOUSE_OUT, hidelarge);
9    thumbnail.addEventListener(MouseEvent.MOUSE_MOVE, showbigger);
10
11   function showlarge(e:MouseEvent):void{
12       largeimage.visible=true;
13   }
14   function hidelarge(e:MouseEvent):void{
15       largeimage.visible=false;
16   }
17   function showbigger(e:MouseEvent):void{
18       xpos=(mouseX-thumbnail.x)/thumbnail.width;
19       ypos=(mouseY-thumbnail.y)/thumbnail.height;
20   }
21
```

The function puts the information from the properties mouseX and mouseY into the variables xpos and ypos, but it does so to make the positions relative to the thumbnail image. Let's look at it in detail.

x=0 x=thumbnail.x

x=thumbnail.x+thumbnail.width

When the mouse cursor moves over the thumbnail, its x-position can range anywhere from the far left edge to the far right edge. Those coordinates are identical to thumbnail.x for the left edge, and thumbnail.x + thumbnail.width for the right edge.

Subtracting thumbnail.x and dividing by thumbnail.width gives you a fraction of how far horizontally the mouse cursor is positioned along the thumbnail image (from 0 to 1).

Tracking variables in the Output panel

The trace() statement is useful for sending information to the Output panel when your Flash project is in Test Movie mode. The trace() statement displays expressions within its parentheses, so you can insert the statement in your code when you need an alert and information on the current values of your variables.

1 Within the function showbigger, add a trace() statement that sends a message to the Output panel when you test your movie.

```
trace(xpos, ypos);
```

```
17    function showbigger(e:MouseEvent):void{
18        xpos=(mouseX-thumbnail.x)/thumbnail.width;
19        ypos=(mouseY-thumbnail.y)/thumbnail.height;
20        trace(xpos, ypos);
21    }
22
```

2   Choose Control > Test Movie > In Flash Professional. Move your mouse cursor over the thumbnail image.

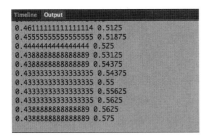

As you move your mouse over the thumbnail image, the Output panel displays the xpos and ypos values. Notice that the xpos value (the first one that appears) is 0 at the left edge and 1 at the right edge. The ypos value (the second one that appears) is 0 at the top edge and 1 at the bottom edge.

Creating more variables for the large image position

Your xpos and ypos variables store the information about the position of the mouse cursor over the thumbnail. You'll use that information to position the large image proportionally under the mask. For example, if the mouse cursor is halfway horizontally across the thumbnail image, then you'll position the large image halfway horizontally under the mask.

Your next task is to create variables to help create the range of x and y values where the large image can be positioned. The position of the mask is the reference point for the position of the large image, so you'll convert the mask to a movie clip for easy access to its x and y positions, and width and height.

1   Unlock the mask layer, if it is locked.

2   Select the rectangular shape of the mask in the mask layer.

3   Choose Modify > Convert to Symbol (F8).

    The Convert to Symbol dialog box appears.

4 Name the symbol **mask**, and choose Movie Clip for Type. Make sure that the registration point for the symbol is located at the top-left corner. Click OK.

Flash converts the mask to a movie clip symbol.

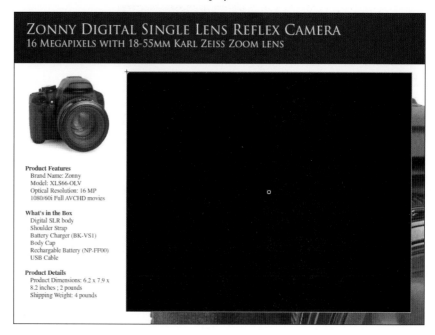

5 In the Properties inspector, enter **mymask** as the instance name.

6   Select the first keyframe of the actions layer and open the Actions panel.

7   At the beginning of your code, after the first two lines where you declare your xpos and ypos variables, enter the following:

```
var xmax:Number
var xmin:Number
var ymax:Number
var ymin:Number
var xrange:Number
var yrange:Number
```

```
actions:1
1      var xpos:Number
2      var ypos:Number
3      var xmax:Number
4      var xmin:Number
5      var ymax:Number
6      var ymin:Number
7      var xrange:Number
8      var yrange:Number
9
10     largeimage.visible=false;
11
12     thumbnail.addEventListener(MouseEvent.MOUSE_OVER, showlarge);
13     thumbnail.addEventListener(MouseEvent.MOUSE_OUT, hidelarge);
14     thumbnail.addEventListener(MouseEvent.MOUSE_MOVE, showbigger);
15
```

The code creates six additional variables for Number data.

8   On the next available line, add the following code:

```
xmax = mymask.x;
xmin = mymask.x+mymask.width-largeimage.width;
xrange = xmax-xmin;
```

```
1      var xpos:Number
2      var ypos:Number
3      var xmax:Number
4      var xmin:Number
5      var ymax:Number
6      var ymin:Number
7      var xrange:Number
8      var yrange:Number
9
10     xmax = mymask.x;
11     xmin = mymask.x+mymask.width-largeimage.width;
12     xrange = xmax-xmin;
13
```

The code creates the limits for the position of your large image under the mask. The first line establishes the maximum x value for the large image—the left edge of the large image shouldn't go farther right on the Stage than the left edge of the mask. Similarly, the second line establishes the minimum x-value for the large image. The xrange variable simply stores the range of possible values.

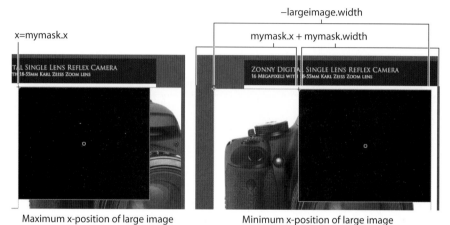

Maximum x-position of large image

Minimum x-position of large image

9 Now add the following code:

```
ymax=mymask.y;
ymin=mymask.y+mymask.height-largeimage.height;
yrange=ymax-ymin;
```

```
1   var xpos:Number
2   var ypos:Number
3   var xmax:Number
4   var xmin:Number
5   var ymax:Number
6   var ymin:Number
7   var xrange:Number
8   var yrange:Number
9
10  xmax = mymask.x;
11  xmin = mymask.x+mymask.width-largeimage.width;
12  xrange = xmax-xmin;
13
14  ymax=mymask.y;
15  ymin=mymask.y+mymask.height-largeimage.height;
16  yrange=ymax-ymin;
17
```

The code creates the y-value limits for the position of your large image under the mask using the same logic as the x-values.

Change the Position of the Large Image

For the last part of this interactivity, you assign new x- and y-values to the large image to change its position.

1 In the Actions panel, add the following code to the function showbigger:

```
largeimage.x=mymask.x-(xpos*xrange);
largeimage.y=mymask.y-(ypos*yrange);
```

```
function showbigger(e:MouseEvent):void{
    xpos=(mouseX-thumbnail.x)/thumbnail.width;
    ypos=(mouseY-thumbnail.y)/thumbnail.height;
    trace(xpos, ypos);

    largeimage.x=mymask.x-(xpos*xrange);
    largeimage.y=mymask.y-(ypos*yrange);
}
```

The horizontal position of the large image starts at the left edge of the mask, but you subtract a proportional amount of its range for its final position.

Similarly, the vertical position of the large image depends on the ypos, which measures the proportional vertical position of the mouse cursor of the small thumbnail image.

2 Choose Control > Test Movie > In Flash Professional. Move your mouse cursor over the thumbnail image.

As you move your mouse over the thumbnail image, the large image under the mask moves proportionally. When your mouse cursor is on the far-left edge of the thumbnail, Flash shows you the far-left edge of the large image. When your mouse cursor is on the far-right edge of the thumbnail, Flash shows you the far-right edge of the large image.

Congratulations! You used variables, more complex mouse events, and movie clip properties to create a sophisticated, dynamic interaction between the user and the graphics on the Stage. The calculations are no more complicated than simple arithmetic. If you know addition, subtraction, multiplication, and division, then you can do similar interfaces.

An Object's Registration Point and the Coordinate Space

With all the calculations you do to position your objects, you need to be especially conscious of the coordinate space and the registration points of your objects that you're using as reference.

When you create your movie clip symbols, you choose the position of the registration point. Most commonly, the registration point is set at the top-left corner or the center of your object.

All measurements, such as the x-value and y-value, are made from that registration point. All transformations, such as rotations or scaling, are made from the registration point as well.

The registration point for the Stage is at the top-left corner. The x-values increase to the right and the y-values increase to the bottom.

Creating a Custom Cursor

When you move your mouse cursor over the thumbnail image, the cursor remains a pointer. But visual cues, such as the cursor turning into a magnifying glass icon, can be an effective aid in usability. When you use Flash's different tools from the Tool panel, the cursor often changes to help you remember the function of the currently selected tool.

Making the custom icon follow the mouse

The custom icon of a magnifying glass has already been created, and is in the Library panel as a movie clip symbol. You'll assign the value of mouseX to the x-property of your custom icon, and the value of mouseY to the y-property of your custom icon to position the icon in the same location as the mouse cursor.

1   Create a new layer and rename it **custom icon**.

2   Drag the movie clip symbol called **cursor** from the Library on to the Stage.

3   In the Properties inspector, name the movie clip instance **cursor**.

4   Select the first keyframe of the actions layer, and open the Actions panel.

5   Inside of the showbigger function, add the following two statements:

```
cursor.x=mouseX;
cursor.y=mouseY;
```

```
function showbigger(e:MouseEvent):void{
    xpos=(mouseX-thumbnail.x)/thumbnail.width;
    ypos=(mouseY-thumbnail.y)/thumbnail.height;
    trace(xpos, ypos);

    largeimage.x=mymask.x-(xpos*xrange);
    largeimage.y=mymask.y-(ypos*yrange);

    cursor.x=mouseX;
    cursor.y=mouseY;
}
```

When the mouse is moving over the thumbnail image, Flash assigns the x- and y-positions of the mouse cursor to the x- and y-positions of the magnifying glass graphic.

Now you need to hide and show the magnifying glass so it only shows up when the mouse is over the thumbnail image.

6   At the top of your code block, add the following statement:

```
cursor.visible=false;
```

```
9
10      xmax = mymask.x;
11      xmin = mymask.x+mymask.width-largeimage.width;
12      xrange = xmax-xmin;
13
14      ymax=mymask.y;
15      ymin=mymask.y+mymask.height-largeimage.height;
16      yrange=ymax-ymin;
17
18      largeimage.visible=false;
19      cursor.visible=false;
20
```

This statement makes the magnifying glass graphic invisible when the project begins.

7   Inside of the function called showlarge, add the following statement:

```
cursor.visible=true;
```

```
17      function showlarge(e:MouseEvent):void{
18          largeimage.visible=true;
19          cursor.visible=true;
20      }
```

This statement makes the magnifying glass graphic visible when the mouse cursor moves over the thumbnail image.

8   Inside of the function called hidelarge, add the following statement:

```
cursor.visible=false;
```

```
21      function hidelarge(e:MouseEvent):void{
22          largeimage.visible=false;
23          cursor.visible=false;
24      }
```

This statement makes the magnifying glass graphic invisible when the mouse cursor moves off of the thumbnail image.

9   Choose Control > Test Movie > In Flash Professional. Move your mouse cursor over the thumbnail image.

The icon of the magnifying glass follows the mouse cursor. When you move your mouse cursor off of the thumbnail image, the magnifying glass icon disappears.

Hiding and showing the mouse cursor

Flash still displays the default pointer, so you need to hide it when it's over the thumbnail and show it again when it's not over the thumbnail. You control the visibility of the default mouse cursor with `Mouse.hide()` and `Mouse.show()`.

1   Within the function called showlarge, add the following statement:

```
Mouse.hide();
```

This statement hides the default mouse cursor.

2   Within the function called hidelarge, add the following statement:

```
Mouse.show();
```

This statement shows the default mouse cursor.

```
17  function showlarge(e:MouseEvent):void{
18      largeimage.visible=true;
19      cursor.visible=true;
20      Mouse.hide();
21  }
22  function hidelarge(e:MouseEvent):void{
23      largeimage.visible=false;
24      cursor.visible=false;
25      Mouse.show();
26  }
```

3   Choose Control > Test Movie > In Flash Professional. Move your mouse cursor over and off the thumbnail image.

The default mouse pointer disappears over the thumbnail image, and the custom magnifying glass icon replaces it. When you move off of the thumbnail image, the mouse pointer returns and the magnifying glass icon disappears.

Note: At the time of this writing, the Flash Player on the Mac OS contains a bug that does not immediately or reliably show the mouse pointer with Mouse.show(). On Windows, there is no problem. Look for future updates to the Flash Player which will address this issue.

Disabling input for the icon

A minor issue remains with the interactivity that you can smooth out. You may notice that, as you move your mouse cursor quickly over the thumbnail image, the large camera image flickers. The graphics of the magnifying glass icon lag behind the motion of your mouse cursor if you move too quickly, and the graphics intersect the mouse cursor (which is hidden). Flash triggers the mouseout event because it detects that the mouse has left the thumbnail image when it crosses over the magnifying glass icon.

To prevent the magnifying glass icon from interfering with mouse events, you can set the property called `mouseEnabled` to false, which disables it from receiving interactive input.

1   At the top of your code block in the Actions panel, add the following statement:

```
cursor.mouseEnabled=false;
```

This statement disables the cursor from receiving any mouse events. The full code should appear as shown in the next figure.

```
actions:1
 1    var xpos:Number
 2    var ypos:Number
 3    var xmax:Number
 4    var xmin:Number
 5    var ymax:Number
 6    var ymin:Number
 7    var xrange:Number
 8    var yrange:Number
 9
10    xmax = mymask.x;
11    xmin = mymask.x+mymask.width-largeimage.width;
12    xrange = xmax-xmin;
13
14    ymax=mymask.y;
15    ymin=mymask.y+mymask.height-largeimage.height;
16    yrange=ymax-ymin;
17
18    largeimage.visible=false;
19    cursor.visible=false;
20    cursor.mouseEnabled=false;
21
22    thumbnail.addEventListener(MouseEvent.MOUSE_OVER, showlarge);
23    thumbnail.addEventListener(MouseEvent.MOUSE_OUT, hidelarge);
24    thumbnail.addEventListener(MouseEvent.MOUSE_MOVE, showbigger);
25
26    function showlarge(e:MouseEvent):void{
27        largeimage.visible=true;
28        cursor.visible=true;
29        Mouse.hide();
30    }
31    function hidelarge(e:MouseEvent):void{
32        largeimage.visible=false;
33        cursor.visible=false;
34        Mouse.show();
35    }
36    function showbigger(e:MouseEvent):void{
37        xpos=(mouseX-thumbnail.x)/thumbnail.width;
38        ypos=(mouseY-thumbnail.y)/thumbnail.height;
39        trace(xpos, ypos);
40
41        largeimage.x=mymask.x-(xpos*xrange);
42        largeimage.y=mymask.y-(ypos*yrange);
43
44        cursor.x=mouseX;
45        cursor.y=mouseY;
46    }
47
```

2   Choose Control > Test Movie > In Flash Professional. Move your mouse cursor over and off the thumbnail image.

The smooth interaction of the mouse motion over the thumbnail and the large image lets your readers examine the detailed image of the camera.

Review Questions

1 What are three different kinds of data types? Give an example of each.

2 How do the movie clip properties `height` and `width` differ from the properties `scaleX` and `scaleY`?

3 Explain the differences between the mouse events `MOUSE_OVER`, `MOUSE_OUT`, and `MOUSE_MOVE`.

4 A movie clip symbol's registration point is at its centerpoint. Imagine that you wanted to dynamically position an instance of the movie clip so that its left edge aligned with the left edge of the Stage. If the instance name of the movie clip is **mymc**, then what ActionScript statement would accomplish this task?

Review Answers

1 Three different data types are Number data, String data, and Boolean data. Number data are numbers, such as –4, 10, 12, or 4.5. String data are characters that are enclosed in double quotes, such as "hello", "john.doe@mydomain.com", or "http://www.adobe.com". Boolean data is either true or false.

2 The movie clip properties `height` and `width` measure the vertical dimension and horizontal dimension of the movie clip instance, in pixels. The `scaleX` and `scaleY` properties measure the vertical proportion or horizontal proportion of the original movie clip. A `scaleX` or `scaleY` of 1 is 100% of the original movie clip's width or height.

3 The `MOUSE_OVER` event happens when the mouse moves over the target.
The `MOUSE_OUT` event happens when the mouse moves away from the target.
The `MOUSE_MOVE` event happens whenever the mouse moves within the target.

4 The correct ActionScript statement is as follows:

```
mymc.x=.5*mymc.width;
```

Since the registration point of the movie clip is at its centerpoint, you need to move the instance half of its width to the right of the left edge of the Stage in order to align their left edges.

10 PUBLISHING TO HTML5

Lesson Overview

In this lesson, you'll learn how to do the following:

- Understand what Toolkit for CreateJS can do

- Create and edit classic tweens

- Follow best practices for creating layers and naming objects

- Recognize unsupported features

- Preview HTML5 animation in a browser

- Insert JavaScript in the Flash Timeline

- Modify publish settings

- Understand the output files

 This lesson will take approximately 60 minutes to complete. If needed, remove the previous lesson folder from your hard drive and copy the Lesson10 folder onto it. Download the project files for this lesson from the Lesson & Update Files tab on your Account page at www.peachpit.com and store them on your computer in a convenient location, as described in the Getting Started section of this book. Your Accounts page is also where you'll find any updates to the chapters or to the lesson files. Look on the Lesson & Update Files tab to access the most current content.

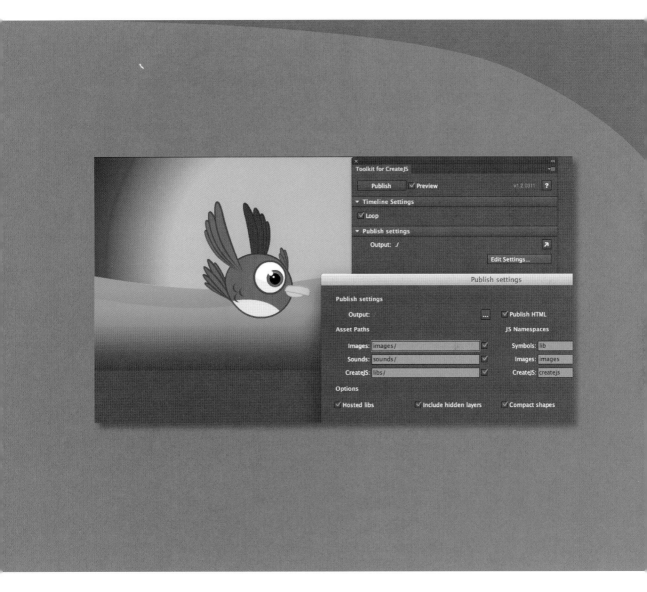

Use the Toolkit for CreateJS to publish your Flash art
and animation assets to HTML5 and JavaScript. The
Toolkit for CreateJS enables a seamless and integrated
workflow for both designers and developers.

Getting Started

● **Note:** If you have not already downloaded the project files for this lesson to your computer from your Account page, make sure to do so now. See "Getting Started" at the beginning of the book.

To begin, view the partially finished project to see how animated assets in Flash Professional translate to HTML5 and JavaScript, viewable in a modern browser on your desktop, or on a mobile phone or tablet.

1   Double-click the 10End.html file in the Lesson10/10End folder to play the animation.

The project is a simple animation of a cartoon bird flying over an endless scrolling landscape.

2   Right-click/Ctrl-click on any part of the animation.

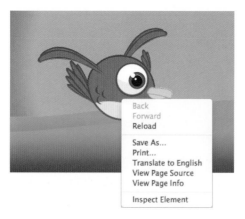

The contextual menu that appears tells you that the animation is HTML content, and not Flash. The graphics and animation, while created in Flash Professional, have been published as HTML and JavaScript for playback without the Flash Player. The animation plays in modern browsers on the desktop and on tablet and mobile devices such as the iPhone or Android phone.

3 Click on the animation.

The bird opens its beak and a speech balloon with a message pops up.

4 Exit your browser.

5 Double-click the 10Start.fla file in the Lesson10/10Start folder to open the initial project file in Flash.

The Flash file already contains the assets for the bird animation. The animation is partially complete, and an instance of the movie clip of the bird animation is on the Stage. In this lesson, you'll add the animation of the bird's tail and the scrolling background with classic tweens, add simple interactivity with JavaScript, and publish the animation as HTML content.

6 Choose File > Save As. Name the file **10_workingcopy.fla** and save it in the 10Start folder. Saving a working copy ensures that the original start file will be available if you want to start over.

What Is Toolkit for CreateJS?

Toolkit for CreateJS, originally an optional extension for Flash Professional, is a way for you to publish HTML5 content from Flash. It allows you to leverage Flash's powerful animation and drawing tools while targeting multiple runtimes—both the Flash Player and HTML5. The Toolkit outputs your animation using a suite of open source JavaScript libraries: EaselJS, TweenJS, and SoundJS.

- EaselJS is a library that provides a display list that allows you to work with objects on the canvas in the browser.

- TweenJS is a library that provides the animation features.

- SoundJS is a library that provides functionality to play audio in the browser.

Toolkit for CreateJS generates all the necessary JavaScript code to represent your images, graphics, symbols, animations, and sounds on the Stage. It also outputs dependent assets, such as images and sounds. You can even include simple JavaScript Timeline commands in the Actions panel, which gets exported in the JavaScript files.

However, the Toolkit for CreateJS is *not* meant to be a soup-to-nuts exporter to convert all Flash content to HTML5 in a single push of a button. It is not an ActionScript-to-JavaScript translator. It is designed to be part of a larger workflow that offers a simple way to output Flash assets for JavaScript. It creates accessible JavaScript files for a developer to continue to add more complex interactivity.

Supported features

● **Note:** Make sure you visit the Adobe CreateJS Dev Center (http://www.adobe. com/devnet/createjs. html) for the latest news and updates to Toolkit for CreateJS.

The Toolkit for CreateJS does not support all Flash Professional features. However, CreateJS is an ongoing effort, and the exporter continues to improve by including more of Flash's capabilities.

Fortunately, the Output panel displays warnings about any features in your Flash file that can't be successfully exported.

Using Classic Tweens

While both motion tweens and shape tweens are supported by the Toolkit for CreateJS, Flash converts those animations to frame-by-frame animations. Classic tweens, an older way of creating animation in Flash Professional, are retained as a runtime tween, which saves file size and allows you to control the animation dynamically via JavaScript. In this section, you'll complete the bird animation with classic tweens.

Classic tweening is an older approach to animation, but it is very similar to motion tweening. Like motion tweens, classic tweens use symbol instances. Changes to the symbol instances between two keyframes are interpolated to create the animation. You can change an instance's position, its rotation, scale, transformation, Color Effect, of Filter effect.

The key differences between classic tweens and motion tweens are as follows:

- Classic tweens require a separate Motion Guide layer to animate along a path.
- Classic tweens don't support 3D rotations or translations.
- Classic tweens are not separated on their own tween layer, but classic and motion tweens share the same restriction that no other object can exist in the same layer as the tween.
- Classic tweens are Timeline-based, and not object-based, meaning you add, remove, or swap the tween or the instance on the Timeline rather than on the Stage.

Adding the tail feathers

The animation of the bird is only partially complete. You'll add the bobbing tail feathers as a classic tween to complete it.

1　Double-click the movie clip instance of the bird on the Stage.

　　Flash takes you to symbol-editing mode for the movie clip symbol called bird_flight.

　　The Timeline contains several different, named layers of the parts of the bird. Each layer contains classic tweens.

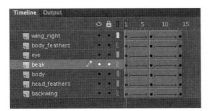

　　The first keyframes show the bird with its wings up, the middle keyframes show the bird with its wings down, and the last keyframes show the bird with its wings up again, to complete the cycle.

2　Choose Control > Loop Playback to enable looping, if it is not already checked.

3　Choose Control > Play, or press the Play button at the bottom of the Timeline.

　　The animation inside the movie clip symbol plays. The bird flaps its wings and bobs up and down.

4　Stop playback.

5　Insert a new layer and name it **tail_feathers**. Drag the new layer to the bottom of the layers.

6 Drag the Graphic symbol called tail_feathers from the Library to the Stage. In the Properties inspector, position the instance at x=23, y=350.

Flash displays an instance of the tail wings behind the bird.

Inserting keyframes

You'll add two additional keyframes for the tail feathers—one for the bird when its wings are up, and another when its wings are down.

1 Select frame 7 of the tail_feathers layer, and insert a new keyframe (F6).

2 Select frame 14 of the tail_feathers layer, and insert a new keyframe (F6).

Flash creates new keyframes at frames 7 and 14, with copies of the symbol instance in each.

Changing the feather instance

Now you'll change the rotation and position of the feather instance in the middle keyframe.

1 Move the playhead to the middle keyframe (frame 7) of the tail_feathers layer.

2 Choose the Free Transform tool and select the tail feathers instance.

Control points appear around the tail feathers.

3 Rotate the tail feathers slightly counterclockwise so the base of the feathers meets the bird's body. You can also use the Transform panel (Window > Transform) to rotate the tail feathers about –15 degrees.

The middle keyframe (frame 7) contains an instance of the tail feathers at a slightly different angle from the first and last keyframes.

Applying a classic tween

Classic tweens are applied to the Timeline between two keyframes.

1 Right-click/Ctrl-click on any frame between the first and second keyframe and choose Create Classic Tween.

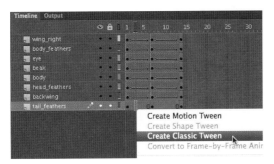

Flash creates a tween between the first and second keyframe, indicated by an arrowhead over a blue background.

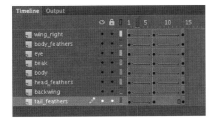

2 Right-click/Ctrl-click on any frame between the second and last keyframe and choose Create Classic Tween.

Flash creates a tween between the second and last keyframe, indicated by an arrowhead over a blue background.

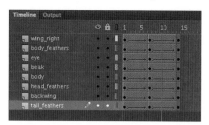

3 Press Enter/Return on your keyboard, or press the Play button under the Timeline to preview the animation.

Flash creates a smooth animation of the tail feathers rotating up and down that matches the animation of the other parts of the bird.

Animating the mountains

Now that you've successfully added a classic tween of the tail feathers to the bird, you'll add the animation of the mountains on the main Timeline.

1 Exit symbol-editing mode by clicking the Scene 1 button at the top of the Edit bar.

2 On the main Timeline, insert a new layer and name it **landscape**. Drag the new layer below the bird layer, but above the sky layer.

3 Drag the Graphic symbol called mountains from the Library to the Stage. In the Properties inspector, position the instance at x=0, y=246 so the bottom edge aligns with the bottom edge of the Stage.

4 Add frames (F5) to all layers up to frame 30.

5 Select frame 30 in the landscape layer, and insert a new keyframe (F6).

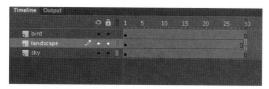

Flash inserts a new keyframe at frame 30 containing a copy of the mountains instance.

6 At frame 30, move the mountain graphic to the left so that x=−800.

The right edge of the mountains instance should be aligned with the right edge of the Stage. The left and right edges of the graphic match up, so when the animation plays as a loop, the effect is a seamless scrolling mountain range.

7 Right-click/Ctrl-click on any frame between the first and second keyframe, and choose Create Classic Tween.

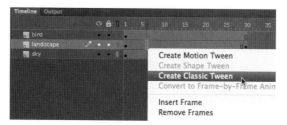

Flash creates a tween between the first and second keyframe, indicated by an arrowhead over a blue background.

8 Press Enter/Return on your keyboard, or press the Play button under the Timeline to preview the animation.

Flash creates a smooth animation of the mountains moving under the flying bird.

9 To add a little more complexity to the animation, add a second layer of mountains. Insert a new layer, called **landscape_back**, and drag it under the landscape layer.

10 Drag another instance of the mountains symbol to the Stage, and in the Properties inspector, make the width (W) 2000 pixels, the height (H) 200 pixels, and position it at x=0, y=200.

11 Insert a new keyframe (F6) at frame 30 of the landscape_back layer.

12 In the end keyframe, move the mountains instance to x=−1000.

13 Right-click/Ctrl-click on any frame between the first and second keyframe, and choose Create Classic Tween.

Flash creates a tween between the first and second keyframe, indicated by an arrowhead over a blue background.

14 Press Enter/Return on your keyboard, or press the Play button under the Timeline to preview the animation.

The second mountain graphic animates from right to left, but it moves a little slower than the one in the foreground, creating a parallax effect.

Best practices and restrictions for exporting classic tweens

A layer with a classic tween can contain only a single symbol instance for its full duration. For example, in the tail_feathers layer, you have three keyframes, each containing an instance of the tail feathers graphic. If you wanted to create a new classic tween with a different symbol instance farther down the Timeline, you'd need to do so in a new layer.

Toolkit for CreateJS exports the layer names and references them in the published JavaScript code. For that reason, provide unique names for all your layers, which will make the exported files easier to read and work with.

The structure of the animation in the bird_flight movie clip and the main Timeline shows the ideal approach to animation using Toolkit for CreateJS. Each body part in a character animation and each part of the scene that moves is a separate instance using Classic tweens.

Exporting to HTML5

The process to export your animation to HTML5 and JavaScript is straightforward and easy. The Toolkit for CreateJS panel, accessible from the Windows menu, contains all the publish settings.

1 Choose Window > Toolkit for CreateJS (Shift+F9).

The Toolkit for CreateJS window appears.

The window provides settings for HTML5 publishing.

2 Make sure the Preview option and the Loop option are checked.

The Preview option, when checked, automatically opens your default browser to show the published animation.

The Loop option makes the animation loop.

3 Click Publish, or choose Command > Publish for CreateJS.

Flash exports the animation as HTML and JavaScript files and plays the animation in your browser.

Understanding the Output files

The default settings create two files, a JavaScript file that contains code that drives the animation, and an HTML file that displays the animation in a browser.

10_workingcopy.ht
ml   10_workingcopy.js

Flash publishes the two files in the same folder as your Flash file.

1   Open the HTML file, called 10_workingcopy.html in a text editor, such as Dreamweaver.

```
1    <!DOCTYPE html>
2    <html>
3    <head>
4    <meta charset="UTF-8">
5    <title>CreateJS export from 10_workingcopy</title>
6
7    <script src="http://code.createjs.com/easeljs-0.6.0.min.js"></script>
8    <script src="http://code.createjs.com/tweenjs-0.4.0.min.js"></script>
9    <script src="http://code.createjs.com/movieclip-0.6.0.min.js"></script>
10   <script src="10_workingcopy.js"></script>
11
12   <script>
13   var canvas, stage, exportRoot;
14
15   function init() {
16       canvas = document.getElementById("canvas");
17       exportRoot = new lib._10_workingcopy();
18
19       stage = new createjs.Stage(canvas);
20       stage.addChild(exportRoot);
21       stage.update();
22
23       createjs.Ticker.setFPS(30);
24       createjs.Ticker.addEventListener("tick", stage);
25   }
26   </script>
27   </head>
28
29   <body onLoad="init();" style="background-color:#D4D4D4">
30       <canvas id="canvas" width="800" height="400" style="background-color:#FFFFFF"></canvas>
31   </body>
32   </html>
```

The HTML file loads the required JavaScript libraries from http://code.createjs.com, which hosts the code. The file also loads the JavaScript code for your animation at 10_workingcopy.js. The HTML file initializes and displays the animation in an HTML5 <canvas> tag.

2   Open the JavaScript file, called 10_workingcopy.js in a text editor, such as Dreamweaver.

The code contains all the information to create the graphics and put them in motion, using the CreateJS JavaScript libraries. Scanning the code, you'll find coordinates and all the specific values required for your content.

Publish Settings

The settings in the Toolkit for CreateJS window lets you change where your files are saved, and how they are saved.

1   Click the Edit Settings button in the Publish Settings section of the Toolkit for CreateJS window.

The Publish Settings dialog box appears.

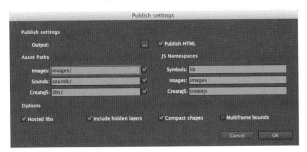

2   Click the Output button to save your published files to a different folder.

3   Change the Asset Paths if you want to save your assets to a different folder. The Asset Paths for Images must be checked if your file contains images, and Sounds must be checked if your file contains sounds. For example, if you replaced the gradient fill for a bitmap image in the sky layer of your 10_workingcopy.fla file, upon export, Flash creates a folder called images that contains the bitmap image.

The CreateJS asset path must be checked if your Hosted libs option (see below) is not checked.

4 The Hosted libs option tells your published file where to find the CreateJS JavaScript libraries. When the Hosted lib option is checked, your published file points to a CDN (Content Distribution Network) at http://code.createjs.com to download the libraries. When the Hosted lib option is not checked, Flash includes the CreateJS JavaScript libraries.

5 For all other options, leave at their default settings which will suit most of your needs.

Inserting JavaScript

● **Note:** For more about the easelJS MovieClip-class JavaScript commands, see the online documentation at http://www.createjs.com/Docs/EaselJS/classes/MovieClip.html.

The optimal workflow is to use the Toolkit for CreateJS to output animated assets from Flash, and then to have a developer integrate additional interactivity with JavaScript.

However, it is possible to add some JavaScript directly to the Flash Timeline, which gets exported to the published JavaScript files.

In the Actions panel, use /* js to begin a block of JavaScript code, and */ to end the block of JavaScript code. Use JavaScript in the Timeline sparingly; to control the Timeline with the easelJS MovieClip class commands play(), gotoAndStop(), stop(), and gotoAndPlay(), for example.

Stopping the playhead

Currently, the bird opens and shuts its beak continuously as it flies. You'll add JavaScript to the Timeline to keep the beak shut until the user clicks on it. You'll give instance names to the animations on the Stage, and add a stop command.

1 Select the movie clip instance of the bird on the Stage.

2 In the Properties inspector, enter **redrobin** for the instance name.

Providing a unique instance name to the movie clip instance allows you to control it with ActionScript as well as with JavaScript.

3 Double-click the redrobin instance.

Flash takes you to symbol-editing mode for the movie clip symbol.

4 Select the bird's beak, and in the Properties inspector, enter **beak** for the instance name.

5 Return to the main Timeline, and insert a new layer and name it **actions**.

6 Select the first keyframe of the actions layer and open the Actions panel.

7 In the Actions panel, enter /* js on the first line.

The backslash and asterisk normally mark the beginning of a multiline comment. The js is a flag for the Toolkit for CreateJS to treat the multiline comment as JavaScript.

8 On the next line, enter the following statement:

```
this.redrobin.beak.stop();
```

The statement targets the movie clip instance called beak, nested inside the movie clip instance called redrobin, and stops the playhead.

Because of something known as "scope," you can't just write redrobin.beak.stop() in JavaScript as you can in ActionScript. In JavaScript, you have to precede the statement with the keyword this, which refers to the current Timeline.

On the next line, enter */ to close the JavaScript code.

9 In the Toolkit for CreateJS window, click Publish, or choose Command > Publish for CreateJS.

Flash exports the animation as HTML5 and JavaScript and incorporates the JavaScript code in the Timeline. The bird flaps and the mountain landscape scrolls, but the bird's beak remains shut because of the `stop()` command that targets the beak Timeline.

Adding a response to a click

Now you'll add an event listener for a mouse click, and move the playhead on the beak's Timeline to display a message.

1 Select the first keyframe of the actions layer and open the Actions panel, if it's not already open.

2 In the Actions panel, add the following statement inside the JavaScript comment:

```js
this.onClick = function() {
  this.redrobin.beak.gotoAndStop("open");
}
```

```
actions:1
1   /* js
2   this.redrobin.beak.stop();
3   this.onClick = function() {
4       this.redrobin.beak.gotoAndStop("open");
5   }
6   */
```

The `onClick` event happens when a user clicks on an element. In this statement, a mouse click results in the playhead of the beak Timeline to move to the frame labeled open.

3 Double-click the beak movie clip symbol in the Library.

You enter symbol-editing mode for the beak movie clip.

4 Insert a new layer and rename it **labels**.

5 Insert a keyframe (F6) at frame 10, and in the Properties inspector, enter **open** as the frame label.

The frame label appears as a tiny flag icon in frame 10 of the labels layer.

6 Insert another new layer and rename it **message**.

7 Insert a keyframe (F6) at frame 10, and drag the symbol called message from the Library to the Stage. Position the graphic in front of the open beak.

When Flash shows the frame labeled open, the beak opens, and the message "Eat at Joes!" appears.

8 In the Toolkit for CreateJS window, click Publish, or choose Command > Publish for CreateJS.

● **Note:** Important! The createJS JavaScript libraries reference Timelines starting with frame numbers at 0 while Flash starts frame numbers at 1. Therefore, frame numbers in your exported JavaScript code are one less than what you would expect to see in Flash. Because of this difference, Adobe recommends that you always use frame labels instead of frame numbers for Timeline navigation.

Flash exports the animation as HTML5 and JavaScript and incorporates the JavaScript code in the Timeline. When you click the animation, the bird's beak opens and the message in the balloon appears.

ActionScript and JavaScript

Because the JavaScript on your Timeline is contained within a multiline comment, your Actions panel can contain both ActionScript and JavaScript. Flash ignores the JavaScript when it compiles the file to a SWF, and it ignores the ActionScript when it exports the file with Toolkit for CreateJS.

```
1    /* js
2    this.redrobin.beak.stop();
3    this.onClick = function() {
4        this.redrobin.beak.gotoAndStop("open");
5    }
6    */
7
8    import flash.events.MouseEvent;
9
10   redrobin.beak.stop();
11   stage.addEventListener(MouseEvent.CLICK, openmouth);
12   function openmouth(e:MouseEvent):void{
13       redrobin.beak.gotoAndStop("open");
14   }
```

Feature compatibility warnings

Pay attention to the messages and recommendations that appear in the Output panel when you publish your animation with Toolkit for CreateJS.

```
Timeline  Output
WARNINGS:
Text support is limited. It is generally recommended to include text as HTML elements (see DOMElement).
Feature not supported: Custom eases. (14)
Feature not supported: Color effects. (4)
Frame numbers in EaselJS start at 0 instead of 1. For example, this affects gotoAndStop and gotoAndPlay calls. (4)
Input and static text fields are published as dynamic text fields.
```

Flash warns you of any incompatible Flash features that will not export or work as expected in the JavaScript runtime.

Review Questions

1 What is the Toolkit for CreateJS?

2 Why is it recommended that animations exported with Toolkit for CreateJS use Classic tweens?

3 What is a Classic tween?

4 How do you incorporate interactivity with JavaScript from your Flash file?

Review Answers

1 The Toolkit for CreateJS is a way for you to publish HTML5 content from Flash. It allows you to leverage Flash's powerful animation and drawing tools and publish to HTML5 and JavaScript for modern browsers. The Toolkit outputs your animation using a suite of open source JavaScript libraries: EaselJS, TweenJS, and SoundJS. Toolkit for CreateJS generates all the necessary JavaScript code to represent your images, graphics, symbols, animations, and sounds on the Stage. It also outputs dependent assets, such as images and sounds. However, the Toolkit for CreateJS is *not* meant to be an exporter to convert all Flash content to HTML5 in a single push of a button. It is designed to be part of a larger workflow that creates accessible JavaScript files for a developer to continue to add more complex interactivity.

2 Although the Toolkit for CreateJS supports motion tweens and shape tweens, they are exported as frame-by-frame animations, and can increase the file size of your exported JavaScript code. Use classic tweens, which are retained as runtime tweens, which saves file size and allows you to control the animation dynamically via JavaScript.

3 Classic tweening is an older approach to animation, but it is very similar to motion tweening. Like motion tweens, classic tweens use symbol instances. Flash smoothly interpolates changes to the symbol instances between two keyframes. You can change an instance's position, its rotation, scale, transformation, color effect, or filter effect.

4 Insert JavaScript on a Flash Timeline by adding the code between /* js and */ in the Actions panel, which represents a multiline comment in ActionScript. Flash ignores the JavaScript code when you compile a SWF for the Flash Player, but it incorporates the JavaScript when you publish with the Toolkit for CreateJS. Limit the JavaScript on the Flash Timeline to simple frame navigation, as most interactivity should be added to the JavaScript after the export process.

11

PUBLISHING FLASH DOCUMENTS

Lesson Overview

In this lesson, you'll learn how to do the following:

- Understand the various Flash runtime environments

- Change publish settings for a document

- Publish a project for the Web

- Understand the output files for Web publishing

- Detect the Flash Player version

- Publish an AIR application for the desktop

- Test mobile interactions in the AIR Debug Launcher

- Recognize USB device and iOS Simulator as additional testing methods

- Configure settings to publish for a mobile device

- Understand how Adobe Scout can analyze Flash content

 This lesson will take 2 hours to complete. If needed, remove the previous lesson folder from your hard drive and copy the Lesson11 folder onto it. Download the project files for this lesson from the Lesson & Update Files tab on your Account page at www.peachpit.com and store them on your computer in a convenient location, as described in the Getting Started section of this book. Your Accounts page is also where you'll find any updates to the chapters or to the lesson files. Look on the Lesson & Update Files tab to access the most current content.

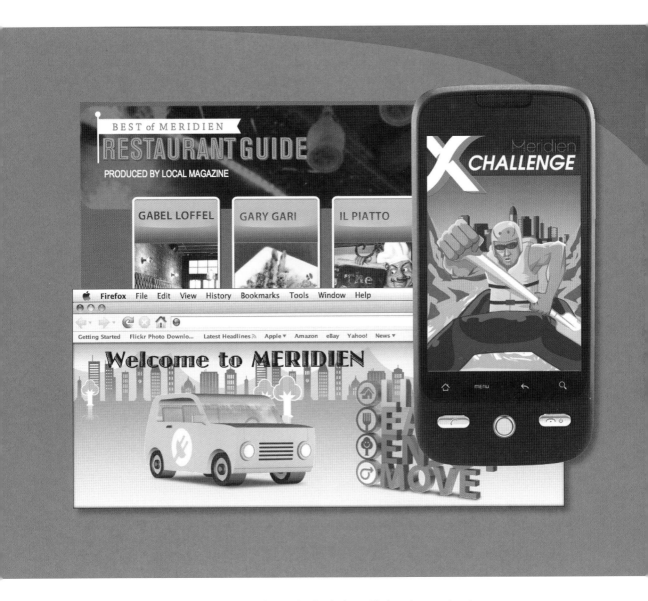

When you've finished your Flash project, test it and publish it in a variety of formats for playback on different devices and environments. Author once and publish (nearly) everywhere with Flash.

Getting Started

● **Note:** If you have not already downloaded the project files for this lesson to your computer from your Account page, make sure to do so now. See "Getting Started" at the beginning of the book.

In this lesson, you'll publish several projects that have already been completed to learn about various output options. The first project is an animated banner for the fictional city of Meridien. You'll publish the project for playback in a desktop browser. The second project is the interactive restaurant guide for Meridien that you completed in a previous lesson. For that project, you'll target Adobe AIR, which creates a standalone application that runs on the desktop outside the browser. Finally, you'll test the interactivity for a third project for a mobile device. You'll also learn about publishing to mobile devices, but won't actually do so, as it not only requires specific hardware, but various developer and provisioning certificates.

1 Double-click the 11Start_banner.fla, 11Start_restaurantguide.fla, and 11Start_mobileapp.fla files in the Lesson11/11Start folder to open the three projects.

The three projects are relatively simple, each having unique Stage dimensions that are suited for their final published playback environments.

2   In the Properties inspector for each project, notice that the Target is set for different options.

The banner ad targets the Flash Player, the restaurant guide targets AIR for Desktop, and the mobile app targets AIR for Android.

The Debugging Process

Before we get to the completed Flash files, consider the troubleshooting process that happens before you publish. Troubleshooting is a skill you develop over time, but it's easier to identify the cause of problems if you test your movie frequently as you create content. If you test after each step, you know which changes you made and therefore what might have gone wrong. A good motto to remember is "Test early. Test often."

One fast way to preview a movie is to choose Control > Test Movie > In Flash Professional (Ctrl+Enter/Command+Return), as you've done in earlier lessons. When your Flash document targets the Flash Player, the Test Movie command creates a SWF file in the same location as your FLA file so you can play and preview the movie directly within the Flash application. It does not create the HTML file necessary to play the movie in a Web browser.

When you believe you've completed your movie or a portion of the movie, take the time to make sure all the pieces are in place and that they perform the way you expect them to.

1   Review the storyboard for the project, if you have one, or other documents that describe the purpose and requirements of the project. If such documents do not exist, write a description of what you expect to see when you view the movie. Include information about the length of the animation, any buttons or links included in the movie, and what should be visible as the movie progresses.

Note: The default behavior for your movie in Test Movie mode is to loop. You can make your SWF play differently in a browser by selecting different publish settings, as described later in this lesson, or by adding ActionScript to stop the Timeline.

2 Using the storyboard, project requirements, or your written description, create a checklist that you can use to verify that the movie meets your expectations.

3 Choose Control > Test Movie > In Flash Professional. As the movie plays, compare it with your checklist. Click buttons and links to ensure they behave as expected. You should click on every possibility that a user may encounter. This process is called QA, or quality assurance. In larger projects, it may be referred to as beta testing.

4 For movies that play with the Flash Player, choose Control > Test Movie > In Browser to export a SWF file and an HTML file required to play in a browser and to preview the movie.

A browser opens, if one is not already open, and plays the final movie.

5 Upload the two files (the SWF and HTML) to your own Web server and give your colleagues or friends the Web site address so they can help you test the movie. Ask them to run the movie on different computers with different browsers to ensure that all the files are included and that the movie meets the criteria on your checklist. Encourage testers to view the movie as though they were its target audience.

If your project requires additional media, such as FLV or F4V video files, skin files for your video, or loaded external SWF files, you must upload them along with your SWF and HTML file in the same relative location as they were on your computer hard drive.

6 Make changes and corrections as necessary to finalize the movie, upload the revised files, and then test it again to ensure it meets your criteria. The iterative process of testing and making revisions may not sound like fun, but it is a critical part of launching a successful Flash project.

Clearing the Publish Cache

When you test your movie by choosing Control > Test Movie > In Flash Professional to generate a SWF, Flash puts compressed copies of any fonts and sounds from your project into the Publish Cache. When you test your movie again, Flash uses the versions in the cache (if the fonts and sounds are unchanged) to speed up the export of the SWF file. However, you can manually purge the cache by choosing Control > Clear Publish Cache. If you want to clear the cache and test the movie, choose Control > Clear Publish Cache and Test Movie.

Understanding Publishing

Publishing is the process that creates the required file or files to play your final Flash project for your viewers. Keep in mind that Flash Professional CC is the authoring application, which is a different environment from where your viewers experience your movie. In Flash Professional CC, you author content. In the target environment, such as a desktop browser or a mobile device, your viewers watch the content when it plays back, or runs. So developers make a distinction between "author-time" and "runtime" environments.

Adobe provides various runtime environments for playing back your Flash content. The Flash runtime for a browser running on the desktop is the Flash Player. Flash Player 11.7 is the latest version and supports all the new features in Flash Professional CC. The Flash Player is available as a free plug-in from the Adobe Web site for all the major browsers and platforms. In Google Chrome, the Flash Player comes pre-installed and updates automatically.

Adobe AIR is another runtime environment for playing Flash content. AIR (Adobe Integrated Runtime) runs Flash content directly from your desktop, without the need for a browser. When you publish your content for AIR, you make it available either as an installer that creates a standalone application, or you can make the application with the runtime already installed. You can also publish AIR applications that can be installed and run on Android devices and iOS mobile devices such as the iPhone or iPad, whose browsers do not support the Flash Player.

Knowing your audience and understanding the target playback environment is essential for your success.

Publishing for the Web

When you want to publish a movie for the Web, you target a Web browser's Flash Player. Flash content for the Web requires a SWF file for the Flash Player and an HTML document that tells the Web browser how to display the Flash content. You need to upload both files to your Web server along with any other files your SWF file references (such as FLV or F4V video files and skins). By default, the Publish command saves all the required files to the same folder.

You can specify different options for publishing a movie, including whether to detect the version of Flash Player installed on the viewer's computer.

Note: When you change the settings in the Publish Settings dialog box, Flash saves them with the document.

Specifying Flash file settings

You can determine how Flash publishes the SWF file, including which version of Flash Player it requires, and how the movie is displayed and plays.

1 Open the **11Start_banner.fla** file.

2 Choose File > Publish Settings, or click the Publish Settings button in the Profile section of the Properties inspector.

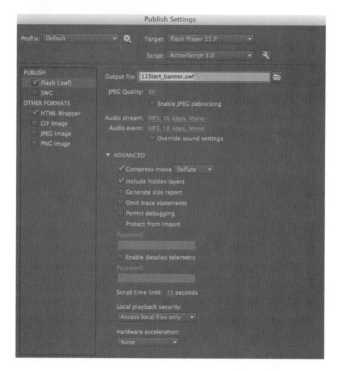

The Publish Settings dialog box appears with the general settings at the top, the formats on the left, and additional options for selected formats on the right.

The Flash (.swf) and the HTML Wrapper formats should already be checked.

3 At the top of the Publish Settings dialog box, select a version of Flash Player. The latest version is Flash Player 11.7.

Some Flash Professional CC features will not play as expected in versions of the player earlier than Flash Player 11.7. If you're using the latest features of Flash, you should choose Flash Player 11.7. Choose an earlier version of the Flash Player only if you're targeting a specific audience that does not have the latest version.

4 Note that the ActionScript settings are for 3.0, which is the latest and only version supported by this release of Flash.

5 Select the Flash (.swf) format on the left side of the dialog box.

The options for the SWF file appear on the right. Expand the ADVANCED section to see more options.

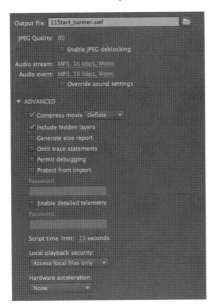

6 If you wish, you can modify the output filename and location by entering a new filename. For this lesson, leave the Output file as **11Start_banner.swf**.

7 If you've included bitmaps in your movie, you can set a global quality setting for JPEG compression levels. Enter a value from 0 (lowest quality) to 100 (highest quality). The value of 80 is the default, which you can leave as is for this lesson.

8 If you've included sound, click on the Audio stream or Audio event values to modify the quality of the audio compression.

The higher the bitrate, the better the sound quality will be. In this interactive banner, there is no sound, so there's no need to change the settings.

9 Make sure the Compress movie check box is selected to reduce file size and download times.

Deflate is the default option. Choose LZMA for better SWF compression. You'll see the biggest improvements in file-size compression if you've built your project with more ActionScript code and vector graphics.

10 Select the HTML Wrapper format on the left side of the dialog box.

11 Make sure that the Flash Only option is selected from the Template menu.

Note: To learn about other template options, select one and then click Info.

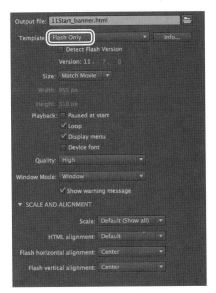

Detecting the version of Flash Player

You can automatically detect the version of Flash Player on a viewer's computer; if the Flash Player version is not the one required, a message will prompt the viewer to download the updated player.

1 If necessary, choose File > Publish Settings, or click the Publish Settings button in the Profile section of the Properties inspector.

2 Select the HTML Wrapper format on the left side of the dialog box.

3 Select Detect Flash Version.

4 In the Version fields, enter the earliest version of the Flash Player to detect.

5 Click Publish, and then click OK to close the dialog box.

Flash publishes three files.

11Start_banner.html   11Start_banner.swf   swfobject.js

Flash creates a SWF file, an HTML file, and an additional file named **swfobject.js** that contains extra JavaScript code that will detect the specified Flash Player version. If the browser does not have the earliest Flash Player version you entered in the Version fields, a message is displayed instead of the Flash movie. All three files need to be uploaded to your Web server to play your movie.

Changing display settings

You have many options for changing the way your Flash movie is displayed in a browser. The Size and Scale settings for the HTML Wrapper work together to determine the movie's size and amount of distortion and cropping.

1 Choose File > Publish Settings, or click the Publish Settings button in the Profile section of the Properties inspector.

2 Select the HTML Wrapper format on the left side of the dialog box.

- Select Match Movie for the Size to play the Flash movie at the exact Stage size set in Flash. This is the usual setting for almost all your Flash projects.

- Select Pixels for the Size to enter a different size in pixels for your Flash movie.

- Select Percent for the Size to enter a different size for your Flash movie as a percentage of the browser window.

3 Click on the Scale and Alignment option to expand the advanced settings below it.

- Select Default (Show all) for the Scale option to fit the movie in the browser window without any distortions or cropping to show all the content. This is the usual setting for almost all Flash projects. If a user reduces the size of the browser window, the content remains constant but is clipped by the window.

- Select Percent for Size and No border for the Scale option to scale the movie to fit the browser window without any distortions but with cropping of the content to fill the window.

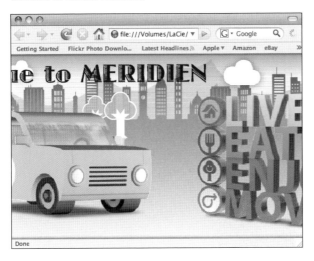

- Select Percent for Size and Exact fit for the Scale option to scale the movie to fill the browser window on both the horizontal and vertical dimensions. With these options, none of the background color shows, but the content can be distorted.

- Select Percent for Size and No scale for the Scale option to keep the movie size constant no matter how big or small the browser window is.

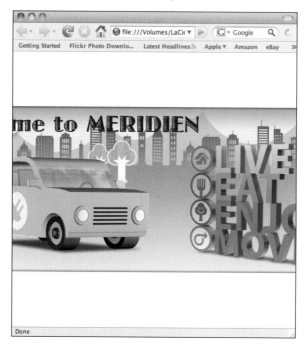

Changing Playback settings

You can change several options that affect the way your Flash movie plays within a browser.

1 Choose File > Publish Settings, or click the Publish Settings button in the Profile section of the Properties inspector.

2 Select the HTML Wrapper format on the left side of the dialog box.

- Select Paused at start for the Playback option to have the movie pause at the very first frame.

- Deselect Loop for the Playback option to have the movie play only once.

- Deselect Display menu for the Playback option to limit the options in the context menu that appears when you right-click/Ctrl-click on a Flash movie in a browser.

Note: In general, it's better to control a Flash movie with ActionScript than to rely on the Playback settings in the Publish Settings dialog box. For example, add a stop() command in the very first frame of your Timeline if you want to pause the movie at the start, or a gotoAndPlay(1) at the end of your Timeline if you want the movie to loop. When you test your movie (Control > Test Movie > In Flash Professional), all the functionality will be in place.

Publishing a Desktop Application

Most desktop computers have the Flash Player installed with their browsers, but you may want to distribute your movie to someone who doesn't have the Flash Player or who has an older version. Perhaps you just want your movie to run without a browser.

You can output your movie as an AIR file, which installs an application on the user's desktop. Adobe AIR is a more robust runtime environment that supports a broader range of technologies.

Viewers must download the free Adobe AIR runtime from Adobe's Web site at http://get.adobe.com/air/.

Creating an AIR application

Adobe AIR allows your viewers to see your Flash content on their desktop as an application.

1 Open **11Start_restaurantguide.fla**.

This is the same interactive restaurant guide that you created in Lesson 6, with a few modifications to the background image.

2 In the Properties inspector, note that the Target is set to AIR 3.6 for Desktop.

AIR 3.6 is the latest version of the Adobe AIR runtime.

3 Click the Edit application settings button (wrench icon) next to the Target.

The AIR Settings dialog box appears.

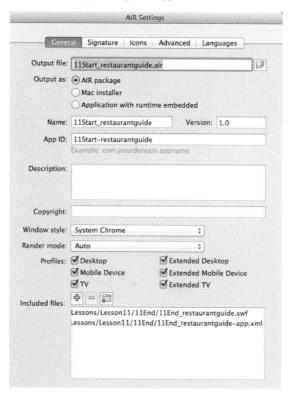

You can also open the AIR Settings dialog box from the Publish Settings dialog box. Click the Player Settings button (wrench icon) next to the Target.

4 Examine the settings under the General tab.

The Output file shows the filename of the published AIR installer as 11Start_restaurantguide.air. The Output as options provide three ways to create an AIR application. The first choice should be selected:

- AIR package creates a platform-independent AIR installer.

- Mac installer/Windows installer creates a platform-specific AIR installer.

- Application with runtime embedded creates an application without an installer or the need for the AIR runtime already on the desktop.

5 In the Name/App Name field, enter **Meridien Restaurant Guide**.

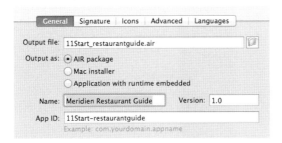

This is the name of your application.

6 In the Window style, choose Custom Chrome (transparent).

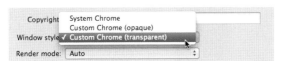

Custom Chrome (transparent) creates an application without any interface or frame elements (known as chrome), and with a transparent background.

7 Click the Signature tab at the top of the AIR Settings dialog box.

Creating an AIR application requires a certificate so that users can trust and identify the developer of the Flash content. For this lesson, you won't need an official certificate, so you can create your own self-signed certificate.

8 Click the New/Create button next to Certificate.

9 Enter your information in the empty fields. You can use **Meridien Press** for Publisher name, **Digital** for the Organization unit, and **Interactive** for the Organization name. Enter your own password in both password fields, and then save the file as **meridienpress**. Click on the Folder/Browse button to save it in a folder of your choice. Click OK.

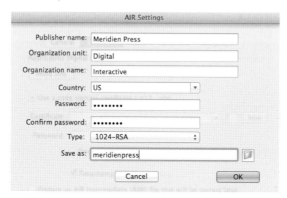

Flash creates a self-signed certificate (.p12) file on your computer.

Flash automatically fills out the path to your .p12 file in the Certificate field. Make sure that the Password field is filled (the password must match the one you used to create the certificate), and that Remember password for this session and Timestamp are checked.

10 Now click on the Icons tab at the top of the AIR Settings dialog box.

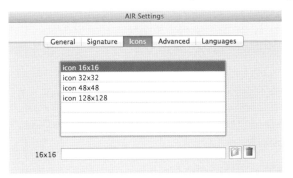

11 Select icon 128x128, and click the folder icon.

12 Navigate to the AppIconsForPublish folder inside the 11Start folder, and choose the restaurantguide.png file provided for you.

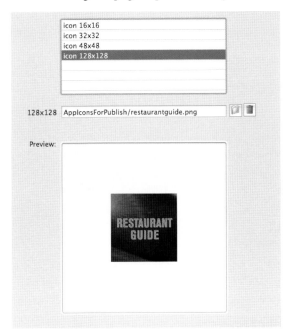

The image in the restaurantguide.png file will appear as the application icon on the desktop.

13 Finally, click on the Advanced tab at the top of the AIR Settings dialog box.

14 Under Initial window settings, enter **0** for the X field and **50** for the Y field.

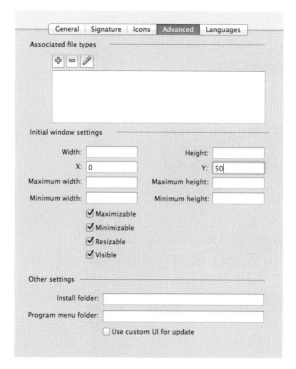

When the application launches, it will appear flushed to the left side of the screen and 50 pixels from the top.

15 Click Publish.

Flash creates an AIR installer (.air).

Installing an AIR Application

The AIR installer is platform-independent, but requires that the AIR runtime is installed on the user's system.

1 Double-click the AIR installer that you just created, **11Start_restaurantguide.air**.

11Start_restaurantguide.air

The Adobe AIR Application Installer opens and asks to install the application. Since you used a self-signed certificate to create the AIR installer, Adobe warns of a potential security risk due to an unknown and untrusted developer. (Since you can trust yourself, you're safe to proceed).

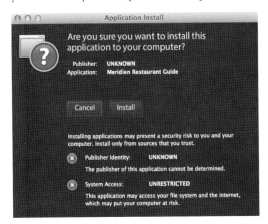

2   Click Install, and then click Continue to proceed with the installation at the default settings.

The application called Meridien Restaurant Guide is installed on your computer and automatically opens.

Notice that the application is positioned at x=0, y=50, and that the Stage is transparent so your graphic elements float over the desktop, much like the appearance of other applications.

3   Quit the application by pressing Alt+F4/Cmd+Q.

Publishing for a Mobile Device

You can also publish Flash content for mobile devices running on Android or on Apple's iOS, such as the iPhone or iPad. To publish Flash content for a mobile device, you target AIR for Android or AIR for iOS to create an application that viewers download and install on their devices.

Testing a mobile app

Creating an app for mobile devices is a little more complicated than creating an application for the desktop, because you have to obtain specific developer certificates for development and distribution. Moreover, you have to factor in the additional time and effort required for testing and debugging on a separate device. However, Flash Professional CC provides several ways to help testing content for mobile devices:

- You can test mobile interactions in Flash's mobile device simulator, the AIR Debug Launcher. The SimController that accompanies the AIR Debug Launcher emulates specific interactions such as tilting the device (using the accelerometer), touch gestures such as swiping and pinching, or even using the geolocation functions.

- For iOS devices, Flash can publish an AIR app to test in the native iOS Simulator, which emulates the mobile app experience on your desktop.

  ● **Note:** The iOS Simulator is part of Apple's XCode developer toolset (https://developer. apple.com/xcode/index.php), available as a free download in the App store.

● **Note:** Testing an app on an iOS device requires that you be part of Apple's iOS Developer program, where you create development, distribution, and provisioning certificates. The certificates allow you to install apps on iOS devices for testing and upload apps to the iTunes store.

- Connect a mobile device to your computer with a USB cable and Flash can publish an AIR app directly to your mobile device.

Simulating a mobile app

You'll use the Adobe SimController and AIR Debug Launcher to simulate mobile device interactions within Flash Professional CC.

1   Open **11Start_mobileapp.fla** if it's not already open.

The project is a simple application with four keyframes that announces an imaginary sports challenge set in our familiar city of Meridien.

The project already contains ActionScript that enables the viewer to swipe the Stage left or right to go to the next or previous frames.

Examine the code in the Actions panel. The code was added using the Code Snippets panel, which includes dozens of code snippets for interactivity on mobile devices.

```
1   stop();
2   /* Swipe to Go to Next/Previous Frame and Stop
3   Swiping the stage moves the playhead to the next/previous frame and stops the movie.
4   */
5
6   Multitouch.inputMode = MultitouchInputMode.GESTURE;
7
8   stage.addEventListener (TransformGestureEvent.GESTURE_SWIPE, fl_SwipeToGoToNextPreviousFrame);
9
10  function fl_SwipeToGoToNextPreviousFrame(event:TransformGestureEvent):void
11  {
12      if(event.offsetX == 1)
13      {
14          // swiped right
15          prevFrame();
16      }
17      else if(event.offsetX == -1)
18      {
19          // swiped left
20          nextFrame();
21      }
22  }
```

2   In the Properties inspector, notice that the Target is set for AIR 3.6 for Android.

Note: On Windows, a security warning may appear when you use the AIR Debug Launcher. Click Allow access to continue.

3   Choose Control > Test Movie > In AIR Debug Launcher (Mobile), which should already be checked.

The project publishes to a new window. In addition, the SimController launches, which provides options to interact with the Flash content.

4 In the Simulator panel, click Touch and Gesture to expand that section.

5 Check the Touch layer box to enable it.

The simulator overlays a transparent gray box over the Flash content to simulate the touch surface of the mobile device.

6 Choose Gesture > Swipe.

Note: Don't move the window that contains your Flash content (Air Debug Launcher, or ADL) when you've enabled the Touch layer. If you do, the Touch layer won't align with the ADL window, and you can't accurately test your mobile interactions.

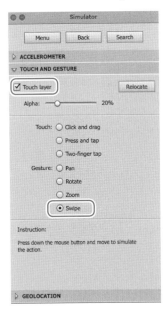

Note: You can change the opacity of the touch layer by changing the Alpha value.

The simulator is now enabled to emulate a swipe interaction. The instructions at the bottom of the panel detail how you can create the interaction with just your mouse cursor.

7 Press down on the touch layer over your Flash content, drag to the left, and then let go of your mouse button.

The yellow dot represents the contact point on the touch layer of the mobile device.

The project recognizes the swipe interaction, and the second keyframe appears.

8 Swipe left and right.

Flash advances ahead one frame, or moves back one frame.

Publishing a mobile app

Lastly, you'll examine the settings in Flash to publish a mobile app for iOS. Publishing an app for Android has similar settings.

While it's beyond the scope of this lesson to present the steps in detail, you'll see the required certificates, assets, and configurations to properly publish and distribute an app to the iTunes store.

1   In Flash, choose File > New, and select AIR for iOS for Type, and click OK.

Flash creates a new Flash file, configured for iOS. The Stage size is set at 640 x 960, and the Target for AIR 3.6 for iOS.

2   Click the wrench icon next to Target.

The AIR for iOS settings dialog box appears.

3   Click on the General tab.

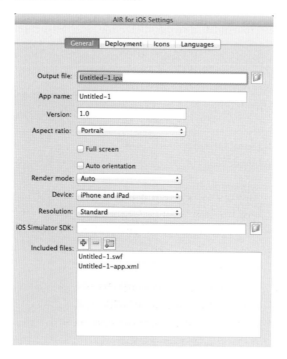

The General tab contains information about the output files and general settings. The actual published file has the extension .ipa. You can choose different aspect ratios (landscape or portrait), and target specific devices (iPhone and/or iPad) and resolutions. The iOS Simulator SDK field is the path to the iOS Simulator file used for testing (Control > Test Movie > On iOS Simulator). The included files contain the two required ones (a .swf and an .xml file), but you can add additional dependent media files, if required for your project. For iOS apps, you can also include PNG files with specific filenames as the default launch image—for example, Default@2x.png—that appears as soon as an app loads.

4   Click the Deployment tab.

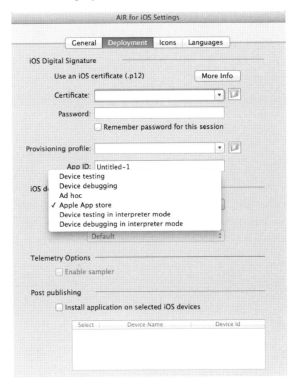

The Deployment tab contains information for testing and distribution. The Certificate field and Provisioning profile are required documents that you create as a certified Apple Developer. It certifies you as a known and trusted developer so Apple and your potential customers can purchase and download your app with confidence.

The iOS deployment types are the various ways you publish your app, such as testing on a connected USB device, testing on a variety of devices (ad hoc), or for final distribution to the iTunes store. Each phase of development requires different certificates and a new round of publishing.

5 Click the Icons tab.

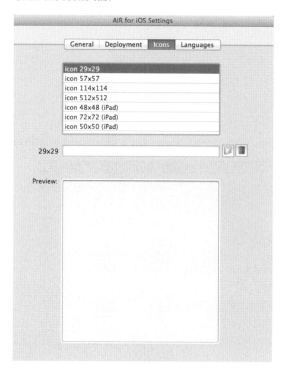

The Icons tab tells Flash what graphics to use for icons to represent your app on the mobile device. You must provide your icon in different resolutions, depending on which device you target.

● **Note:** For more information about publishing Flash content to AIR for iOS or Android, visit the Adobe AIR Developer Center at http://www.adobe.com/devnet/air.html. Tutorials, tricks and tips, and sample files are available for download.

6 Click the Languages tab.

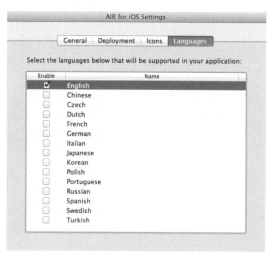

The Languages tab contains support for different languages.

Testing Flash content through Adobe Scout

Adobe Scout is an advanced tool for analyzing your Flash content and its performance. Use Scout to profile and optimize any Flash content, whether it runs in a browser or on a mobile device.

Scout is a standalone application available through the Creative Cloud (http://gaming.adobe.com/technologies/scout/). Scout gives you a peek behind the scenes of the Flash Player—information such as CPU and memory usage, or how the frame rate of your movie is keeping up or falling behind.

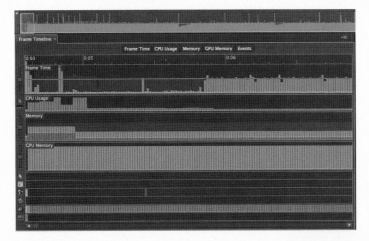

There are two basic ways to use Scout: When you run any SWF, detailed information about it automatically appears as a new session in Scout.

However, because of security, Scout displays only basic information about the SWF. For more advanced information, you must enable detailed telemetry. To enable detailed telemetry, click the Enable detailed telemetry option in the Publish Settings dialog box of your Flash file.

Once enabled, the published SWF allows Scout access to more detailed metrics. For more information about using Adobe Scout, visit the Adobe site.

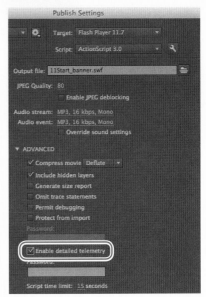

Next Steps

Congratulations! You've made it through the last lesson. By now you've seen how Flash Professional CC, in the right creative hands (your hands!), has all the features to produce media-rich, interactive projects that run on multiple platforms. You've completed these lessons—many of them from scratch—so you understand how the various tools, panels, and ActionScript work together for real-world applications.

But there's always more to learn. Continue practicing your Flash skills by creating your own animation or interactive site. Get inspired by seeking out Flash projects on the Web and exploring apps on mobile devices. Expand your ActionScript knowledge by exploring the Adobe Flash Help resources and other fine Adobe *Classroom in a Book* manuals.

Review Questions

1 What's the difference between author-time and runtime?

2 What files do you need to upload to a server to ensure your final Flash movie plays in the Flash Player in Web browsers?

3 How can you tell which version of Flash Player a viewer has installed, and why is it important?

4 What are the various ways you can test a Flash file for a mobile device?

5 What is a code-signing certificate, and why do you need one for an AIR application?

Review Answers

1 Author-time refers to the environment in which you build your Flash content, such as Flash Professional CC. Runtime refers to the environment in which your Flash content plays back for your audience. The runtime for your content can be the Flash Player in a desktop browser or an AIR application on the desktop or on a mobile device.

2 To ensure that your movie plays as expected in Web browsers, upload the Flash SWF file and the HTML document that tells the browser how to display the SWF file. You also need to upload the swfobject.js file, if one was published, and any files your SWF file references, such as video or other SWF files; be sure that they are in the same relative location (usually the same folder as the final SWF file) as they were on your hard drive.

3 Select Detect Flash Version in the HTML tab in the Publish Settings dialog box to automatically detect the version of Flash Player on a viewer's computer.

4 You can test your Flash project for a mobile device by testing it in the Air Debug Launcher (Control > Test Movie > In AIR Debug Launcher (Mobile). The accompanying SimController allows you to simulate various mobile interactions, such as pinches and swipes. You can also test your Flash project by publishing it directly to a connected USB device (Android or iOS). Lastly, you can test an iOS app in the native iOS Simulator (Control > Test Movie > On iOS Simulator).

5 A code-signing certificate is a certified document that acts as your digital signature. You purchase one from a certification authority. It provides a way for your audience to authenticate your identity so they can confidently download and install desktop AIR applications, or AIR apps for Android or iOS.

INDEX

corners, adding to shapes, 52
cropping video, 233–239
Ctrl key. *See* keyboard shortcuts
cue points, using in video encoding, 239
cursor, customizing, 302–306
curves
    adding anchor points, 63
    creating, 61–63
    deleting anchor points, 63
    editing, 63
    Pen tool, 61–62
custom icon
    disabling input for, 305–306
    following mouse with, 302–305

D

data types
    Boolean, 294
    Number, 294
    String, 294
debugging process, reviewing storyboard,
        333–334
deleting
    anchor points, 63
    fills, 50
    layers, 20
    shape hints, 160
    sound files, 226
    strokes, 50
desktop application, publishing, 343–349
destination keyframes. *See also* keyframes;
        property keyframes
    frame labels, 198–199
    inserting, 195–197
    straight quotes ('), 199
display options
    blending effects, 96
    visible property for movie clips, 95–96
documents, creating, 11–12. *See also*
        XFL documents
dot operator (.), using in ActionScript 3.0, 188
Double Identity project
    adding frames, 115
    animating 3D motion, 138–140
    animating filters, 118–121
    animating position, 110–113
    animating transformations, 122–125
    animating transparency, 116–118

animation duration, 113–115
described, 109–110
easing, 133–136
frame-based selections, 116
frame-by-frame animation, 136–138
motion presets, 125
moving keyframes, 115
nesting animations, 131–133
pacing, 113–115
path of motion, 126–129
PNG sequences, 142
previewing animation, 113–114
property keyframes, 121
span-based selections, 116
sprite sheets, 142
swapping tween targets, 129–130
testing, 141
timing, 113–115
viewing, 108
drawing modes
    Merge, 54
    Object, 54
    Primitive, 54

E

EaselJS commands, documentation for, 324
EaselJS library, described, 311
eases of motion tweens, setting, 135–136
easing
    explained, 133
    shape tween, 169–170
    splitting motion tweens, 133–134
Edit bar, identifying, 12
educators, resources for, 7
embedded video, using, 253–256
equals sign (=), using with variables, 295
event handlers for buttons
    checking for errors, 195
    event listener and function, 192–194
event handling, process of, 192
event listeners
    adding for buttons, 192–195
    adding for mouse click, 326–327
    adding for mouseout, 290–291
    adding for mouseover, 290–291
    adding to movie clips, 268–269
events, defined, 192

Ink Bottle tool, using, 53
installing
    AIR application, 343–348
    Flash Professional, 4
instances, naming rules, 185
interactive movies, 175
iOS Simulator, obtaining, 350

J

JavaScript
    and ActionScript, 328
    code blocks, 324
    event listener for mouse click, 326–327
    exporting to, 321–324
    inserting, 324–327
    output files, 322
    publish settings, 323–324
    stopping playhead, 324–326
JavaScript open source libraries
    EaselJS, 311, 324
    SoundJS, 311
    TweenJS, 311
JavaScript project
    adding tail feathers, 313–314
    animating mountains, 317–320
    applying classic tween, 315–316
    changing feature instance, 314–315
    classic tweens, 312
    inserting keyframes, 314
    Toolkit for CreateJS, 311–312
    viewing, 310–311
JPEG images, importing into library, 16

K

keyboard shortcuts. *See also* function keys
    Actions panel, 266
    Clear Keyframe, 24
    Copy command, 51
    Lock Guides, 93
    Paste in Center command, 51
    previewing movies, 333
    Properties inspector, 28
    Rulers, 92
    Select All, 138
    undoing steps, 34–35
    ungrouping shapes, 59

keyframes. *See also* destination keyframes;
        property keyframes
    creating, 22–23
    destination, 195–199
    distributing in tweens, 114
    establishing for shapes, 147–148
    and frames, 23
    identifying, 22
    inserting in HTML5 project, 314
    moving, 24, 115, 150
    removing, 24

L

large image. *See* camera image
layer folders
    adding layers to, 26
    collapsing, 26
    creating, 25–26
layers. *See also* Timeline
    adding to Timeline, 18–20
    cutting, 27
    deleting, 20
    duplicating, 27
    identifying, 12
    modifying into Masked layers, 164
    organizing in Timeline, 24–27
    pasting, 27
    rearranging, 20
    renaming in Timeline, 18
    in Timeline, 18
lesson files
    copying, 5
    using, 6
Library panel
    accessing, 15
    adding items to Stage, 17
    described, 15
    features, 16
    importing items to, 16
line styles
    controlling, 60
    customizing, 59–61
    decorative, 59–60
linear gradient, explained, 55
looping animations
    duplicating keyframes, 154
    inserting into movie clips, 155–156
    Loop Playback option, 154
    previewing loops, 154–155

M

movie clips
adding event listeners to, 268–269
alpha property, 288
controlling, 274–275
data types, 288
height property, 288
name properties, 288
properties, 288
read-only, 288
rotation property, 288
scaleX property, 288
scaleY property, 288
visible property, 288
visual properties of, 287–290
width property, 288
x property, 288
y property, 288
movie samples, copying, 5
movies. *See also* animations; videos
creating HTML files, 41–43
creating SWF files, 41–43
interactive, 175
previewing, 36, 333
publishing, 41–43
saving, 38–41
moving keyframes, 24

N

nested animations, creating, 131–133
Number data type, explained, 294

O

Object Drawing mode, explained, 54
objects
aligning, 69–70
grouping, 59
Onion Skin Outlines, using with
animations, 160
Option key, using with control points, 51
Output panel, sending information to, 296
Oval tool, using, 49–50

P

pacing of animations, changing, 113–115
Paint Bucket tool, using, 53
panel groups, moving, 30

panels
described, 9
displaying as icons, 30
docking, 30
grouping, 30
moving, 30
opening, 30
toggling, 14
undocking, 30
parentheses [()], using in ActionScript 3.0,
188
Paste in Center command, using with
shapes, 51
path of motion
changing rotation of path, 127
changing scale of path, 127
editing, 128
manipulating directly, 128
moving, 126
orienting objects to, 129
Pen tool, using for curves, 61–62
perspective angle, explained, 103–104
photo layers, adding to photo folder, 26
Photoshop files
editing, 83
importing, 80–83
Play option, accessing, 141
PNG sequences, generating, 142
previewing
animations, 36
movies, 36, 333
Primitive Drawing mode, explained, 54
project samples, copying, 5
ProLoader objects
overlapping, 276
positioning, 272
removing from Stage, 273
unloading content from, 273
using with external content, 266–268
Properties inspector
features, 27
identifying, 12
opening, 28
positioning objects on Stage, 28–29
property keyframes, 121. *See also* keyframes
Publish Cache, clearing, 334
publish settings, changing, 333
Publish Settings dialog box, displaying, 336

training centers, contacting, 7
transformations
    animating, 122–125
    global, 102
    local, 102
    resetting, 102–103
transition animations, creating, 205–207
transparencies
    adding shadows, 65–66
    animating, 116–118
    creating, 64–66
    modifying alpha value of fill, 64–65
Tween layers, explained, 109
tween targets, swapping, 129–130. *See also* motion tweens
TweenJS library, described, 311
tweens, distributing keyframes in, 114. *See also* shape tweens

U

undoing steps, 34–35
updates
    checking for, 44
    setting preferences for, 44
URLRequest object, using with external content, 266–268

V

vanishing point, explained, 103–104
variables
    assigning values to, 295–296
    creating, 293–294
    creating for camera image, 297–300
    strictly typed, 294
    tracking in Output panel, 296–297
    using equals sign (=) with, 295
vector art, converting to bitmap art, 60–61
vector graphics, converting bitmap images to, 84
video encoding
    adjusting length, 238–239
    advanced options, 240–242
    audio options, 240–242
    cropping video, 233–239
    cue points, 239
    Export Settings dialog box, 234–235

video files
    adding to Media Encoder, 231–232
    changing status in Queue, 233
    converting to Flash video, 232–233
video playback, controlling, 246
videos. *See also* animations; external video; Flash video; movies
    channels, 247
    embedded, 253–256
    exporting from Flash, 256–260
    Output settings, 234
    preset browser settings, 234
    preventing overlapping audio, 249
    processing in Watch Folders panel, 234
    and transparency, 246–249
visible property, changing for camera image, 289–290

W

Watch Folders panel, using with videos, 234
Web publishing
    Bitmap properties dialog box, 338
    changing display settings, 340–342
    Enable detailed telemetry option, 338
    Flash file settings, 336–339
    Flash Player version, 339–340
    HTML Wrapper format, 338
    playback settings, 343
    requirements, 335
    template options, 339
Web sites. *See also* resources
    Adobe AIR Developer Center, 356
    Adobe AIR runtime, 3, 343
    Adobe Certified programs, 7
    AIR Developer Center, 356
    Flash Professional installation, 4
    QuickTime software, 3, 231, 258
    system-requirement updates, 4
    Toolkit for CreateJS updates, 312
Windows, installing Flash Professional on, 4
workspace
    choosing, 13
    Edit bar, 12
    layers, 12
    Properties inspector, 12
    saving, 13–14
    Stage, 12
    Timeline, 12
    Tools panel, 12

X

XFL documents. *See also* documents
    modifying, 40–41
    saving, 39–40

Z

Zonny DSLR Camera project
    creating variables, 293–294, 297–300
    custom cursor, 302–306
    data types, 294
    event listener for mouseout, 290–291
    event listener for mouseover, 290–291
    graphics setup, 282–284
    hiding large image, 291–292
    making image invisible, 289–290
    mapping mouse movements, 293
    mask for camera detail, 284–287
    naming movie clip instances, 289
    project file, 281–282
    registration point, 302
    repositioning large image, 300–301
    showing large image, 291–292
    text setup, 282–284
    tracking variables, 296–297
    values for variables, 295–296
    viewing, 280–281
    visual properties of movie clips, 287–288

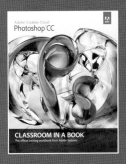

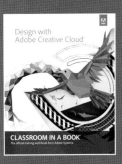

The fastest, easiest, most comprehensive way to learn
Adobe Creative Cloud™

Classroom in a Book®, the best-selling series of hands-on software training books, helps you learn the features of Adobe software quickly and easily.

The **Classroom in a Book** series offers what no other book or training program does—an official training series from Adobe Systems, developed with the support of Adobe product experts.

To see a complete list of our Adobe Creative Cloud titles go to:
www.adobepress.com/adobecc

Adobe Photoshop CC Classroom in a Book
ISBN: 9780321928078

Adobe Illustrator CC Classroom in a Book
ISBN: 9780321929495

Adobe InDesign CC Classroom in a Book
ISBN: 9780321926975

Adobe Dreamweaver CC Classroom in a Book
ISBN: 9780321919410

Adobe Flash Professional CC Classroom in a Book
ISBN: 9780321927859

Adobe Premiere Pro CC Classroom in a Book
ISBN: 9780321919380

Adobe After Effects CC Classroom in a Book
ISBN: 9780321929600

Adobe Audition CC Classroom in a Book
ISBN: 9780321929532

Adobe SpeedGrade CC Classroom in a Book
ISBN: 9780321927002

Digital Video with Adobe Creative Cloud Classroom in a Book
ISBN: 9780321934024

Design with the Adobe Creative Cloud Classroom in a Book
ISBN: 9780321940513

AdobePress